The Ethics of
Environmental Concern

ROBIN ATTFIELD

The Ethics of Environmental Concern

Columbia University Press
New York
1983

Printed in Great Britain

Library of Congress Cataloging in Publication Data

Attfield, Robin.
    The ethics of environmental concern.

    Bibliography: p.
    Includes index.
    1. Human ecology—Moral and ethical aspects.
I. Title.
GF80.A88   1983   179'.1   83-7217
ISBN 0-231-05798-9
ISBN 0-231-05799-7 (pbk.)

Contents

Preface

My thanks go to Peter Singer for discussion of a paper related to this book, to Robert Young and Nigel Dower for bibliographical assistance, to Derek Parfit for encouragement, to Tom Regan and Mary Midgley for their comments on chapter 8, and to the Cardiff Philosophical Society, and particularly its student members, for comments on chapter 6. An enormous debt of gratitude is also due to Thomas McPherson for commenting on the first draft of the entire book, to Andrew Belsey for comments on some chapters of that draft and on the entire second draft, and also to the publishers' reader. Their advice and criticisms have proved invaluable; but, like the others here mentioned, they cannot be held responsible for the final text, and would each profoundly disagree with at least some of it.

I am also grateful to the staff of the Library of University College, Cardiff for their tireless help in locating much of the material referred to, to Jean Barber for typing the second draft of chapter 6, and particularly to my wife, Leela Dutt, for encouragement and for reading the entire first draft, as well as enduring the composition of the book at the same time as composing a novel herself.

Introduction

This is an unusual book. It is an exercise neither solely in philosophy nor solely in history, nor certainly in any other single discipline. Part One is predominantly but not exclusively a study in the history of ideas, while Part Two is a philosophical investigation into normative ethics and some of its applications. This sort of structure is dictated by the subject of environmental ethics; indeed a similar structure was employed by John Passmore in his book *Man's Responsibility for Nature*, the one authoritative treatment of environmental ethics so far produced.

In Part One moral traditions are explored, for no satisfactory ethic can be put forward which disregards them. In environmental ethics our moral traditions are often held to be so deficient as to need to be superseded: such views are held, I believe, because our traditions have just as often been misrepresented, and embody ampler resources than they are credited with by Passmore and others.

Attitudes and ideas alone cannot explain or resolve our problems, however. In chapter 1 I review some much more material explanations of our ecological problems (an interdisciplinary undertaking if ever there was one), but conclude that such explanations, though important, are incomplete unless people's underlying beliefs are also studied.

In subsequent chapters attention is focused on traditions of belief common to the areas of the world where ecological problems are most intense, and in particular on Judaeo-Christian beliefs and on the ideas of the Enlightenment. In the ancient and continuous Jewish and Christian tradition of Stewardship I find the makings of an ethic suited to our problems, even though belief in man's dominion has often been misinterpreted to suggest that people may treat nature as they please. But at least as important a source of current problems as this convenient travesty of our religious tradition has been the secular belief in perpetual progress of the last two hundred years. Even so, aspects of this very belief can also contribute to an environmental ethic, including the heightened awareness of obligations to posterity and the realization that society can change its course.

In Part Two moral principles are re-examined. Scientific discoveries have opened up new opportunities and new perils, and have also disclosed many of the side-effects of our actions on the complex systems of nature; and our moral horizons have to be broadened to take this into account. Thus the effects of our deeds on other species and on future people require us to be more explicit about our responsibilities in their regard, and to take them more seriously. If, as I maintain, all worthwhile life is of intrinsic value, our obligations must be reassessed. No longer can we discount future people's interests or disregard the interests of fellow-creatures. It also turns out that some of the central traditions of our culture have not disregarded them either; and this gives hope that the principles of a satisfactory environmental ethic can secure acceptance, where proposals for a totally new ethic have no such prospect.

Legitimate ecological concern thus exceeds the limited preoccupation of what has been called 'the shallow ecology movement' with the problems of pollution and resource-depletion as they affect the developed world for the next fifty years. It extends to the life-support systems of the Third World, of the further future, and of nonhuman species. Yet I do not accept, with the so-called 'deep, long-range ecology movement', the view that our principal loyalty should be focused not on fellow-humans or fellow-creatures but on the biosphere as an organic whole, the constituents of which are only, supposedly, of value insofar as they contribute to its stability. Environmental ethics can only proceed by reasoning outwards from received moral judgements about familiar cases to their implications and to analogous cases in the future or in the nonhuman realm; it cannot discard the traditional concern for individuals in favour of an irreducible concern for biotic systems and expect a hearing.

This is not, of course, to suggest that individual agents should be free to treat the natural world as they please; nor is it to suggest that we cannot take into account the countless future people of whose individual identity we can have no knowledge. Indeed the principles for which I shall be arguing embody considerable constraints in the interests of contemporary and future people, as well as of nonhuman creatures. Nor am I suggesting that ecosystems do not matter: they

are morally as significant as the individual creatures which depend
on them.

Many articles and collections of papers have been published on
topics in environmental ethics and its historical background. Though
it has not been possible to consider all of these, and no claim can be
made to any kind of comprehensiveness, I have attempted to present
a consistent critique of a good number of the more significant ones,
and thereby to introduce their merits as well as their demerits to the
reader, in the hope that he or she can take up the subject from
there. In doing so I have tried to bear in mind the interests both of
philosophers and non-philosophers, but in case some readers find
difficulty with some passages in the later chapters I have also
attempted to include enough signposts in the text to enable them to
follow the main direction of the argument. This said, the argument
must in the end, as Passmore remarks at a similar point, speak for
itself or not at all.

1

Ecological Problems

Ecological problems have been defined as problems arising 'as a practical consequence of man's dealings with nature',[1] where 'nature' is used of the nonhuman environment of man. Ecology is the science of the complex interplay of natural organisms and natural systems, and brings to light, among other things, the long-term, distant and unexpected consequences of these dealings. Transactions with nature usually have multiple side-effects, and it is wise when considering how to cope with them to keep this fact to the fore: designating the problems as 'ecological' is one way of giving it due recognition. The choice of phrase also reminds us that the problems may be more far-reaching than the frustrated aspirations of one generation of humans to be encompassed by a pleasant environment, important as this can be.

Perceptions of problems

Agreement is less than universal about the identification of ecological problems, but the following would be widely agreed to be examples: pollution; diminishing natural resources; the increasing size of the human population; the destruction of wildlife and wilderness; losses of cultivable land through erosion and the growth of deserts; and the endangering of the life-support systems of the planet. It is not universally realized how human activity causes deserts to spread or life-support systems to be subverted: but such inadvertence would be an unimportant source of disagreement about the problems, were it not an ingredient of the problems itself.

The significant disagreement concerns how to solve the problems, and also, more basically, what makes them problems. Problems are sometimes understood, as by John Passmore,[2] as intolerable costs to humans which human action can eliminate or, at any rate, alleviate.

Among those who understand problems in this way, some are concerned principally with costs to humans already alive, while others are prepared to take into account the next fifty or a hundred years, and yet others the distant future. Those who understand problems like this are likely to be satisfied with solutions which effectively safeguard the interests of those humans on whom they focus their attention.

But problems may also be seen where there is actual or possible harm to living organisms in general. Here some extend their purview to the welfare of sentient animals, others to the interests of all living organisms, while yet others concentrate on species, ecosystems or the biosphere as a whole. Occasionally, nonhuman interests are given precedence over human interests in general: the extreme position is that which goes further still and presents humanity as a cancerous growth upon nature, and the human species as constituting the problem itself. Holders of any of these alternative conceptions of the nature of problems will naturally be less satisfied with man-centred solutions, and particularly ones confined to the short-term future. Thus, different views of what makes a problem reflect not only different estimates of possibilities, likelihoods and the limits of tolerance, but also disagreements about moral principles and about what is of value in itself.

Here it is useful to distinguish, with Arne Naess,[3] the shallow ecology movement and its deep, long-range counterpart (though it should be realized that there are many positions between the two). Naess characterizes the shallow ecology movement as being concerned with medium-term human interests, interests for all that often disregarded in traditional economics, and in particular with the interests of people in developed countries.

By contrast the deep movement takes into account distant future generations, the Third World, nonhuman species and, at times, the biosphere as a whole, sometimes regarding them all as having independent moral standing. For example, the term 'conservation' is applied to the concerns and activities of both movements: but, while the shallow movement seeks in the main to conserve mineral and energy resources, and extends the notion of resources to quarriable mountains and cultivable forests, the deep movement is less than happy to regard nonhuman species and their wild habitats as nothing but resources, and is at least equally concerned to preserve wilderness and the fragile equilibrium of natural ecosystems.

Both kinds of conservationist are in conflict with adherents of unstinted growth and of the 'technological fix', people who believe that whatever natural resources are expended can without too much difficulty be replaced through human ingenuity and substitution technology: but even those who allow there to be a problem of conservation clearly differ as to what precisely is bad about the disruptive effects of human action upon the environment, and also therefore as to what attitudes cause the problems and how to solve them.

The deep ecology movement, however, itself incorporates a variety of disparate emphases. Thus those opposed to the use of nuclear energy often argue from the effects of its use on the long-term future, but are sometimes less concerned with the preservation of wildlife, especially when they advocate estuarial barrages as an alternative energy source. Similarly, preservationists concerned for the survival of rare species and for ecological balance are sometimes prepared to countenance culling the members of plentiful species by means such as seal-hunts which inflict a great deal of suffering upon individual animals, while animal welfare and animal rights campaigners can be indifferent to the elimination of plant species except where animals' habitats are destroyed thereby.

There again, the deep movement might be thought to have affinities with those who preach catastrophe resulting from 'over-population'. Themes common to these people and to deep ecologists include the need to safeguard human life in a hundred years' time, and the damaging effects upon nonhuman nature of swelling human numbers. Yet those who favour a reduction in the size of the human population often do so partly from a fear that people in the West will be swamped by multitudes from elsewhere; and to this extent they are scarcely the natural allies of believers in the value of each worthwhile life, whether human or nonhuman, let alone of those who believe in the equality of animals with like capacities whatever their species. Indeed Naess himself makes no mention of concern for the restriction or reduction of population in his depiction of the deep, long-range ecology movement, perhaps regarding such a concern as elitist rather than egalitarian (though he is concerned about levels of crowding among mammals in general). Nevertheless those who are concerned about 'overpopulation' would doubtless lay claim to ecological depth.

Many of the tendencies within the deep ecology movement have been influenced both at the levels of theory and of inspiration by Aldo Leopold's *A Sand County Almanac*, and in particular by his call for a new, environmental ethic. Leopold calls for a recognition of the obligations which are owed to all members of the biotic community (what he calls 'the land'),[4] and to the biosphere as an organic whole: thus he holds that 'a thing is right when it tends to promote the integrity, stability and beauty of the biotic community. It is wrong when it tends otherwise.'[5] The suggestion here is that our traditional ethic lacks resources equal to our problems, and needs a drastic revaluation. This suggestion will be considered through a study of traditional attitudes (in Part One) and by a consideration of principles of obligation and value (in Part Two).

Believing, as I do, that matters of morality admit of truth, I am reluctant to conclude that we can devise or invent a new ethic; and, even if we could invent one, I do not see how it could establish its credibility unless it were not a new departure but an extension, analogical or otherwise, of existing patterns of moral thought. The case for a new ethic should rather consist in exhibiting principles which have not always been recognized but which are nevertheless implicit in our moral traditions, or, perhaps, in morality itself, and which it is important now to acknowledge. If the necessary principles are found to hold a place within our traditions already, then what is required is not so much a replacement of moral traditions (if that were possible), or even their supplementation with new principles, as the more promising endeavour of developing in a more consistent manner themes to which at least lip-service has long been paid.

Despotism, Stewardship and ethical innovation

In the only extended philosophical treatment of ecological problems yet to appear, *Man's Responsibility for Nature,*[6] John Passmore examines Western moral traditions and historical attitudes to nature, and in the course of his subsequent survey of the problems of pollution, resources, population growth and preservation defends the view that no new ethic is needed to cope with the problems, so long as the traditional belief that man has dominion over nature and that people may manipulate their natural environment in their own interests is interpreted in a suitably humble way. What needs to be rejected is the attitude and tradition of Despotism, an interpretation of the Biblical belief in man's dominion according to which everything is made for man, nothing else is of any intrinsic value or moral importance, and people may treat nature in any way that they like without inhibition. Instead we should accept that natural processes are not devised or guaranteed to serve humanity, and that manipulating them requires skill and care. Science, technology and cost/benefit analysis should not be abandoned, but we should not be indifferent to animal suffering, and should bear in mind the consequences of our actions upon our immediate descendants to the limited extent to which Passmore believes they can be foreseen. In the Western tradition of Stewardship Passmore finds a belated interpretation of belief in man's dominion which supplies the seeds of such a chastened position: and because there are such 'seeds' within traditional morality, there is no need to turn to mystical or irrationalist metaphysics or ethics to solve ecological problems.

Passmore's position has been shrewdly criticized by Val Routley,[7] who holds that his triumph over any form of new ethic is too easily won. In part this is because the only alternative ethical positions which he entertains either treat nature as sacred or at least recognize rights throughout the animal and vegetable kingdoms; he neglects to consider the view that there are obligations or responsibilities *concerning* natural objects or people in the distant future, which would not always be obligations owed to them as individuals or involve the recognition that they have *rights*. In part his triumph is too easy because the Stewardship tradition is incompatible with belief in man's dominion if, as Routley believes, that belief holds that nature may be manipulated entirely in the human interest; for this tradition involves obligations to care for the plants and animals of the earth, obligations not deriving from human interests. If there are such obligations, then consistency requires a considerable overhaul of the belief in man's dominion. But the basic unsoundness in Passmore's case lies in his tendency not to count as real any problem which is not a problem for human interests; if so, it is unsurprising that the man-centred ethic which he favours is found to be adequate to their solution. For if nothing could count as a problem which would require a revision of traditional morality for its solution, the discovery that problems recognized as such on this basis can all be solved within the Western moral tradition is an unsurprising hollow victory.

The nature and extent of responsibilities with regard to future people and nonhuman creatures are discussed in later chapters. For the time being it suffices to say that the mere possibility that there are such responsibilities discloses a weakness in Passmore's case. (In chapters 6—9 I shall argue for more extensive obligations than Passmore recognizes, but ones in keeping with the Stewardship tradition.) As to Routley's point about the inconsistency between this tradition and the belief in man's dominion, she is right if her characterization of that belief is granted. But this kind of construal is, as I shall contend in chapters 2—4, a misinterpretation of belief in man's dominion. To some extent, as I argue there, Passmore misinterprets that belief, particularly by underestimating the antiquity and pervasiveness of the Stewardship tradition over the centuries; but when Routley writes as if the Stewardship tradition is out of keeping with belief in man's dominion it is she who misinterprets this belief. If so, then there may be little need for radical departures from the older principles of our moral traditions. Routley's point about the need for an overhaul for the sake of consistency still stands, however (granted the parallel existence of the Despotism tradition). And, as I shall contend, so does the need to reject the wholly man-centred ethic at which she protests, and which she believes to be the dominant assumption of Western moral traditions.

In subsequent writings Passmore has been much more ready to propose revisions of moral (and, to some extent, metaphysical) principles,[8] though in the Preface to the second edition of *Man's Responsibility*[9] he concedes only that these writings are 'more philosophically explicit'. Some of the issues which arise in these more recent papers are discussed in chapters 3 and 4 below. But it is worth observing at this stage how he now understands both the problems and the principles more broadly.[10] Thus he now thinks that pollution can affect nonhuman species in a way that makes it difficult to invoke existing moral principles to condemn the pollutor; that a stronger emphasis than traditional principles seem to permit on obligations to future people is necessary if resources are to be preserved; and that our attitudes to nature and the environment form a major obstacle to the solution of problems such as the preservation of species.

This recent combination of views could, of course, be cited as evidence for Routley's view that theories of what the problems are and of how to solve them are prone to fit together with a noncontingent closeness. Fortunately, however, this need not always be so. For one thing, people can intuitively sense that something is amiss and that there is a problem, without having any clear grasp of the principles which may have been violated and may need to be reaffirmed, and even on reflection they may be in genuine doubt about which these are. A good example is the problem of endangered species, which is certainly a problem in terms of human interests (losses to medical and agricultural research; foreclosure of a source of aesthetic pleasure and of scientific curiosity), but which seems more of a problem than these grounds alone would warrant.[11]

There can also be a gap between value-theory and moral

principles. Thus it may be agreed that something is an evil (e.g. skin-cancer, whoever the sufferer may be), but not agreed what obligations we may have in its regard (e.g. an obligation to prevent its occurrence in future people unknown to ourselves, as long as it is probable that our acts or omissions in the present will make a significant difference in the matter). So we do not in all cases need to await agreement on principles (much less on social solutions in which they are applied) before particular problems can be recognized as such. Further instances in the area of ecology are the problems of pollution and resource-depletion.

As to Routley's 'hollow victory' criticism, the question of whether Passmore's book falls foul of it need not be settled here. In his second edition he rejects the view that, if Naess' classification of ecological philosophies is adopted, he is a 'shallow ecophilosopher', on the grounds that he has been concerned all along with developing countries as well as developed ones, and also with the destruction of animal species and of wilderness. This being so, he may perhaps be deemed to have changed more over principles and ethical solutions than over the profundity of the problems. At the same time it should be added that he also rejects the attribution of ecological 'depth' to his later writings if depth implies an acceptance of primitivism or mysticism, or the rejection 'of any preference for human interests over the interests of other species';[12] to avoid such attributions he is glad to call himself 'shallow'. Yet his principles have clearly become deeper with time.

What is much more important is the fact that there is considerable scope for reasoning and for persuasion about both problems and principles, even if perceptions of each are often informed by perceptions of the other. Reasoning can be conducted on the basis of acknowledged moral judgements and principles about comparable topics which allow analogies (and disanalogies) to be drawn, or by drawing out the implications of the acceptance of either principles as binding or of problems as problematic. There is also at least the possibility that examining the historical roots of our attitudes to nature and of our problems will allow better-founded judgements to be reached, whether by eliciting the resources of our traditions, by exposing ancient errors which remain influential, or by broadening the perspective within which the issues are tackled.

In any case it is high time for a re-examination of these issues. Like Passmore I begin with a study of Western traditions, partly to set the record straight, and partly to develop an account of the Stewardship tradition, which I find a deeper-rooted seed, and, like some metaphysical variants within Western traditions, more profound and more fruitful than Passmore does. Next I survey some more recent roots of contemporary attitudes to nature held in both Western and Eastern Europe which seem to explain those attitudes much better than Genesis does. Thereafter, instead of using Passmore's method of arguing from the problems to the principles which account for their being problematic and need to be invoked to solve them, I investigate directly what principles can consistently and most defensibly be held over our responsibilities with respect to future generations and nonhuman creatures, and what their bearing is on current ecological problems.

But before investigating either traditions or principles of value or of obligation, I shall now turn to the task of setting the more widely acknowledged problems in their historical context by examining their causes. Despite the difficulties about conflicts of value, there is in fact widespread agreement that pollution, the depletion of resources, population growth and the destruction of wild species and their habitats constitute problems: medium-term human interests suffice to make them such. Moreover the fact that they are problems for long went unrecognized. Taken together, these circumstances suggest the importance of understanding the causes of the problems and the factors which perpetuate them. Granted the conflicts of values which exist over the problems, it should not be assumed that unearthing their causes is a simple empirical matter, any more than discovering their solutions is; but it should not be assumed either that these endeavours are radically flawed by these disputes, as if they were in principle irresolvable.

In a book about environmental ethics it is worthwhile to make an attempt to locate the causes of our ecological problems. If we can arrive at even a tentative grasp of the causes, in the sense of the factors but for which the problems would not have reached their current state, we shall understand them better, and we may even be able to discover how, by reducing or reversing some of the contributing factors, the problems may be resolved or at least alleviated. There is a danger here of assuming that all the problems have one and the same cause, and a counterpart danger of rejecting as a cause any factor which fails to explain everything. There may well be no single cause for the various problems, but it is still worth looking into the theories which purport to disclose one. There is also the danger that the disclosure of material or efficient causes may obscure the importance of explanations which turn on beliefs and attitudes: material and efficient factors may take effect only where people have mostly failed to see the problems as problems, or have held questionable attitudes and beliefs such as the attitude of Despotism or the belief in the inevitable and providential character of material progress. But a study of the causes of ecological problems can serve to bring out the need to scrutinize just such underlying attitudes, and this is what I believe that it does do in fact.

In the rest of this chapter, therefore, I shall consider the theories that the network of our interrelated ecological problems is caused by population increases, by affluence, by technology, by capitalism and by economic growth. An adequate treatment of these themes would involve a good deal more natural science and social science than I am qualified to deploy, and indeed more than is suited to a study in the fields, mainly, of moral philosophy and the history of ideas. But philosophy is a great deal more susceptible of application to contemporary public issues than used to appear in the heyday of linguistic analysis, as journals such as *Ethics* and *Philosophy and Public Affairs* bear witness; and when it is so applied it needs to draw upon the methods and the understandings of other disciplines. Indeed it is clearly necessary to do so in the course of the present attempt to throw light on the theories and the principles by which problems may be understood and tackled. What follows is obviously open to revision by specialists in the various disciplines concerned; yet if that were enough to deter nonspecialists, no interdisciplinary enquiry could ever begin. But on the issue of the causes of ecological problems just such an enquiry is needed.

The population theory. On this theory the various ecological problems (other than the increase in human population itself) are brought about by the striking upturn in human numbers, or at least would not exist as we know them but for this upturn. World population has been held (prematurely, as it turns out) to be doubling every 35 years,[13] and so, correspondingly, would be the waste products of human economic activity and of humans themselves, and the food, energy and mineral resources which they consume. The increase in pollution and the retreat of wilderness coincide with the increase in population, as does the erosion of overworked tillage and overgrazed pasturage, and the depletion of fossil fuels and minerals. In general, it is held, the nonhuman environment cannot sustain, or be expected to continue to sustain, the increasing rates of population growth; and the problems cannot be resolved unless not only the rate of growth ceases to grow but also population growth itself ceases altogether. Indeed, for preference, there should be some reduction. Each extra person takes an extra toll on the earth's resources, and that is why the burden on those resources has become excessive.

It is difficult to hold that there is *nothing* of merit in this theory. There must, after all, be some level of human population beyond which further increases cannot be sustained by the natural environment: the earth and its several regions have a finite carrying capacity. But the theory too readily assumes that each human being and each human community contribute to the deterioration of the environment. In fact, many communities in many parts of the world have preserved the fertility of the land which they live off over long periods, often enhancing it by techniques such as drainage and terracing; and their own waste products, rather than poisoning the land, have re-entered its natural cycles. Such a harmonious relation to the land could indeed be upset by the pressure of numbers, but this has not happened yet on a global scale (though it could happen if present rates of increase were to persist for long enough). Even the Sahelian region of sub-Saharan Africa, the natural balance of which was upset during the droughts of the 1970s, has reached its present state through colonial policies and a sharp increase in the number of cattle rather than of humans.

Meanwhile the most aesthetically offensive of our ecological problems, pollution, is principally located in the western world, where population growth has been much less striking than it has in the Third World; and the same applies to the depletion of fossil fuels and minerals, at least insofar as their extraction largely reflects the economic activity of the companies and governments of the wealthier countries. Population growth in these countries certainly magnifies the effects of these activities, but, as Barry Commoner has pointed out, pollution and the exhaustion of mineral resources would still take place without it.[14] Thus, though population growth is not irrelevant to their explanation, ecological problems are not greatest where it is most noticeable, and vary with factors quite independent of it.

More will be said (in chapter 7) about the intrinsic value of human lives. But enough has been said already to cast doubt on the belief that each human is an ecological liability, and on theories that bad ecological effects are bound to accrue wherever it is held that extra human lives are welcome. I have not denied that the eventual stabilization of the human population is a necessity if global famine and global war are to be averted, or if our ecological problems are to be resolved. But I do maintain that the theory which sets these problems down to population growth is to be rejected as unduly shallow. To put matters technically, population growth is part of a sufficient condition for some such problems but it is not their necessary condition. At the same time we should reject some of the assumptions about the supposed negative value of people which derive their plausibility solely from the population theory. Pernicious as their activities sometimes are, people are not a cancer.

The affluence theory. This theory does at least concern one of the blatant features of those societies whose activities do seem to underlie most pollution, most of the extraction of minerals and a large amount of the destruction of wildlife and wilderness. It notes that the startling increase in levels of pollution in the post-1945 period has coincided with a marked increase in gross national product per head in Western societies, and in particular in the United States, and concludes that the single most significant factor promoting ecological stress is an increase in individual affluence and consumption.[15] Increased rates of consumer demand and consumer wastefulness would then lead, via increased consumption of fuel and the discarding of products which cannot be re-used, to environmental deterioration. The theory is graphically illustrated by calculations of the large number of slaves which would be equivalent to the power of the gadgetry possessed by the average American.

The affluence theory does not, of course, pretend to explain population growth. Indeed there is evidence from societies such as Japan of a marked fall in the birth-rate coincident with the increase in that society's affluence and the social provisions and sense of security which it has facilitated. There is, moreover, good reason to believe that rapid population growth is actually caused not by affluence but by poverty, lack of development, high rates of infant mortality, and the accompanying sense of insecurity.[16] If so, provision of the basic necessities for development and self-help may well be the best (or indeed the only) way to arrest rapid population increases in poor countries.

But this possible solution of the population problem in no way implies that affluence needs to be spread worldwide. Indeed such a development would probably bring ecological catastrophe long before it was complete. For, though affluence does not explain the population problem, it would appear to exacerbate most of the other developments of ecological concern. In that case those who accept that current Western consumption of fuel and minerals and current Western production of synthetic and non-biodegradable 'goods' is excessive and ecologically burdensome would have reason to aim, like Patrick Rivers,[17] at a simpler style of life: and the spread of such a symbolic life-style could have some impact on the mode of production and consumption in the society where they were adopted.

Commoner, however, rejects the affluence theory. He points out that in the same post-war period as that in which pollution has increased so markedly there has been no matching increase in the average consumption in the United States of shoes, clothing or housing, and that there was actually a slight decrease in the average consumption of carbohydrate and protein. He grants that individuals have had to spend more on these items, but maintains that '*per capita* production of goods to meet major human needs' has 'not increased significantly between 1946 and 1968' and has 'even declined in some respects'.[18] Average consumption of household amenities and leisure items, he admits, has indeed increased, as has domestic fuel consumption, but not enough to account for the increase in levels of pollution. This increase is rather to be explained by the use of the new production technologies.[19]

This rejection of the affluence theory leaves lingering doubts. Thus the increased use of cars and of labour saving devices is undeniably a mark of affluence and has quite certainly had an environmental impact. Again, it might be supposed that consumers who purchase the products of advanced technology have some responsibility for its persistence and growth, just as consumers of the products of factory-farms have some responsibility for their perpetuation. Here Commoner would reply that they have little choice, at least over most food, clothing and shelter, and that their connivance cannot be the single most important factor in environmental deterioration. And with this way of articulating a rejection of the affluence theory I should largely agree. Far more important factors are to be found in the new technology, the associated economic forces, and the readiness of those concerned to ignore any costs which do not figure in the balance-sheet of one's own enterprise. If, however, the connivance of consumers makes any difference at all, as surely it does, then consumer revolts and efforts at simpler and less wasteful patterns of life will not be altogether futile.

The technology theory. As Commoner points out,[20] neither the increase in the population of the United States nor the per capita increase in production, nor even their product, suffices to account for the intensification of pollution. He would not deny that if this product were to persist at current rates for any considerable period the environmental effects would be serious, but its impact would largely be due, in his view, to the newer methods of production, involving, for example, detergents, aluminium, plastic and inorganic fertilizers in place of soap powder, wood, steel and manure. Similarly, disposable packaging has replaced returnable bottles, petrol contains more lead, and chlorine production — important in the synthesis of organic chemicals — has involved an enormous increase in the consumption of mercury. Thus the new technology, which has many times the environmental impact of the old, is the crucial missing factor accounting for the difference between the percentage increase in production and the much greater percentage increase in pollution.

To theories such as Commoner's, Sir Fred Catherwood[21] replies that modern technology has sometimes brought environmental benefits. Aluminium, he claims, is less wasteful than steel because of its longer life and its suitability for reuse; and modern methods of sewage treatment and water purification have also brought obvious gains. In general, he adds, modern technology has greatly increased the resources available to mankind and raised the standard of living of the common man. But the benefits of technology are not the present issue. Commoner's claim is that for many cases its costs are intolerable; and over many of the instances which he cites the claim cannot be gainsaid.

The technology theory is not primarily intended to explain such problems as the global increase in population (though even to this the technology of disease control must have made a key contribution), but it does, in Commoner's exposition, explain the recent poisoning of land, air and water, the elimination of much wildlife (through pesticides) and the depletion of many of the earth's mineral resources. It does not, however, explain the considerable ecological damage resulting from human activity prior to 1945,[22] nor does it explain why at this particular time and place these particular processes were adopted. If, however, these developments cannot themselves be explained, efforts to reverse them may well miscarry. We need to know, if possible, the causes of the pollutant processes, or they may survive attempts to make them harmless, or even take on a more serious character, as a result of the very same hidden forces which launched them in the first place. So, until we have explained the rise of the new technology, we have done little more than move the explanatory problem one stage along without solving it.

Nevertheless Commoner's theory is important. It allows us to focus more clearly on the immediate explanation of some of our more recent ecological problems; and it suggests thereby which societies may need to change, and which methods of production should be spurned by consumers and planners who believe that current ways of life are doing unjustified harm either to the present generation of humans, or to other species, or to people of future generations.

The capitalism theory. In large measure the new technology was introduced because it was more profitable: synthetic fibres and detergents gave better returns on capital than cotton or soap powder. Similarly, the best (or only) way for farmers in the West to make profits from arable land has been the heavy and unabating use of fertilizers and pesticides, despite the effect of the run-off on human health and the way in which non-biodegradable substances accumulate as they pass through natural food-chains.

The theory to be considered, then, is that capitalism requires as a condition of both prosperity and survival the employment of the most profitable technology available, and that firms competing on the open market cannot afford to forego the extra profits which high technology offers. Those which fail to maximize profits will, it might be held, be out-manoeuvred by competitors who have no inhibitions. Only if profits are made and maximized will there be sufficient capital to renew or replace old equipment, and thereby to maximize future profits, as firms must do on pain of falling behind or perishing. Thus capitalism is the cause of increased pollution and the depletion of minerals, as these phenomena are often the unintended by-products of the business methods required by the capitalist system.

It is also widely held that capitalism is dependent upon economic growth, and radically incompatible with the kind of steady-state, no-growth society which people concerned about ecological problems often advocate, at least as an eventual desideratum. Capitalism seems, as Commoner remarks,[23] to depend on the accumulation of capital, and there would probably be little such accumulation in a steady-state economy. Again, capitalism seems because of its very nature to involve a search for new means of making profit, and if such means were precluded by the rules of a steady-state society, it might well atrophy and wither, or, more plausibly, resist to the death the inauguration of such a dispensation. This close dependence of capitalism upon economic growth is, however, disputed, and it is possible to imagine a centrally organized but mixed economy with strict regulations governing reinvestment and also, to prevent disregard of effects on the environment, governing productive techniques. It is even possible to imagine multinational corporations being subjected to similar rules as a result of international agreements. The scenario is very far removed from that of contemporary big business, yet it remains a possibility, however slender.

For present purposes, however, I must leave on one side the extent and nature of the modifications which would be necessary for a society where growth was restricted. The present question is rather whether capitalism as it has been found hitherto has caused pollution and other ecological problems. And part of the answer is that other economic systems have permitted pollution too, including that of the USSR.[24] Hence the overthrow of capitalism would not be guaranteed to resolve our ecological problems: capitalism is not their necessary condition. On the other hand the orientation of capitalism towards the most profitable form of production, however destructive of natural life or natural resources and however costly on any account other than that of company profits and shareholders' dividends, suggests that very considerable modifications to the capitalist system would be required before ecological problems could be overcome. Something similar, no doubt, holds good for centrally controlled economies in which private enterprise has been abolished: economic policy, at any rate, would need a thorough overhaul there too, if natural resources are to be conserved, if wilderness and wildlife are to be left intact, and if the land, the air and the waters are not to be poisoned.

The growth theory. The theories based on population, affluence and capitalism do not seem to explain the problems before us, while the technology theory explains a subset of them, only to pose much the same explanatory problem again at one remove. Indeed ecological problems seem to pervade both Western capitalist societies and Eastern European communist ones; both kinds of society are inclined to seek short-term or medium-term benefits, whether for the whole community or, more often, for circumscribed groups within it, at the cost of considerable damage to the natural environment, to nonhuman species and to their own descendants.

These considerations suggest the need for a broader theory of the cause of our ecological problems. A candidate is the theory that they result from exponential or geometrical growth, growth in particular with respect to five crucial factors — population, food production, industrialization, pollution and consumption of non-renewable resources — and from the interplay of these five kinds of growth. This is the thesis of *The Limits to Growth*,[25] the authors of which hold that the limits to the growth of these factors will automatically be reached within the next hundred years, unless the people of the world alter the current trends and 'establish a condition of ecological and economic stability that is sustainable far into the future'.[26] This comprehensive theory clearly incorporates many of the partial causes so far considered, and supplements them by its greater emphasis on *economic growth*.

Neither population increases nor capitalism explain the problem alone, for the problems sometimes arise independently of them; and neither affluence nor modern technology explain them sufficiently, but seem rather to be symptoms of something more general. Economic growth, however, explains the impact upon nature of the affluent capitalist West and also of the rapidly industrializing communist countries, and together with the growth in human numbers does make global problems such as the current ones all too predictable.[27]

Now it may be granted to this theory that industrialization, pollution and consumption of non-renewable resources are growing exponentially, and that even if food production is not doing so, it is, like population, with which it is keeping pace, still growing steadily. Whether the continuation of current trends would produce the forms of global catastrophe predicted to take place before the end of the next century is disputed,[28] but there is no need to enter into that controversy here. For the case can scarcely be disputed that the continuation of exponential economic growth, allied to a continuation of steady population growth, must prove catastrophic; and from this it follows that economic growth must cease to be exponential, and that preferably the rate of population growth must diminish even more than it has in the 1970s.

It does not follow, however, that either population growth or economic growth is bad, or that the solution to our problems consists in the complete abandonment of both. Nor is it clear that economic growth, any more than population growth (or even in combination with it), constitutes a complete explanation of our problems, without any account being taken of the attitudes or the beliefs which perpetuate it.

Thus Mesarovic and Pestel resist the view that all growth is of an undifferentiated type, and in their Second Report to the Club of Rome[29] urge the need for 'organic' or differentiated growth, the world being viewed as a system of diverse interacting regions, which need to co-operate globally, with growth in some regions and the abandonment of growth in others, if regional (but potentially global) catastrophes are to be avoided. A pattern of economic activity sustainable far into the future is certainly part of their goal, but it is not clear that this need be a pattern of no overall growth whatever. On this view, then, not all growth is bad, though the continuation of exponential growth certainly is. This conclusion is further supported by Thomas Derr,[30] who points out that in economic growth lies the only realistic hope for the poor that global injustices will be remedied.

Just as not all economic growth is bad, so too an explanation of our problems which stops short at economic growth is incomplete and partial. What attitudes give rise to the goal of perpetual growth and perpetuate it as a goal? Unlike the present-day societies of the Western and communist worlds, more traditional societies have often lacked such attitudes. Perhaps, then, a part of the explanation is to be found in the deep-rooted attitudes common to both socialist societies and the West. In the next four chapters I consider theories which claim to find the explanation in their common religious, moral and metaphysical traditions.

NOTES

1   John Passmore, *Man's Responsibility for Nature,* London: Duckworth, 1974 (hereinafter *MRN*), p. 43.
2   *MRN*, pp. 43—5.
3   Arne Naess, 'The Shallow and the Deep, Long-range Ecology Movement. A Summary', *Inquiry,* 16, 1973, 95—100.
4   Aldo Leopold, *A Sand County Almanac and Sketches Here and There*, New York: Oxford University Press, 1949, pp. 203f. The call for such a new ethic has been echoed in Richard Routley, 'Is There a Need for a New, an Environmental Ethic?', *Proceedings of the XVth World Congress of Philosophy,* Varna, 1973, 205—10.
5   Leopold, *A Sand County Almanac*, pp. 224f.
6   See n. 1. A second edition, with a new Preface and Appendix, appeared in 1980.
7   Val Routley, Critical Notice of John Passmore, *Man's Responsibility for Nature, Australasian Journal of Philosophy,* 53, 1975, 171—85.
8   See his 'Attitudes to Nature', in Royal Institute of Philosophy (ed.), *Nature and Conduct,* London and Basingstoke: Macmillan Press, 1975, 251—64; 'The Treatment of Animals', *Journal of the History of*

Ideas, 36, 1975, 195—218; 'Ecological Problems and Persuasion', in Gray Dorsey (ed.), *Equality and Freedom,* Vol. II, New York: Oceana Publications and Leiden: A. W. Sijthoff, 1977, 431—42. The claim that Passmore's metaphysic is revised in 'Attitudes to Nature' is argued in R. and V. Routley, 'Nuclear Energy and Obligations to the Future', *Inquiry,* 21, 1978, 133—79, at n. 12, pp. 175f.

9   *MRN,* 2nd edn, pp. viiif.

10   'Ecological Problems and Persuasion', at pp. 438—41.

11   For a discussion of this issue yielding slightly different conclusions from my own, see Alastair S. Gunn, 'Why Should We Care about Rare Species?', *Environmental Ethics,* 2, 1980, 17—37. See also chapter 8 (below).

12   *MRN,* 2nd edn, p. ix.

13   See Paul R. Ehrlich and Anne H. Ehrlich, *Population, Resources, Environment, Issues in Human Ecology,* San Francisco: W. H. Freeman, (2nd edn) 1972, chapter 2. The structure and overall outlook of this book reflect the theory here depicted (though Paul Ehrlich's more recent work suggests a change of emphasis). Cf. John Breslaw, 'Economics and Ecosystems', in John Barr (ed.), *The Environmental Handbook,* London: Ballantine/Friends of the Earth, 1971, 83—93, p. 92: 'The essential cause of environmental pollution is over-population, combined with an excessive population growth rate'. The current paragraph also reflects broadly the published views of Garrett Hardin and to some extent those of Kenneth Boulding. For a criticism of their prescriptions, see Richard Neuhaus, *In Defense of People, Ecology and the Seduction of Radicalism,* New York: Macmillan and London: Collier-Macmillan, 1971.

14   See further Barry Commoner, *The Closing Circle,* London: Jonathan Cape, 1972, pp. 125—39. For Hardin's view on the Sahel, see Garrett Hardin and John Baden (eds), *Managing the Commons,* San Francisco: W. H. Freeman, 1977, 112—24.

15   This theory is presented and criticized by Commoner in *The Closing Circle,* pp. 136—9.

16   Cf. Susan George, *How the Other Half Dies,* Harmondsworth: Penguin Books, 1976, chapter 2; Peter Donaldson, *Worlds Apart,* London: BBC, 1971, pp. 46—52; Judith Hart, *Aid and Liberation,* London: Gollancz, 1973, *passim.*

17   Patrick Rivers, *Living Better on Less,* London: Turnstone Books, 1977.

18   Commoner, *The Closing Circle,* p. 139.

19   See ibid. p. 144 and generally pp. 140—77.

20   Ibid. p. 140.

21   Sir Frederick Catherwood, *A Better Way, The Case for a Christian Social Order,* Leicester: Inter-Varsity Press, 1975, pp. 104—11.

22   Yet the pre-1945 problems were sufficient to give rise to the first conservationist movement in America. See Pete A. Y. Gunter, 'The Big Thicket: A Case Study in Attitudes toward Environment', in

William T. Blackstone (ed.), *Philosophy and Environmental Crisis,* Athens: University of Georgia Press, 1974, 117–37, p. 124. More strikingly, the theory does not explain the blight caused by the original industrial revolution, or the deforestation of much of the Scottish Highlands in the nineteenth century.

23 Commoner, *The Closing Circle,* p. 274.

24 See ibid. pp. 277–81. For an interesting discussion of the prospects for the limitation of growth in capitalist and communist societies, see chapter 3 of Robert L. Heilbroner, *An Inquiry into the Human Prospect,* London: Calder & Boyars, 1975.

25 Donella H. Meadows *et al., The Limits to Growth,* a report for the Club of Rome's Project on the Predicament of Mankind (1972), London and Sydney: Pan Books, 1974.

26 Ibid. p. 24.

27 See further Edward J. Mishan, *The Costs of Economic Growth,* Harmondsworth: Penguin Books, 1969.

28 See H. Cole *et al., Thinking About the Future: A Critique of The Limits to Growth,* London: Chatto & Windus and Sussex University Press, 1973. The rate of growth of the world population seems to have been decreasing throughout the 1970s: see editorial, *New Internationalist,* 79, September 1979.

29 Mihajlo D. Mesarovic and Eduard Pestel, *Mankind at the Turning Point,* London: Hutchinson, 1975; see pp. 1–5, 55.

30 Thomas Sieger Derr, *Ecology and Human Liberation,* Geneva: WSCF Books, 1973, pp. 89f.

2

Man's Dominion and the Judaeo-Christian Heritage

In this chapter I shall consider the theory that the source of our ecological problems is to be found in the Judaeo-Christian belief that mankind was created to have dominion over nature, a belief which, according to the theory, can be interpreted as implying that humans may treat their natural environment as they like. This theory has to confront the objection that ideas cannot have such a causal efficacy, and also seems to imply that the attitude to nature of the medieval West was improperly exploitative: having considered these difficulties, the second of which I claim to have substance, I proceed to consider whether the theory correctly interprets the Biblical belief in man's dominion, or whether the Old and New Testaments embody, on the contrary, the makings of a much gentler and more enlightened attitude to nature. In the next chapter I consider the evidence for these various attitudes from subsequent Christian history, and in the following chapter I survey the significance for these matters of Judaeo-Christian beliefs about the nature of man. These chapters prepare the way for the presentation of a moral theory in later chapters, as well as throwing light on the resources of Western traditions for coping with ecological problems, which I claim to be much ampler than is usually supposed.

Religion as the source of the problems

What Lynn White calls 'the historical roots of our ecological crisis' are held by him (in an essay with the phrase just quoted as title[1]) to be located in the Judaic and Christian doctrine of creation. More specifically they lie in the belief that man was made in God's image and shares in God's transcendence of nature, and that the whole natural order was created for the sake of humanity. In the more recent past the roots of the crisis may be detected in the alliance of science and technology, only finally cemented in the nineteenth century; but the beliefs implicit in Genesis, or rather in the activist, Western interpretation of Genesis, underlie those distinctive products of the West, science and technology.

Well before the rise of modern science in the sixteenth and seventeenth centuries the medieval West was technologically far ahead of the other cultures of the day, uninhibitedly harnessing natural forces for human ends: moreover this characteristically Western phenomenon was no accident, but embodied the very beliefs newly accepted when paganism was overcome by Christianity. In place of the respect for the guardian spirits of groves, streams and hills afforded by pagan animism, 'Christianity made it possible to exploit nature in a mood of indifference to the feelings of natural objects'. Indeed 'the spirits *in* natural objects, which formerly had protected nature from man, evaporated . . . and the old inhibitions to the exploitation of nature crumbled'.[2] Such being their roots, science and technology are unfit to solve our current problems; rather the remedy must lie in religion, and we should either replace Christianity, the root cause of the problems, with a new religion such as Zen Buddhism, or, failing that, modify it by adopting the pan-psychism of St Francis, according to which all creatures, whether animate or inanimate, have souls and are designed for the glorification of their Creator.

White's paper has, as Passmore observes, exercised widespread influence,[3] partly because of the delayed but increasing impact of Aldo Leopold's call for a new ethic, an ethic still, in his view, lacking in the West, governing man's relation to the land and the whole biotic community associated with it.[4] In particular, White's view that technology, the immediate cause of some of our ecological problems, cannot be expected to solve them alone, commands wide agreement, but there is less agreement about the nature and extent of the other social and moral changes required. More specifically his theory about the religious source of our problems and the corresponding need for a religious remedy has been challenged, not only over his theological interpretations, but also over his historical method.

One possible objection in the area of historical method is that it is fallacious to locate the causes of a phenomenon in its origins, for attitudes, like institutions, may be perpetuated for reasons quite other than those which originated them. Thus it would be a fallacy to represent as the cause of our largely post-1945 ecological problems such ancient Hebrew beliefs as may have originated the Western attitude to nature. This objection, however, has no force, for White can document the persistence of similar beliefs (how similar remains to be seen) among patristic and medieval writers and among more recent scientists, and a concomitant activist attitude to the natural environment. It is certainly odd that the same attitude also pervades a post-Christian age, and also societies such as that of Japan which have never been significantly Christian: but this could be because in the former case there has been no motive for a change of belief about the superiority and the dominance of man, and because in the latter case such was the prestige of Western technology that beliefs such as these could be imported with little or no resistance. White is thus immune from the fallacy of origins.

A more serious charge, however, concerns the extent of his reliance on ideas to explain social phenomena. 'It is difficult,' writes F. B. Welbourn,[5] 'to give so much primacy to the causal efficacy of ideas.' Welbourn's own view is that the function of ideas in history is to legitimize actions and institutions which are to be explained by more material considerations: thus new-found technological power may have been justified after the event by 'suitably selected and interpreted ideas'.[6] Now, it should certainly be granted that religious ideas are often pressed into service as justifications of social and technological developments. Nevertheless I should wish, with White, to question whether either modern science or modern technology can be explained solely by the structure of society or by economic forces and without reference to belief in an orderly creation and in the propriety of using and moulding it for human benefit.

The connection between science and the doctrine of creation is a close one, as I have argued elsewhere:[7] belief in creation implies the possibility of natural science and belief in man's dominion implies that its pursuit is, for some at least, a humanitarian duty. These implications of central Christian doctrines were, admittedly, neglected (but not universally disregarded) for many centuries, but the connection was explicitly argued in the early seventeenth century by Francis Bacon, and later that century the central features of his method were adopted by the Royal Society. Two hundred years later, and against the background of the same beliefs, science began to be applied systematically to technology and medicine, and the Baconian programme began to be fully realised (but without some of the safeguards which Bacon would have favoured); and, although belief in Christianity has waned, belief in the propriety of harnessing natural forces for human benefit has not.

There is also the problem of explaining, on Welbourn's view, why the growth of technology has been so specifically a Western phenomenon, if characteristic Western beliefs and attitudes are not to be invoked. Science and technology elsewhere, as Stanley L. Jaki and White himself have shown, either failed to develop despite promising beginnings, or were directed to devotional and spiritual purposes.[8] Thus, short of some other explanation of the distinctive progress of technology in the West, ideas may play an indispensable role in the explanation of this (and other) social and historical developments, even if they seldom constitute sufficient conditions alone. Accordingly White's theory is not to be rejected on grounds of historical method or of historical materialism: indeed the invocation of traditional ethical and religious attitudes may do much to illuminate ecological problems and the principles required for their solution.

Nevertheless reservations need to be expressed about those passages in which White elicits from his discoveries about medieval technology the attitudes to nature which they bespeak. Remarking on the invention of the eight-oxen plough in Northern Europe in the seventh century and the changes which it brought to agricultural practice, he claims that a crucial change in man's relation and attitude to the soil took place therewith; 'once man had been part of nature; now he became her exploiter'.[9] A similar tone pervades his remarks on the Carolingian calendars of shortly before AD 830, wherein 'passive personifications' of the months were replaced by scenes of 'ploughing, harvesting, wood-chopping, people knocking down acorns for pigs, pig-slaughtering'. Of this change White observes: 'They show a coercive attitude to natural resources . . . Man and nature are now two things, and man is master.'[10]

These comments betray an exaggerated view of the moral and metaphysical significance of new ploughs and new calendars. It is beyond my present scope to question White's conclusions about the social changes which accompanied the introduction of the new plough.[11] But if his comments on their significance are taken seriously it should be inferred that until around AD 800 people in the West regarded themselves as no different from the rest of nature, despite the conflicting account of their Christian beliefs presented by White himself,[12] and that thereafter a grasping, coercive and improper attitude prevailed towards natural organisms, minerals and wilderness. The passages in White's book in which this interpretation is put forward are isolated and untypical ones, and the facts which White presents simply will not bear such an interpretation. Moreover, if an exploitative attitude to nature is fully embodied in heavy ploughing, wood-chopping and acorn gathering, just as much as in the heedless pollution of rivers by mercury compounds and of the atmosphere by strontium 90, it must be asked whether White is concerned about the same attitude to nature as, for example, Barry Commoner, and whether what he is concerned about is really exploitative at all.

White presents no further arguments for the view that these changes embody an improperly exploitative view, yet there seems to be no alternative interpretation of his remarks. (He cannot merely be remarking that man began at that time to exploit nature, in the non-pejorative sense of 'exploit', for on his own account such mere *use* of nature had been current for centuries.) But if the new uses to which nature was put in North-West Europe around AD 800 constitute (improper) exploitation, so, it would seem, must all the other ingenious contrivances of medieval technology which White proceeds to describe with such care and apparent admiration. If so, it is difficult to understand his attitude to his own subject-matter as a historian. The belief that gunpowder might best have been left alone would be understandable, but does White really hold the same about the power of wind and water, the three-field rotation system, and the nutritive powers of broad beans and chickpeas? If not, he may still persuade us that people in North-West Europe in the ninth century were more ready to mould nature for human advantage than those elsewhere, but he cannot persuade us that the changes they made in this direction were for the most part regrettable. Indeed if such developments are what a new religion is required to curtail or prevent, then White seems to have mischaracterized what is needed.

Old Testament attitudes

It is now appropriate to ask whether, as Passmore and Welbourn claim, White has mischaracterized the Old Testament also, and with it at least the roots of the belief which he considers to underly our ecological problems. According to Genesis, God created mankind to have 'dominion over the fish of the sea, and over the fowl of the air, and over the earth and over every creeping thing that creepeth upon the earth',[13] and authorized man to 'Be fruitful and multiply and replenish the earth and subdue it'.[14] White's comment is 'God planned all of this [his creation] explicitly for man's benefit and rule: no item in the physical creation has any purpose save to serve man's purposes.' To what extent will the Old Testament bear this interpretation?

It is generally agreed that on the Old Testament view nature is not sacred. The Creator and his creation are radically distinct, it is idolatrous to worship the latter, and so there is nothing sacrilegious in treating creatures as resources for human benefit. Indeed the passages about man's dominion authorize just that, within certain limits. On the other hand the belief that nature may properly be used by mankind does not, as Passmore points out, justify an irresponsible attitude to nature.[15] At most it removes one possible inhibition to such an attitude: but this inhibition is surely an undesirable one, at least if alternatives can serve instead. For belief in the sacredness of nature makes medical and scientific research not only wrong but actually impious, and this ban would include the science of ecology itself. Against such a view Christian defenders of science such as Boyle have quite properly appealed to the Bible, as Passmore reminds us.[16] The possibility of alternative inhibitions is already implicit in Genesis 1, which authorizes exclusively a vegetarian diet. Only after the Fall and the Flood were human beings authorized to eat flesh,[17] as if the society which transmitted and edited the Genesis narratives was uneasy about meat-eating and sensed that a special justification was needed.

Though the Old Testament eventually allowed flesh to be used for human food, the Laws of Leviticus and Deuteronomy in fact set considerable limits to human dealings with nature, affecting, for example, the treatment of fruit-trees, oxen, mother birds and fallow land.[18] Similarly the Book of Proverbs declares that 'A righteous man regardeth the life of his beast.' Nor, as Welbourn points out, is pagan animism the only form of religion to have imposed restraints on people's treatment of plants and animals; indeed monotheistic religions have a similar capacity, as he ably shows. Thus White's remarks that according to Christianity God intends man to exploit nature 'for his proper ends'[19] and that with the Christian defeat of paganism 'the old inhibitions to the exploitation of nature crumbled'[20] are at best misleading, insofar as Christians have not forgotten the Old Testament. (White cannot be taken as limiting the divine mandate to man's *morally* 'proper ends', as it is supposed to constitute the pernicious root of our ecological problems, rather than merely to authorize behaviour which is morally justified.)

The point can be taken further if White's claim that the Old Testament represents nature as being created solely for man is considered. As soon as this claim is examined, it collapses. In Genesis 1, plants are intended as food for beasts, fowls and reptiles as much as for mankind; and after the Flood all these kinds of creatures are alike instructed to breed and be fruitful. In Job, God is said to send rain for the plants and the uninhabited wilderness (38:25ff), and to have made the wilderness for the wild ass (39:5ff). Still more impressively, Psalm 104 catalogues God's concern for nature and all creatures, among which man figures no more prominently than the birds and the wild beasts. Passmore indeed traces the belief that everything was made for man not to the Old Testament but to Stoic and earlier Greek sources,[21] from which it seems to have been derived by the third century Christian Origen;[22] as we shall see, the influence of Stoicism in this regard did not prevail over that of the Old Testament to anything like the extent which Passmore supposes.

The truth seems to be that the tradition which holds that in God's eyes the nonhuman creation has no value except its instrumental value for mankind has Greek rather than Hebrew sources,[23] and is only one, and not the only (or even, perhaps, the predominant) view of the value of creatures of other kinds to have been held by Christians; not, as White calls it, 'orthodox Christian arrogance'.[24] Indeed even to call it 'Greco-Christian arrogance', as Passmore thinks may be in order,[25] is to go beyond the evidence, as most ancient Greeks and many (perhaps most) Christians have held no such view (see chapter 3). Moreover, since Christians familiar with the Old Testament would assume that in God's eyes various creatures other than humans are of intrinsic value, White must be mistaken in holding that according to Christianity in general man is intended to regard nature as raw material for his own ends alone.

Views such as White's about the supposed Judaeo-Christian origins of belief in the duality of man and nature and in perpetual progress receive some discussion in chapters 4 and 5. Here it remains to consider how far the biblical belief in mankind's dominion is even compatible with the view of man as despot which Passmore regards as the dominant Western tradition, though one only put into practical effect in a thorough-going manner since the time of Bacon and Descartes. For, though he subjects White's theory to considerable qualification, Passmore holds that the Old Testament leaves open the possibility of an attitude of absolute despotism towards nature on the part of mankind: and he believes that this ability has actually occupied the centre of the stage till recently within Christianity.[26] I shall claim in reply that the despotic attitude is a possible interpretation of the Old Testament only by means of selective quotation and disregard for Hebrew thought.

The interpretation of belief in mankind's dominion as involving man as steward or bailiff of creation, charged by God with responsibility for its care, is claimed by Passmore to be largely a recent view, and to have originated (at least among Christians) in the seventeenth century.[27] If he is right, then the predominant Christian belief has been that, except for practices specifically forbidden by God, people are entitled to deal with nature without further limitations and in whatever way they please, like an absolutist prince of the Holy Roman Empire subject only to the largely theoretical constraints of the Emperor.

But the biblical dominion of man is no despotism. If Genesis authorizes mankind to rule nature, it authorizes only the kind of rule compatible with the Hebrew concept of monarchy: and, though the Hebrews were aware of other nations having absolute monarchs, their own kings were never so regarded. Rather they were considered to be answerable to God for the well-being of the realm,[28] and if they failed in their responsibilities, God would send a prophet to anoint another. The attitude ascribed to David at I Chronicles 29:11—14[29] epitomizes that proper to a king; David there attributes all power to God, and acknowledges before God that he and his people cannot even offer up gifts which have not first, like everything else, been bestowed through God's grace. Not surprisingly kings often deviated from the spirit of this humble prayer; but what is at stake is the characteristic Hebrew concept of kingship and dominion, not the practice of all who implicitly accepted the ideals implicit in it. Nor was it only kingship which the Hebrews expected to be exercised responsibly: the same view was taken of the ordinary ownership of property.[30]

John Black derives from Genesis 2:15 a more direct argument for the view that man's dominion was interpreted as the responsible exercise of a circumscribed trust or mandate, and not as despotism. The second or Yahwist account of the creation there relates that 'the Lord God took the man, and put him into the garden to dress it and keep it'.[31] Black interprets 'dress' as meaning to 'till' for both pleasure and profit, and 'keep' as 'protect from harm'. Thus man is put into the world to look after it for God, and, as Black points out, to preserve it as a source of pleasure, and not only as good for food (Genesis 2:9). Passmore[32] considers this authorization to have been superseded by man's expulsion from the garden, which was cursed for his sake; yet the original mandate of dominion, conferred before the Fall, was repeated after it, and the new circumstances then arising can scarcely have been understood to have disburdened humanity of all prior obligations, or to have granted people the privilege of acting as they liked. Living by the sweat of one's brow need not involve the exploitation of nature, as we have seen in connection with heavy ploughing in the seventh century.

Thus, as C. J. Glacken remarks about the belief in man's dominion expressed in Psalm 8, once the background of the Old Testament is understood, the words are much less amenable to being interpreted as arrogant than they may at first glance appear.[33] On the contrary, Glacken, unlike Passmore, is inclined to the conclusion that in the Bible man was 'a steward of God'.[34] In any case the evidence cited above makes it clear that the Old Testament cannot be reconciled with either the anthropocentric view that everything was made for mankind or the despotic view that people are free to treat nature and nonhuman creatures as they please. Moreover for the writers of the New Testament the Old Testament precisely constituted the Scriptures; any Old Testament tenet not explicitly superseded in the new dispensation was for them authoritative. (Admittedly Christians were released in the New Testament from subservience to the details of the Law of Leviticus and Deuteronomy: yet these books themselves continued to be cited as Scriptural.) Thus, short of clear indications to the contrary, the New Testament position will have been identical over the matters under discussion with that of the Old, a position incompatible with the arrogant one ascribed to Christianity by Passmore and others.

New Testament attitudes

In actual fact Jesus, as Passmore grants, stood in the Old Testament tradition when he taught that God cares for sparrows (Matthew 10:29, Luke 12:6). Here, and also when Jesus talked of 'the lilies of the field' (Matthew 7:28–30), the emphasis is on the greater value of people; yet the words chosen about the lilies suggest that God takes delight even in plants, and that their value is an independent one.

Consider the lilies of the field, how they grow; they toil not, neither do they spin: And yet I say unto you, That even Solomon in all his glory was not arrayed like one of these. Wherefore, if God so clothe the grass of the field, which to day is, and to morrow is cast into the oven, shall he not much more clothe you, o ye of little faith?[35]

Earlier (Mark 1:12f), Jesus spent 40 days in the wilderness in the company of wild beasts; and several times he asked his disciples to sail to the other side of the Lake of Galilee to have solitude and escape the multitude (Mark 4:35; 6:45; 8:13). These passages suggest that he regarded nature not only as a resource but also as an asylum and a source of renewal, just as the passage about the lilies suggests that he appreciated natural beauty.

As to the treatment of animals, Passmore believes that his concern was solely for the preservation of human property.

. . . the other familiar Old Testament prohibitions (against cruelty to animals) . . . sometimes rest on the fact that asses and oxen were a valuable form of property, just as when Luke reports Jesus as asking the Jews 'Which of you shall have an ass or an ox fallen into a pit and will not straightway pull him out on the Sabbath day?'[36]

But this is to beg the question about Jesus' attitude to animals, and, come to that, about the attitude of the Old Testament writers also. The human interest in domestic animals was obviously one reason for protecting them, but it need not have been the only one. Indeed in the Parable of the Lost Sheep (Luke 15:4—7) the marginal benefit of retrieving the hundredth sheep was, all things considered, slight if not negative, but the shepherd still recovered the beast: and, though it is impermissible to argue unrestrictedly from the actors within a parable to the intention of the teller, yet in this case the explicit comparison of the shepherd's care for the sheep to God's loving concern for sinners suggests that we can take it that Jesus was endorsing the shepherd's attitude. Thus Jesus understood and sympathized with disinterested care of animals. Indeed the Johannine Jesus declares (John 10:11) that the good shepherd, by contrast with the hireling, actually lays down his life for the sheep (a passage which, whether historical or not, must have influenced its readers' attitudes to actual flocks as well as to the pastoral care of Christ for his followers).

The only evidence for his holding a despotic view consists in the narratives of his reported treatment of the Gadarene swine (Matthew 8:28—34; Mark 5:1—20; Luke 8:26—39) and of the barren fig-tree (Mark 11:13f, 20—4). Certainly these passages were later used, as by Augustine, as dominical authority for ruthlessness towards animals and plants.

Christ Himself shows that to refrain from the killing of animals and the destroying of plants is the height of superstition for, judging that there are no common rights between us and the beasts and trees, he sent the devils into a herd of swine and with a curse withered the tree on which he found no fruit.[37]

But this passage tells us more about Augustine (whose other views, however, belie his remarks here — see chapter 3) and his polemical powers in castigating his former associates, the Manichaeans, than they do about Jesus. It is peculiarly hard to know how to interpret passages relating nature-miracles; but in these two cases I commend the view of Stephen Clark about the pigs: 'I suspect that there is a parable lurking behind the trivia (who, after all, was keeping *pigs*?)'[38] In the case of the fig-tree, we actually have a version at Luke 13:6—9 of a parable which could easily have been transformed into the Markan narrative. (Similar changes of stories told by Jesus into stories about Jesus seem to be present between the Parable of Dives and Lazarus (Luke 16:19—31) and the raising of Lazarus (John 11:1—44), and between parables about wedding feasts, wedding guests and new wine (Matthew 22:1—14; 25:1—13; Mark 2:19—22) and the miracle performed at Cana in Galilee (John 2:1—11).) Similarly the symbolic significance of swine could well betoken a parable underlying the story about the pigs presented in the three synoptic gospels; which will, if so, have accidentally given the impression of dominical authority for attitudes which, for all that we can tell, Jesus himself would not have shared.

Where attitudes to nature are concerned, the New Testament departed from the Old over its eventual annulment of the distinction between clean and unclean animals (Acts 10, 11), and over its abolition of animal sacrifices in a passage (Hebrews 10:1—18) which speaks with evident distaste of the idea of sins being taken away by 'the blood of bulls and goats'. There is also Paul's stray question implying that God does not care for oxen (I Corinthians 9:10f). Yet when Paul was actually focusing his attention on the subject of nonhuman creatures, rather than delving for the symbolism behind Scriptural proverbs, he held that every creature was in travail awaiting release from decay and participation in the liberty of the sons of God (Romans 8:21f). Passmore indeed allows that Paul intends here that both human and nonhuman creatures are waiting on God,[39] and therefore can hardly ascribe to him nothing but an instrumental attitude to the nonhuman creation. Indeed in another epistle the whole of creation is presented as caught up in the drama of salvation (Colossians 1:15—20). The same broad vision, moreover, is present in Revelation, where the tree of life (22:2) symbolizes the final restoration of the original tree of life of Genesis 2:9, and with it a restoration of the original Garden.

These and other passages altogether preclude a despotic reading of the New Testament; nor is it defensible to hold that the New Testament view of the nonhuman creation was discontinuous (except momentarily) with that of the Old. Even if the stewardship of vineyards and the tending of flocks symbolizes in the New Testament care for the Church rather than for the earth, as Passmore maintains,[40] the benign understanding of nature required by the symbolism must have reinforced the gentle and responsible attitudes to nature which the Old Testament was known to urge.

Passmore for his part sums up the Christian attitude to nature as follows:[41]

What can properly be argued, however, is that Christianity encouraged certain special attitudes to nature: that it exists primarily as a resource rather than as something to be contemplated with enjoyment, that man has the *right* to use it as he will, that it is not sacred, that man's relationships with it are not governed by moral principles.

About the third of these attitudes (that nature is not sacred), and it alone, I should agree with Passmore's ascription, though even here it is appropriate to remark that all terrestrial and celestial bodies are said at I Corinthians 15:40 to have a glory of their own. The remaining attitudes are, as we have seen, foreign to the Christianity of the Bible. Genesis, the Book of Psalms, Job and the gospels bespeak an awareness of nature's beauty; and the awareness, present in both the Old and the New Testament, of the independent value of nonhuman creatures implies constraints upon the treatment of such creatures at least as far-reaching as those which the Old Testament makes explicit. Mankind's dominion is responsible to God, who regards all creation as very good (Genesis 1), and it is entirely mistaken to read into this recognition of the power with which human moral agents are entrusted an absence of moral constraints in its exercise. God is concerned in the Bible with the well-being of other creatures besides mankind (Psalm 104), and people accordingly have obligations to care for nature and not to subvert its integrity by subordinating it ruthlessly to their own purposes. Though the Bible does not set out these obligations in the form of principles, it nevertheless precludes the despotic and anthropocentric attitudes

which White and Passmore alike consider its most natural interpretation; indeed it may well be held to contain, explicitly or
implicitly, many of the ingredients necessary for a responsible
environmental ethic.

NOTES

1 Lynn White Jnr, 'The Historical Roots of our Ecological Crisis', in
   John Barr (ed.) *The Environmental Handbook*, 3—16, reprinted from
   Science, 155 (37), 10 March 1967, 1203—7.
2 Ibid. pp. 11f.
3 *MRN*, p. 5.
4 Aldo Leopold, *A Sand County Almanac with Other Essays on
   Conservation*, New York: Oxford University Press, (2nd edn) 1966,
   p. 238.
5 F. B. Welbourn, 'Man's Dominion', *Theology*, 78, November 1975,
   561—8, p. 561.
6 Ibid. p. 562.
7 Robin Attfield, *God and The Secular: A Philosophical Assessment of
   Secular Reasoning from Bacon to Kant*, Cardiff: University College
   Cardiff Press, 1978, chapter 1.
8 Stanley L. Jaki, *Science and Creation*, Edinburgh: Scottish Academic
   Press, 1974; Lynn White Jnr, *Medieval Technology and Social Change*,
   Oxford: Clarendon Press, 1962. See especially pp. 86, 130f.
9 White, *Medieval Technology*, p. 56. Similar sentences appear at p. 9
   of White's article in *The Environmental Handbook*.
10 At pp. 56f of White's book, replicated closely at p. 9 of his article.
11 But White's methods and findings have been severely criticized by
   R. H. Hilton and P. H. Sawyer in *Past and Present*, 24, April 1963,
   90—100.
12 *The Environmental Handbook*, pp. 10f.
13 Genesis 1:26.
14 Genesis 1:28.
15 *MRN*, p. 9. See further Ian G. Barbour, 'Attitudes Toward Nature and
   Technology', in Ian G. Barbour (ed.), *Earth Might Be Fair*, Englewood
   Cliffs, NJ: Prentice-Hall, 1972, 146—68.
16 *MRN*, p. 11.
17 *MRN*, p. 6.
18 Welbourn, 'Man's Dominion', p. 564.
19 *The Environmental Handbook*, p. 11.
20 Ibid. p. 12.
21 *MRN*, p. 14.
22 *MRN*, p. 16.
23 Thus C. J. Glacken, *Traces on the Rhodian Shore, Nature and Culture
   in Western Thought from Ancient Times to the End of the Eighteenth*

Century, Berkeley, LA and London: University of California Press, 1967, pp. 42—62. In the Preface to his first edition Passmore rightly praises Glacken's work as a 'vast storehouse of learning'.

24   Thus White, *The Environmental Handbook,* p. 16.

25   *MRN,* p. 17. Parallel qualifications are in place over Peter Singer's accounts of Hebrew and Christian views of man and the animals in chapter 5, 'Man's Dominion, a Short History of Speciesism', of his *Animal Liberation, A New Ethic for Our Treatment of Animals,* London: Jonathan Cape, 1976. See Robin Attfield, 'Western Traditions and Environmental Ethics', in Robert Elliot and Aaron Gair, *Environmental Philosophy: A Collection of Readings,* Brisbane: University of Queensland Press, due to appear in 1983.

26   *MRN,* p. 9.

27   *MRN,* pp. 29f. At p. 185 he holds that its fullest implications were only first seen by Kant.

28   See Andrew Linzey, *Animal Rights: A Christian Assessment of Man's Treatment of Animals,* London: SCM Press, 1976, p. 15, where he cites the support of Claus Westermann, *Creation,* London: SPCK, 1974, p. 52.

29   Cited by Thomas Sieger Derr, *Ecology and Human Liberation,* p. 73.

30   Ibid. p. 70.

31   Cited by John Black, *Man's Dominion,* Edinburgh: Edinburgh University Press, 1970, p. 48.

32   *MRN,* p. 31. Cf. Westermann, *Creation,* p. 82, whose account I follow.

33   Glacken, *Traces on the Rhodian Shore,* p. 166. See also John Austin Baker, 'Biblical Attitudes to Nature', in Hugh Montefiore (ed.), *Man and Nature,* London: Collins, 1975, 87—109. See also James Barr, 'Man and Nature: The Ecological Controversy in the Old Testament', *Bulletin of the John Rylands Library,* 55, 1972, 9—32; my disagreements with parts of this article will be clear to its readers and mine.

34   Glacken, *Traces on the Rhodian Shore,* p. 168.

35   Matthew 7:28b—30 (Authorized Version). See further J. Donald Hughes, *Ecology in Ancient Civilizations,* Albuquerque: University of New Mexico Press, 1975.

36   Passmore, 'The Treatment of Animals', p. 196.

37   Quoted ibid. p. 197.

38   Stephen R. L. Clark, *The Moral Status of Animals,* Oxford: Clarendon Press, 1977, p. 196.

39   'The Treatment of Animals', p. 198.

40   *MRN,* p. 29.

41   *MRN,* p. 20.

3

The Tradition of Stewardship

It is worthwhile to investigate further whether the central religious and ethical tradition of our culture has been despotic or environmentally responsible. Even if the Bible is not despotic as to its writers' view of nature (as was argued in chapter 2), the teaching of its adherents could still have been so; and if it had been so, then the causes of our ecological problems would be easier to understand, and we should be obliged to depart from this teaching as radically as possible. If, however, as I shall argue in this chapter, the Judaeo-Christian tradition has historically stressed responsibility for nature, and that not only in the interest of human beings, and if its secular critics have often echoed this emphasis, then whatever the causes of the problems may be, our traditions offer resources which may, in refurbished form, allow us to cope with these problems without resorting to the dubious and implausible expedient of introducing a new environmental ethic.

Classical Christian attitudes

Christian attitudes to nature have in fact been much more diverse than their critics suppose. Thus the belief that everything was made for mankind was held by some Christians such as Origen, Peter Lombard, Aquinas and Calvin, but was expressly rejected by others such as Augustine, Descartes, John Ray, Linnaeus and William Paley, and by the Jewish philosopher Maimonides, and was implicitly rejected by many others, such as Alan of Lille, whose high view of nature was anything but an instrumental one.[1]

The Eastern Church, at any rate, seems to have adhered to a compassionate view of nonhuman species. Thus a prayer for animals of Basil the Great accepted, probably on the strength of Romans 8, that God had promised to save both man and beast. There is also

34

the testimony of St Chrysostom, who in the fourth century wrote of the beasts as follows: 'Surely we ought to show them great kindness and gentleness for many reasons, but, above all, because they are of the same origin as ourselves',[2] and apparently regarded this as a requirement of justice.[3] There are many stories of saintly gentleness to animals, and it has been claimed that in Eastern Orthodoxy 'awareness of man's cosmic vision has never been lost to sight, has never ceased to be an integral part of man's redemption'.[4] Thus St Isaac the Syrian in the seventh century urged compassion for all creatures, and 'a heart which could not bear to see or hear any creature suffer hurt, or the slightest pain'.[5] The secular state too accepted (at least in theory) that there is a *jus naturae*, a law which nature has taught all animals, as well as a *jus gentium* which is peculiar to humans, by admitting this distinction of the third century jurist Ulpian into the *Institutes* of Justinian.[6] The recognition of motives such as self-defence and the care of the young as falling under the *jus naturae* suggests that animals were accorded some degree of moral acknowledgement, even if nothing as clear-cut as moral entitlements. Indeed John Rodman has contended that this understanding of the *jus naturae* tradition was widely accepted until it was redefined in a 'hominicentric' way by Hugo Grotius in *De Belli ac Pacis* (1625).[7]

Even in the West, St Bonaventure wrote of St Francis: 'When he considered the origin of all things, he would be filled with overwhelming pity, and he called all creatures, no matter how lowly, by the name of brother or sister, because as far as he knew, they had sprung from the same original principle as himself.'[8] And Nicholas Arseniev has shown how echoes of Francis' cosmic vision persisted, at least among some of his early followers.[9] On the other hand the Stoic view that irrational creatures lack rights heavily influenced Origen, as Passmore has shown,[10] as also did the Stoic belief that nature exists only to serve mankind's interests. Passmore also finds this influence in the anti-Manichaean passage of Augustine already cited in chapter 2, where the view is ascribed to Christ that there are no moral ties between man and animals.[11] But Augustine also rejected the belief that nonhuman creatures have instrumental value only, and that everything was made to satisfy mankind's need or pleasure. Each creature, he held, has value in itself in the scale of creation.[12] Indeed, as I have argued much more fully elsewhere,[13] his position, seen in the round, was far from reflecting 'Greco-Christian arrogance'.

It is instructive, moreover, to trace two traditions depicted by

Passmore, the Stewardship tradition (involving the belief that people are entrusted with a duty to preserve the earth's beauty and fruitfulness) and the tradition of Cooperation with Nature (embodying the view that mankind should endeavour to develop and perfect the natural world in accordance with its potentials) — traditions of which Passmore discovers no trace between pagan antiquity and the seventeenth century. But in fact both views were held widely among Christians in the patristic period in both East and West. Thus, as Glacken points out, Basil's understanding of man as the furnisher and perfecter of creation was further stressed in the West by Ambrose and in the East by Theodoret;[14] and Augustine's praise of improvements to nature and his belief that man participates in God's work through sciences like agriculture as well as in the arts led to the deliberate application of this teaching in the monasteries of the Benedictine rule.[15] As to the belief that man's role is that of God's steward of creation, this view may also be found in the patristic period. Indeed Glacken locates it in *The Christian Topography* of the sixth century traveller, Cosmas Indicopleustes,[16] and implicitly in Basil, Ambrose and Theodoret. Moreover the belief that the land should be improved seems throughout the Middle Ages to have been taken for granted, without this preventing active measures to conserve the forests;[17] while Christian writers such as Albertus Magnus have long since given warnings against damaging the landscape.[18] There is strong evidence, then, against the claim made by Walter H. O'Briant that the Judaeo-Christian tradition regards man as 'apart from nature', and gives people a careless attitude towards the environment, being preoccupied with the salvation of the soul and unconcerned about a world which is not their true home.[19] Some strands of Christian teaching could have fostered such a view, but the underlying metaphysic can scarcely enjoin it, granted the concern to enhance natural beauty and fruitfulness shown by such a representative figure as Bernard of Clairvaux,[20] and the compassion for other creatures evinced by St Isaac the Syrian, one of those desert fathers often associated with the kind of other-worldliness which O'Briant deprecates.

But it is in the matter of the treatment of animals that the accusation that Christianity embodies a despotic view is most insistent. In this area Peter Singer, in *Animal Liberation* and other writings,[21] has supplemented the evidence adduced by Passmore and has drawn even blacker conclusions. I have argued elsewhere[22] that his charges of despotism and anthropocentrism conflict with a good deal of the evidence, though it must be granted that until the

Reformation there was no opposition to practices such as bull-fighting, and that even since then the Christian and other opponents of cruelty to animals have had an uphill struggle.[23] Christianity, however, abolished animal sacrifices,[24] and, though the spectacles of the arena involving contests between animals were not banned when gladiatorial contests were abolished, the continuing ban on attendance by Christians must have contributed to their disappearance in their ancient form.[25] At the same time in both East and West the veneration of the saints, associated in many cases with kindliness to animals, encouraged a gentle attitude,[26] an attitude evidenced also both in the prayers for sick animals in the medieval Roman liturgy[27] and in medieval bestiaries.[28]

Thus though nonhuman creatures were usually omitted in the West from the scheme of salvation, they were not omitted from the moral reckoning of the patristic and medieval period. (Indeed when, as occasionally, they were put on trial, too great a degree of responsibility was imputed.) Domestic animals, of course, continued to be used as beasts of burden, and cattle were still killed for food; but a case has to be made out before these practices are accepted as exploitative, as opposed to the abuses which sometimes accompany them. (Singer himself does not object to killing and replacing animals which lack self-consciousness.[29]) There again, Basil's prayer for 'the humble beasts who bear with us the heat and burden of the day'[30] suggests that beasts of burden were not always treated oppressively.

Thus in the patristic and medieval periods there was a widespread sense of responsibility for the care of the earth and for the completion of God's work of creation, together with an underlying sense that animals should be treated with kindliness and were of more than merely instrumental value. Aquinas, however, held an instrumentalist view of animals,[31] and taught that cruelty to animals is wrong mainly because of the adverse consequences upon the character of the perpetrator and the loss of property to their human owner.[32] Yet he allowed that irrational creatures 'can be loved from charity as good things we wish others to have, in that from charity we cherish them for God's honour and service. Thus does God love them from charity':[33] a sentiment sometimes taken to imply that we should love them, if not for themselves, then because God does. He also contended that Paul's question about whether God cares for oxen implies no more than that God has no regard for them as rational creatures, not that they fall outside the sphere of his providence.[34] Indeed he expects the just man to feel pity at their suffering, lest he should fail to feel compassion for fellow-men.[35]

Such teaching at any rate allowed Scholastics in the seventeenth century to maintain the reality of animals suffering against the Cartesians;[36] it should also be remarked that some of Aquinas' modern followers, such as Maritain and Journet,[37] have been able to accept nonderivative duties to animals without abandoning his overall metaphysical system. Though his doctrines have often encouraged a despotic attitude to animals, they were not, in fact, ineradicably despotic.

Early modern attitudes

It was, however, Calvin who explicitly resuscitated the New Testament metaphor of Stewardship, which he applied both to a person's possessions[38] and to the care of the earth as a whole, decrying the 'plundering of the earth of what God has given it for the nourishment of man' as frustrating God's goodness.[39] Calvin's version of the Stewardship tradition was anthropocentric, but in the next century Sir Matthew Hale (who was, according to Passmore, one of the earliest Christian adherents of this ancient tradition)[40] gave it an ampler interpretation, somewhat reminiscent of Chrysostom, Basil, Ambrose and Theodoret. Hale, in a notable and much-quoted passage, concluded that 'the End of Man's Creation was, that he should be [God's] Viceroy . . . Steward, *Villicus*, Bailiff, or Farmer of this goodly farm of the lower World', and was endowed with this 'dominion, trust and care' to restrain the fiercer animals, defend the tame and useful ones, to conserve and cultivate plant species, and 'to preserve the face of the Earth in beauty, usefulness and fruitfulness'.[41] Passmore's comment on Hale's view that there is such a duty is that it is not a typically Christian view, but embodies a Pelagian emphasis on what can be accomplished by the human will, an emphasis which plays down original sin.[42] Certainly Calvin stressed original sin more than Hale, but he too stood in the Stewardship tradition and acknowledged that man's dominion is subject to moral limitations; and as to the claims about Pelagianism, such a charge would make the patristic adherents of the Stewardship view and of Cooperation with Nature Pelagians too, including even Augustine![43] There was, in fact, considerable continuity between such seventeenth-century advocates of stewardship and the further adornment of creation as Hale and John Ray on the one hand,[44] and the fathers and monastic communities of the early centuries of the Church, as reviewed above, on the other. It should also be stressed that Hale and Ray, like Basil and Chrysostom (and indeed

Augustine), but unlike Calvin, accepted the intrinsic value of nonhuman creatures.

Now Passmore ascribes the inauguration of a more actively despotic attitude to Francis Bacon and René Descartes, an approach on which, 'since everything on earth is for man's use, he is at liberty to modify it as he will'.[45] Undoubtedly both Bacon and Descartes advocated and pioneered new methods in the investigation of nature. But to what extent did they adhere to the attitude just mentioned, and to what extent did it become accepted as a legitimate Christian view in the period which followed?

Both Bacon and Descartes commended the systematic study of nature so as to improve the human lot.[46] Bacon in particular consciously reinterpreted the doctrine of dominion over nature, which he held to have been twice forfeited, once by Adam's fall and then again by a fall into ignorance. To some degree, he held, it could be recovered through a patient and humble investigation of nature. He opposed those versions of religion which held that natural causes should be treated as sacred and left uninvestigated, holding that God was honoured rather by their study than by wilful ignorance in the face of apparent mystery.[47] Moreover his emphasis was one of technological optimism:[48] 'Now the true and lawful goal of the sciences,' he wrote, 'is none other than this: that human life be endowed with new discoveries and powers.'[49] Indeed in a work of fiction he ascribes to the scientific community of New Atlantis the goal of increasing human power in every possible way.[50]

These passages raise, without answering, the question of whether Bacon simply favoured the alleviation of disease, poverty and famine, or commended uncompromising ruthlessness in the interests of any community equipped with power based on knowledge, at whatever cost to other humans and other creatures. There are certainly times at which he seems to approach the latter view, at any rate when he apparently endorsed the practice of experimenting on live animals in the interests of the progress of surgery.[51] Yet Bacon was also deeply concerned about the misguided uses to which knowledge might be put, and was adamant that neither contemporary nor future people should have to suffer as a result of its pursuit or its applications. Thus in the Dedicatory Epistle of *The Great Instauration* he wrote:

Lastly, I would address one general admonition to all — that they consider what are the true ends of knowledge, and that they seek it not either for pleasure of the mind, or for contention, or for superiority to others, or for profit, or fame, or power, or any of those inferior things, but for the benefit and use of life, and that they perfect and govern it in charity. For it was from lust of power that the angels fell, and from lust of knowledge that man fell; but of charity there can be no excess, neither did angel or man ever come in danger by it.[52]

These are not the words of an advocate of the belief that 'man is at liberty to modify everything on earth as he will'. Rather Bacon was in effect acknowledging constraints on acts which might harm either our fellows or our descendants, and on the kind of motives which have in actual fact prompted exploitation of man and nature.

Ethically, then, Bacon may well have had anthropocentrist leanings, but his opposition to uncharitableness towards people suggests that he could have endorsed Calvin's strictures on 'plundering the earth', though not, perhaps, the duty to preserve the beauty of nature, as well as its usefulness, as recognized and advocated by Hale. Only through the kind of misinterpretation which borders on wilfulness could Bacon be cited in justification of the employment of technology in the heedless pursuit of profit or sectional advantage.

It was, however, the aim of Descartes to 'find a practical philosophy by means of which, knowing the force and the action of fire, water, air, the stars, heavens and all other bodies which environ us, as distinctly as we know the different crafts of our artisans, we can in the same way employ them in all those uses to which they are adapted, and thus render ourselves the masters and possessors of nature.'[53] A despotic attitude is certainly implicit in this interpretation of dominion over nature, an attitude which becomes even more evident over his understanding of animals and other nonhuman species. For Descartes went so far as to maintain that nonhuman creatures lack conscious thought and can be regarded as automata.[54] He does not seem, as Passmore asserts, to have held that animals cannot feel:[55] 'I do not deny sensation, in so far as it depends on a bodily organ', he wrote. But the same passage concludes with a declaration that since animals lack thought, there can be no 'suspicion of crime when [people] eat or kill animals'.[56] Indeed Descartes and several of his followers practised vivisection in the course of their researches.

Yet Descartes held no brief for the unbridled pursuit of power or gain. Defending a decision to delay the publication of his findings, he wrote:

although it is true that each man is obliged to procure, as much as in him lies, the good of others, and that to be useful to nobody is popularly speaking to be worthless, it is at the same time true that our cares should extend further than the present time, and that it is good to set aside those things which may possibly be adapted to bring profit to the living, when we have in view the accomplishment of other ends which will bring much more advantage to our descendants.[57]

The benefits which Descartes hoped to confer on posterity were advances in medicine, which he saw as among the greatest benefits with which human life could be endowed; such pursuits justified the time spent on them much more than 'those which can only be useful to some by being harmful to others'.[58] In theory at least, then, Descartes would have opposed activities aimed at short-term gain which also undermined the life-support systems of our planet; though it may fairly be observed that he foresaw the dangers of science and technology less clearly than either the seventeenth-century critics of his mechanist view of nature were to do, or indeed than had been done by Francis Bacon. There again, Descartes' metaphysic, which will be further discussed in chapter 4, was undoubtedly unsuited to the resolution of ecological problems.

Passmore further contends that Descartes' system in no way depended on revelation, and plays down the traditional emphasis on human limitations and the need for humility: hence it could be inherited unreflectively by a post-Christian Europe and exported readily to non-Christian cultures elsewhere.[59] No doubt elements of his system have been pressed into service in this way; but Descartes himself stressed our dependence on revelation in theology in general and in particular in matters of our inability to discover God's purposes 'by the powers of the mind',[60] and of the requirement of humility to reflect on our faults and the feebleness of our nature.[61] These elements in his system, however, were discarded by some later mechanists who abandoned his theology, such as La Mettrie, D'Holbach and Diderot.[62] Thus Descartes' own remarks suggest that the duty to make the world a better place to live in belongs to a faith involving answerability to God: but it was comparatively easy for some of his followers to omit the traditionally Christian elements in his thought, and to stress his rationalism and his mechanism without the theological and moral constraints with which he tempered them. This is not to imply, however, that the attitude of the French Enlightenment was uniformly more ruthless than Descartes': thus such an advocate of science and a sceptic about revelation as

Voltaire could still reject the view that animals lack feelings and thought, and contend that animals' powers were God-given;[63] while other *philosophes* replaced duties to God with duties to posterity (see chapter 5).

Meanwhile in England the founders of the Royal Society, which received its charter in 1662, set out to employ the methods of Bacon's *Novum Organum* somewhat after the manner of the scientific community in his *New Atlantis*.[64] Their scientific method, like that which he advocated, was secular and autonomous, but they nevertheless perceived their enterprise as a religious duty whereby the Creator was glorified and his workmanship disclosed and published abroad.[65] They rejected the view that nature was 'venerable' and therefore not to be controlled, modified, or understood:[66] but the modifications of the natural environment which they favoured were moderate ones, such as the adornment of the countryside with fruitful fields, orchards and woods, as advocated by John Ray, who was a close associate of the Society's members.[67] Indeed in one of the earliest publications by a member after its foundation, *Silva, or a Discourse on Forest Trees*, John Evelyn warned his readers against excessive deforestation, and exhorted them to take seriously both the theory and the practice of silviculture, so that the nation would be deprived neither of the resources of the woods nor of their beauty. Evelyn, indeed, was concerned about the air of conurbations as well as about the preservation of the forests, and anticipated many later ecological writings in his *Fumifugium*, a study of atmospheric pollution in cities.[68] Accordingly at any rate the first generation of Baconian scientists would have rejected the view that 'man's relations with [nature] are not governed by moral principles'. (It should, however, be acknowledged that Evelyn also participated in experiments on living animals,[69] like several members of the Society.)

The subsequent period

The humanitarian movement, which successfully altered attitudes and practice in matters of slavery, punishment, working conditions and also the treatment of animals gathered strength in the following century, though there had been predecessors of its concern in matters of animal welfare such as Philip Stubbes (1583)[70] and the Massachusetts legislature (1641).[71] In these matters the movement was fostered in its early stages by Christian moralists such as Locke, Wollaston, Balguy and Hutcheson, and in general by Quakers,

Methodists and Evangelicals, as well as by sceptics such as
Montaigne, Shaftesbury, Voltaire, Hume and Bentham.[72] Thus
Passmore's view that theological doctrines retarded this movement,
while sustained by some of the evidence, is in conflict with much of
the rest: for the Christian humanitarians were motivated by a
profound belief in Christian charity, and by their religious con-
victions in general, and not in spite of them.[73] Thus Alexander Pope
wrote in 1713 about vivisection that 'The more entirely the inferior
creation is submitted to our power the more answerable we should
seem for our mismanagement of it.'[74] Further examples of Christians
concerned to avoid harm to animals are the philosopher Gottfried
Wilhelm Leibniz,[75] and the Anglican poet William Cowper,[76] who
held that the true appreciation of nature was sullied by the detestable
cruelty of blood-sports, from which he rescued a hare. Though the
victory of humanitarianism is less than complete in matters of the
treatment of animals, it has long been beyond dispute, both among
religious believers and others, that it is wrong to treat nonhuman
animals as nothing but means to human ends, and it has become a
religious and secular commonplace that they should not be treated
oppressively.[77]

It is becoming clear that whatever has caused our ecological
problems, they cannot be set down to Judaeo-Christian attitudes to
nature. This conclusion is further supported by the reasoning of
Lewis W. Moncrief.[78] Moncrief holds that Lynn White is mistaken to
regard the Judaeo-Christian tradition as causing an exploitative
attitude to nature, at any rate directly, and stresses the cultural,
technological and social forces which have more directly fostered
this outlook. Thus he ascribes our ecological 'crisis' directly to
urbanization, increased wealth, increased population and to the rise
of the private ownership of resources; and these factors in turn are
set down to capitalism (with science and technology in attendance)
and the growth of democracy. The connection between all this and
the Judaeo-Christian tradition is at most that this tradition may have
encouraged capitalism and democracy: but the empirical evidence
for this link, Moncrief holds, is slender. (It should be observed that,
as Moncrief has in mind democracy in a property-owning form, the
link for which he believes the evidence to be wanting would have to
be between the Judaeo-Christian tradition and capitalism; even if
this tradition fosters democratic self-management, as in some of its
forms it undoubtedly does, the link here is irrelevant unless the
tradition supports capitalism too.) To this critique of White's position
William Coleman has responded by maintaining that the theologian

and scientist William Derham, and the apologetic tradition to which he belonged, supply just the empirical evidence which Moncrief believes to be required and missing.[79] Derham, he alleges, gave the blessing of Christianity both to capitalistic enterprise and to science-based technology, and thus White's claims are vindicated, albeit in connection with the period just after 1700, and not with the medieval technology of a millennium earlier.

But, as Coleman admits, other Christians of the period were outspoken in their condemnation of avarice, and Isaac Barrow, Newton's mentor, wrote that, though man could and should use God's terrestrial gifts, he should do so only to meet his daily needs, and under no circumstances so monopolize them as to hinder the satisfaction of the needs of others.[80] Nor do Christian writers of the decades following, such as Swift, retract the traditional strictures on greed and self-aggrandizement. Indeed, as I have argued in 'Christian Attitudes to Nature', Coleman exaggerates both the extent of Derham's blessing on capitalism and its influence. There was no question of 'a divine command to steel ourselves for a ruthless assault upon nature',[81] though there was a somewhat uncritical extension of the legitimate areas of stewardship to all the various callings, trade and war included (and with no qualification about the slave-trade), which contemporary society regarded as respectable. Yet the evidence proffered by Coleman for the link, doubted by Moncrief, between Christianity and untrammelled capitalism, remains too scanty to sustain Coleman's reapplication of White's thesis to the early modern period. Additional evidence, it may be thought, is supplied by Locke's second *Treatise of Civil Government*, with its justification of private property and enclosures; yet even Locke's justification embodied significant constraints, sufficient severely to limit the pursuit of economic growth if they were to be put into effect at the present time. (These constraints are discussed further in chapter 6.)

The actual attitude of the churches, or at least of the Church of England, to the new capitalism may, as R. H. Tawney held,[82] have been one of resignation verging on indifference. Coleman, who maintains, as against this view, that Derham's position was in fact symptomatic of an attitude of actual favour, has not sufficiently made out his case. Indeed the areas to which Christian social teaching was applied at this time seem to have contracted in some quarters to those of individual piety and the prevention of social disorder, though the Evangelicals, Quakers and Methodists upheld the lively concern of their Puritan forebears for social justice (as related above). Undoubtedly there was an insufficient condemnation of the greed and injustice implicit in the excesses of the new capitalism, and an insufficient advocacy of community and fraternity. Yet the awareness of answerability to God was not lost; indeed it was widely appealed to in the nineteenth century by humanitarians and by Christian Socialists. It has also been applied more recently to ecological problems in such works as the 1974 Report of the Doctrine Commission of the Church of England, published in Hugh Montefiore's *Man and Nature*[83] alongside a number of essays in which responsibility for the care of nature is the common theme.

Thus there has been a strong tradition in Europe and lands of European settlement, a tradition of Judaeo-Christian origins but not confined to adherents of Judaism and Christianity, of belief that people are the stewards of the earth, and responsible for its conservation, for its lasting improvement, and also for the care of our fellow-creatures, its nonhuman inhabitants. This tradition, far from being merely modern, has been a continuous one, at any rate among Christians, from the Bible, via Basil, Chrysostom, Ambrose, Theodoret and Bernard of Clairvaux, to Calvin, Hale and Ray and to modern writers like Black and Montefiore. And, though some of its adherents, such as Calvin, have regarded nonhuman creatures as of instrumental value only, or, like the Puritan Philip Stubbes and the Catholic Cardinal Manning, as meriting our care simply because they are loved by God,[84] it has more usually been held that cruelty and injustice in their regard are wrong in themselves, and that these creatures are of intrinsic value, this being, perhaps, the reason for God's love. Variants of this tradition, indeed, have at most times played a leading role in our culture. Accordingly, as Val Routley recognizes,[85] the Stewardship tradition is not confined to human interests, but is concerned with much else besides; indeed the same holds good of the related tradition of Cooperation with Nature (see above), the variant of the Stewardship tradition in which human agents have the role of perfecting the created order by enhancing its beauty and actively conserving and improving its fertility on a sustainable basis.

These traditions, taken together, are at least as representative of Christian history as any despotic view, and may well be considered to offer materials from which an environmental ethic equal to our current problems can be elicited, without the need for the introduction of a new ethic to govern our transactions with nature. Indeed in our existing moral thought and traditions (whether religious or secular) the roots may be found from which, with the help of the findings of ecological science, a tenable environmental ethic can grow.

NOTES

1 On Maimonides, Aquinas, Calvin and Descartes, see *MRN*, pp. 12, 113, 13 and 20; on Peter Lombard, see Passmore, 'Attitudes to Nature', p. 253; on Augustine, Alan of Lille, Linnaeus and Paley, see Glacken, *Traces on the Rhodian Shore*, pp. 198, 216—18 and 424. On Origen see Glacken, pp. 185f, and *MRN*, p. 16; on Ray see Glacken, p. 424 and *MRN*, pp. 21f.

2 C. W. Hume, *The Status of Animals in the Christian Religion*, London: Universities Federation for Animal Welfare, 1957, p. 26, cited by Andrew Linzey, *Animal Rights: A Christian Assessment of Man's Treatment of Animals*, London: SCM Press, 1976, p. 103, n. 22.

3 Thus he declared that 'Even in the case of creatures which lack reason and perception men ought not to deviate from the considerations of what is just and unjust.' This quotation, from Grotius' *De Jure Belli ac Pacis*, I:I:xi, is cited by John Rodman, 'Animal Justice: The Counter-revolution in Natural Right and Law', *Inquiry*, 22, 1979, 3—22, p. 8.

4 A. M. Allchin, *Wholeness and Transfiguration Illustrated in the Lives of St Francis of Assisi and St Seraphim of Sarov*, Oxford: SLG Press, 1974, p. 5; quoted by Linzey, *Animal Rights*, p. 103, n. 22.

5 Nicholas Arseniev, *Mysticism and the Eastern Church* (1925), trans. Arthur Chambers, London and Oxford: Mowbray, 1979, cites this passage at p. 88.

6 Rodman, 'Animal Justice', p. 3.

7 Ibid. pp. 3, 10 and 20, n. 2.

8 Otto Karrer (ed.), *St Francis of Assisi, The Legends and the Lauds*, trans. N. Wydenbruck, London: Sheed & Ward, 1977, at p. 161; a passage cited by Linzey, *Animal Rights*, p. 103, n. 22.

9 Arseniev, *Mysticism and the Eastern Church*, p. 102.

10 *MRN*, p. 16.

11 *MRN*, pp. 111f; 'The Treatment of Animals', p. 197.

12 Glacken, *Traces on the Rhodian Shore*, p. 198.

13 Robin Attfield, 'Christian Attitudes to Nature', *Journal of the History of Ideas*, 44, 1983.

14 Glacken, *Traces on the Rhodian Shore*, pp. 192, 299, 300.

15 Glacken, *Traces on the Rhodian Shore*, pp. 200, 299f., 304—6. On the Benedictine attitude to nature, see ibid., pp. 302—4, and Robert Nisbet, *The Social Philosophers*, London: Heinemann, 1974, pp. 326—8, esp. 327, and 334. See also René Dubos, 'Franciscan Conservation and Benedictine Stewardship', in David and Eileen Spring

(eds), *Ecology and Religion in History,* New York, Evanston, San Francisco and London: Harper & Row, 1974, 114—36.

16 Glacken, *Traces on the Rhodian Shore,* pp. 300f.

17 Ibid. pp. 313—46.

18 Ibid. p. 315.

19 Walter H. O'Briant, 'Man, Nature and the History of Philosophy', in William T. Blackstone (ed.) *Philosophy and Environmental Crisis,* Athens: University of Georgia Press, 1974, 79—89.

20 Glacken, *Traces on the Rhodian Shore,* pp. 213f; Dubos, 'Franciscan Conservation and Benedictine Stewardship', p. 133.

21 Peter Singer, *Animal Liberation, A New Ethic for Our Treatment of Animals,* London: Jonathan Cape, 1976, chapter 5, 'Man's Dominion, a Short History of Speciesism', pp. 202—34; see also his *Practical Ethics,* Cambridge: Cambridge University Press, 1979, p. 77, and his 'Not for Humans Only: The Place of Nonhumans in Environmental Issues', in K. E. Goodpaster and K. M. Sayre (eds), *Ethics and Problems of the 21st Century,* Notre Dame and London: Notre Dame University Press, 1979, 191—206, pp. 192f.

22 Robin Attfield, 'Western Traditions and Environmental Ethics'; in Robert Elliot and Aaron Gair (eds), *Environmental Philosophy. A Collection of Readings,* Brisbane: University of Queensland Press, due to appear in 1983.

23 The story is told in E. S. Turner, *All Heaven in a Rage,* London: Michael Joseph, 1964.

24 Eusebius, 'Oration in Honour of Constantine on the Thirtieth Anniversary of his Reign', 2, in Maurice Wiles and Mark Santer (eds), *Documents in Early Christian Thought,* Cambridge: Cambridge University Press, 1975, p. 232.

25 H. H. Milman, *The History of Christianity from the Birth of Christ to the Abolition of Paganism in the Roman Empire* (3 Vols.), London: John Murray, 1840, Vol. 3, p. 460.

26 Glacken, *Traces on the Rhodian Shore,* pp. 309—11; also W. E. H. Lecky, *History of European Morals from Augustus to Charlemagne* (1869), London: Longmans, Green, 1913, Vol. II, p. 171.

27 C. W. Hume, *The Status of Animals in the Christian Religion,* pp. 94—8.

28 T. H. White (trans. and ed.), *The Book of Beasts,* London: Jonathan Cape, 1954, especially the Appendix, p. 247; cited by A. R. Peacocke, *Creation and the World of Science,* Oxford: Oxford University Press, 1979, p. 278.

29 'Killing Humans and Killing Animals', *Inquiry,* 22, 1979, 145—56, pp. 152f; *Practical Ethics,* p. 104.

30 John Passmore, 'The Treatment of Animals', *Journal of the History of Ideas,* 36, 1975, 195—218, p. 198.

31 Thomas Aquinas, *Summa Contra Gentiles,* trans. Anton Pegis *et al.,* (5

Vols.), Garden City, NY: Image Books, 1955—57, III:II:112(1).

32 Ibid., III:II:113. In 'Western Traditions and Environmental Ethics', I have argued that this summary of Aquinas' position may be an incomplete one (see n. 47 there).

33 *Summa Theologiae,* (60 Vols.), London: Eyre and Spottiswoode, and New York: McGraw-Hill, 1964, 2:2, q. 25, a3.

34 *Summa Theologiae,* 1, q. 103, a5, ad2. See further 'Western Traditions and Environmental Ethics', section I.

35 *Summa Theologiae,* 2:1:102, a6, ad8.

36 Pierre Bayle, 'Rorarius', in *Historical and Critical Dictionary* (1697), trans. and ed. Richard H. Popkin, Indianapolis and New York: Bobbs Merrill, 1965, 213—54, pp. 221—31.

37 Passmore, 'The Treatment of Animals', p. 206, and n. 43 there.

38 'Let every one regard himself as the steward of God in all things which he possesses': John Calvin, *Commentary* on Genesis 2:15; quoted, from a translation of 1847, by F. B. Welbourn at 'Man's Dominion', *Theology,* 78, 1975, 561—8, p. 563.

39 A passage cited by André Bieler, *La Pensée economique et sociale de Calvin,* Geneva: Georg, 1959, at pp. 432—35, and translated by Thomas Sieger Derr in *Ecology and Human Liberation,* Geneva: WSCF Books, 1973, p. 20.

40 *MRN,* pp. 29—31, 185.

41 Sir Matthew Hale, *The Primitive Origination of Mankind,* London, 1677, cited by Glacken, *Traces on the Rhodian Shore,* p. 481, by Black, *Man's Dominion,* pp. 56f, and by Passmore at *MRN,* p. 30.

42 *MRN,* pp. 30f.

43 See sections III and IV of 'Christian Attitudes to Nature'.

44 See John Ray, *The Wisdom of God Manifested in the Works of Creation,* London, 11th edn, 1743, 164f; a passage cited by Glacken *Traces on the Rhodian Shore,* p. 484, by Coleman 'Providence, Capitalism and Environmental Degradation', p. 31, and in section IV of 'Christian Attitudes to Nature'.

45 *MRN,* p. 17.

46 Both philosophers are discussed in much greater detail in chapter 1 of Robin Attfield, *God and The Secular,* Cardiff: University College Cardiff Press, 1978. Passmore discusses them in *MRN,* pp. 18—21.

47 Thus *Novum Organum* I:89. See *The New Organon,* ed. Fulton H. Anderson, Indianapolis and New York: Bobbs-Merrill, 1960, pp. 87—9.

48 *MRN,* p. 19.

49 *Novum Organum,* I:81.

50 *The New Atlantis,* in Francis Bacon, *The Advancement of Learning and the New Atlantis,* ed. Arthur Johnston, Oxford: Clarendon Press, 1974, p. 239.

51 Ibid. p. 241 (from *The New Atlantis*).

52 In *The New Organon,* pp. 15f.

53 René Descartes, *Discourse on Method*, Part VI, from Elizabeth S. Haldane and G. R. T. Ross (trans.), *The Philosophical Works of Descartes*, Cambridge: Cambridge University Press, 1967, Vol. I, p. 119.

54 The passages of Descartes on these topics are conveniently gathered together in Tom Regan and Peter Singer (eds), *Animal Rights and Human Obligations*, Englewood Cliffs, NJ: Prentice-Hall, 1976, pp. 60—6.

55 'The Treatment of Animals', p. 204.

56 Regan and Singer, *Animal Rights and Human Obligations*, p. 66.

57 Haldane and Ross, *The Philosophical Works of Descartes*, Vol. I, p. 122; from *Discourse on Method*, Part VI.

58 Ibid. p. 130; from *Discourse on Method*, Part VI.

59 *MRN*, p. 21.

60 Haldane and Ross, *The Philosophical Works of Descartes*, Vol. I, p. 271; *Principles of Philosophy*, Third Part, Principles I—III. On Descartes on revelation, see 'God and Nature in the Philosophy of Descartes' by David C. Goodman, in *Towards a Mechanistic Philosophy*, Milton Keynes: Open University Press, 1974, 5—43, pp. 13f.

61 Haldane and Ross, *The Philosophical Works of Descartes*, Vol. I, p. 402; *The Passions of the Soul*, Article CLV.

62 See 'The Enlightenment: Deists and 'Rationalists'', by David C. Goodman, in *Scientific Progress and Religious Dissent*, Milton Keynes: Open University Press, 1974, 33—68, pp. 49—52, 60—6. Rodman ('Animal Justice', p. 9) represents La Mettrie as standing in the *jus naturae* tradition against those like Grotius and Püfendorf who played down the similarities between the behaviour of humans and animals. But La Mettrie in fact contended that humans, animals and indeed plants are all alike because they are all machines. Even his book *Les Animaux plus que machines* (La Haye, 1751) was intended to show that humans have souls, and are non-mechanical, *no more than animals*.

63 From his entry 'Animals' in *Philosophical Dictionary*; presented in translation by Regan and Singer, *Animal Rights and Human Obligations*, pp. 67f.

64 See Margery Purver, *The Royal Society: Concept and Creation*, London: Routledge & Kegan Paul, 1967.

65 Thus Robert Boyle entitled one of his works *The Christian Virtuoso* (London, 1690).

66 *MRN*, p. 11; see also Attfield, *God and The Secular*, chapter 1.

67 See the passage cited in n. 44 (above), which echoes some of the words of Basil's *Hexaemeron*. On William Coleman's treatment of Ray, see 'Christian Attitudes to Nature', section IV.

68 Glacken, *Traces on the Rhodian Shore*, pp. 485—94.

69 Turner, *All Heaven in a Rage,* p. 46.

70 Ibid. p. 35.

71 Lawrence Stone, *The Family, Sex and Marriage in England, 1500—1800,* London: Weidenfeld & Nicolson, 1977, p. 237.

72 On Locke, see Robert S. Brumbaugh, 'Of Man, Animals and Morals: A Brief History', in Richard Knowles Morris and Michael W. Fox (eds), *On the Fifth Day, Animal Rights and Human Ethics,* Washington DC: Acropolis Books, 1978, 6—25, pp. 17 and 25, n. 4. On Wollaston, Balguy and Hutcheson (Christians all) see 'The Treatment of Animals', p. 209, which mentions efforts by Evangelicals at pp. 209—11. For Quakers cf. John Woolman's statement of 1772 in *Christian Faith and Practice in the Experience of the Society of Friends*, London: London Yearly Meeting of the Society of Friends, 1960, para. 478. On Methodists, see Turner, *All Heaven in a Rage*, p. 50. On Montaigne, Hume and Bentham, see 'The Treatment of Animals', pp. 208ff and 211. Shaftesbury is mentioned by Norman S. Fiering, 'Irresistible Compassion: An Aspect of Eighteenth Century Humanitarianism', *Journal of the History of Ideas*, 37, 1976, 195—218, p. 202, and Voltaire in *Animal Liberation,* p. 220.

73 Cf. the couplet from a hymn of Isaac Watts (1674—1748), an Independent, 'Creatures as numerous as they be/Are subject to Thy care;' in *The Baptist Hymn Book*, London: Psalms and Hymns Trust, 1962, hymn 58. (Parts of the present paragraph appear also in 'Western Traditions and Environmental Ethics'.)

74 Turner, *All Heaven in a Rage,* p. 48.

75 See the story of Leibniz's concern for a tiny worm which he had been observing, as related by Immanuel Kant, *Lectures on Ethics,* trans. Louis Infield, New York: Harper & Row, 1963, pp. 239—41.

76 William Cowper, *The Task*, Ilkley and London: Scolar Press, 1973, Book III, pp. 106—9.

77 Turner, *All Heaven in a Rage*, pp. 114, 120, 151, 161.

78 Lewis W. Moncrief, 'The Cultural Basis for our Environmental Crisis', *Science,* 170, 508—12; reprinted in *Ecology and Religion in History,* 76—90.

79 William Coleman, 'Providence, Capitalism and Environmental Degradation', *Journal of the History of Ideas,* 37, 1976, 27—44, p. 37.

80 Ibid. p. 38.

81 Ibid. p. 35.

82 Ibid. p. 28.

83 Hugh Montefiore (ed.), *Man and Nature,* London: Collins, 1975.

84 Turner, *All Heaven in a Rage*, pp. 35, 165.

85 Val Routley, Critical Notice of *Man's Responsibility for Nature, Australasian Journal of Philosophy,* 53, 1975, 171—85, p. 174.

4

Nature and the Place of Man

From what we have seen so far, our moral traditions already embody an ethic on which humans are the stewards and guardians of nature, an ethic which derives from the Judaeo-Christian tradition and is apparently well-suited to our current ecological problems. But it remains appropriate to enquire whether our underlying view of reality and our traditional interpretations of the scheme of things are sufficiently suited to our problems, or whether, as a number of writers have maintained, we need a new way of regarding mankind and the world, or, in other words, a new metaphysics. Latterly John Passmore has claimed that the elaboration of a new metaphysics suited to environmental problems is 'the most important task which lies ahead of philosophy';[1] John Rodman has urged a holistic ethic based on 'the nature of things';[2] Henryk Skolimowski has advocated, as the counterpart of the ecological humanism which he commends, an evolutionary cosmology which gives rise to an ethic of reverence for life;[3] and, as we have seen in chapter 3, Walter H. O'Briant has criticized the 'religious' view of 'man apart from nature' in favour of a more organic view of the universe, mankind included. To what extent, it should be asked, should our traditional metaphysics be rejected or revised, and what range of metaphysical positions can prove equal to current insights and problems?

No comprehensive treatment of these issues can be attempted here; yet it is worthwhile to stand back so as to make sure, if possible, that the principles of value and obligation presented in other chapters are not vitiated by adherence to a fundamentally inappropriate metaphysics. I shall first investigate O'Briant's critique; this will involve a brief historical survey of Judaeo-Christian metaphysical positions. I shall then consider which metaphysical views satisfy the requirements of evolutionary theory, ecological science and belief in the intrinsic value of forms of nonhuman as well as human life.

Theistic anthropology

In his essay 'Man, Nature and the History of Philosophy',[4] O'Briant depicts two views of man and nature in our culture, the religious view of 'man *apart from* nature' and the scientific view of 'man *a part of* nature'. In the Judaeo-Christian tradition man alone is made in the image of God and alone has a rational soul, something which sets him apart from all other creatures. Man has dominion over the other creatures, according to O'Briant's interpretation, in the sense that they 'were put here by the Creator for man's use and enjoyment'.[5] Though his body is material his soul is immaterial and incorruptible: in this tradition man is sometimes regarded as comprising a union of body and soul, and sometimes as consisting in the soul alone, a supernatural being temporarily imprisoned in a natural body.

On the scientific view, by contrast, man differs from the other animals not in kind but in degree. He is an animal among his fellow animals, and has no dominion over them except insofar as his intelligence makes him their effective superior. As an animal he is mortal, and made of matter like everything else, for there is no soul and no Creator, nor anything else which cannot be investigated empirically. Indeed there may be nothing more distinctive about man that the relative absence of body hair.

The religious view, O'Briant believes, is in need of radical reform. As we have seen, he believes that its preoccupation with the salvation of the immortal soul has issued in the view that the natural world is not our home, and indeed that 'our animal nature is vile and contemptible':[6] also it involves a 'careless attitude' toward the environment. The connection is that religious beliefs about salvation make people see themselves as exempt from the consequences of past misbehaviour, and not ultimately a part of the world at all. So people have felt 'comfortable in raping and pillaging this earthly abode'.[7] Not that O'Briant commends the 'scientific view' which he describes, with its empiricism, its mechanism and its scepticism about values; rather he favours the ontology of philosophers such as Leibniz who refuse to admit a radical distinction between the living and the nonliving. But he is clear that our religion and our metaphysics need revision, as well as our ethics, if we are to solve the problems affecting ourselves and our environment.[8]

O'Briant's characterization of the scientific view will not be discussed here. Many different metaphysical and ethical views have, in fact, been held by scientists; for my own part I have attempted elsewhere[9] to set out the logic of the relations between theism and empirical science, and in chapter 5 I shall return to the bearing upon ecological matters of belief in technological progress. As to our religious tradition, I shall here assume, on the strength of the preceding chapters, that the Bible does not take the dominion of man to imply that all other creatures were made solely for man's use and enjoyment, and that Jews and Christians have not standardly construed it in this sense. I shall also assume that as Leibniz, whose metaphysics O'Briant favours, believed both in God as creator and in the immortality of the soul, not all those holding such beliefs are thought to hold exploitative attitudes or to suffer from metaphysical arrogance.

In connection with O'Briant's account of the 'religious view' it should next be remarked that belief in the immortality of the soul is not, in general,[10] a biblical belief — nor a centrally Christian one, Leibniz notwithstanding. Prior to the latest stages of its composition (e.g. Job 19:25−27, 2 Maccabees 7:23, 28f), the writers of the Old Testament did not believe in personal survival of death, and the passages about man's creation in God's image must be interpreted otherwise. The author of Ecclesiastes could even claim that 'a man hath no pre-eminence above a beast' as man and beast die alike, and alike return to their native dust.[11] (On this passage Black[12] comments that the very biblical elements which it has been most difficult to assimilate into orthodox Christianity may have a peculiar appeal in the twentieth century: be this as it may, the passage is a striking affirmation of human kinship with the beasts.) The New Testament writers, for their part, affirm a belief in eternal life and in the resurrection of the body, rather than in a soul possessed of natural immortality: and so does the 'Apostles' Creed'. Even Paul's distinction between flesh and spirit concerns not, as has often been supposed, different elements of a person or even different sets of desires, but rather two opposed ways of life, one in accordance with God's will and the other heedless of it.[13] In general the Bible does not take a radical dualist view of man as composed of a separable body and soul; rather the soul is what gives life to a body, though 'soul' is sometimes metaphorically used of the quality of a person's moral or spiritual life.[14]

Belief in a separable and naturally immortal soul entered Christianity rather from Platonism, but the ideas of Platonizing

Christians such as Origen had to compete not only with the Hebraic view but also with that of Aristotle on which the soul is the form of the body.[15] Indeed the Christological controversies of the fourth and fifth centuries can be regarded as a struggle between the Platonizing tradition of Alexandria, in which the Word constituted the soul of Christ, and the more Aristotelian view of the Antiochenes, on which Christ's body was informed by a human soul, without which he could not have been a man. On this view it was with a complete human, and not just a body, that the Word was united.[16] At this stage, though all Christians believed in life after death, not all took this qualitatively to differentiate mankind from the beasts, as we have seen over Basil the Great, Chrysostom and Francis in chapter 3.[17]

In more recent centuries the single most influential view has been that of Aquinas.[18] As an Aristotelian, Aquinas held that plants have vegetative souls and animals sensitive souls, but contrasted with these the rational soul of man which, as it can operate without reliance on bodily organs, can exist independently of the body. But a disembodied soul is not a person, and is confined to the powers of intellect, will and memory. A soul is properly the form of a body, and there can be no human life without either body or soul. A man is not, as Plato held, a soul using a body, nor is a body a substance in its own right, for without a soul it perishes. Rather a man is an ensouled body; and human life can only be restored after death if God resurrects a body for the disembodied soul to inform.

These views allowed Aquinas to acknowledge that man is generically akin to the animals, even though specifically different. His actual attitudes to animals have been explored already in chapter 3: it remains only to observe that his instrumentalist view was not required by his beliefs either about the human soul or about the bodily and sensitive nature which men and animals share. Indeed O'Briant seems right to exempt versions of Christianity on which people are, like other animals, essentially composed of the union of a body and a soul from the charge of contempt for animals and for our animal nature. The Thomist metaphysic, indeed, does not require the despotic attitude to animals held by Aquinas himself; and as to human nature (and the nature of creatures in general) Aquinas believed that God's providential activity does not overthrow or destroy it, but preserves it with a view to its perfection.[19]

Nevertheless Christians have at times thought of man as nothing but a soul. Such seems to have been the view of the heretical Christian, Origen, who believed that souls were fallen angels, punished by being made to inhabit mortal bodies;[20] these beliefs, however, were not readily accepted in face of the common belief of Christians that God had taken on flesh for the sake of man's salvation without being defiled thereby. Nor, as we have seen in chapter 3, did the efforts of Eastern monasticism to mortify the flesh issue invariably in contempt for nature.

The belief that man survives death as a soul, albeit as a soul which in life is closely attached to the body, exercised a widespread impact, not least among Christians, through the advocacy of Descartes, in whom O'Briant finds an alternation between the 'religious' and the 'scientific' view.[21] Descartes regarded bodies, both human and animal, as mechanisms; but construed the subject of reason and will as an immaterial substance, which was not subject to dissolution at death, and in which human immortality was located. Unlike Aquinas, Descartes derived the soul's immortality from its immaterial nature; and in this he was followed by many writers such as Samuel Clarke and Richard Price[22] who saw no other way of reconciling Christian beliefs about life after death with science.

Descartes' dualism and his view of animals as automata lead, as we have seen, to an insensitivity towards beasts. But it did not in his own case engender otherworldliness or irresponsibility in moral matters. Nevertheless it was prone to produce in some of his philosophical heirs a disparagement of the body and of the joys of this life, as sometimes in that in many ways enlightened figure, Richard Price.[23] In a period when the doctrine of the natural goodness of creation often went understressed, the Cartesian distinction between mind and matter must at times, as O'Briant implies, have led to a sense that man was not truly at home on earth, and that as far as his true interests were concerned the natural order was as dispensable as his natural body. Indeed, as William Blackstone has written, 'There is no room for an ecological ethic within the Cartesian metaphysic.'[24]

Doubts should be expressed, though, about whether these attitudes have actually led to improper exploitation of the environment (if this can be considered separately from the matter of the treatment of animals). The link suspected by O'Briant is that if salvation is in another world and God's forgiveness exempts people from the consequences of their sins, then these consequences can be disregarded. This criticism of Christianity as 'antinomian' is an age-old one, and has at other times been focused on sayings such as Augustine's 'Love God and do as you like'. Yet with negligible exceptions Christianity has always stressed the need for sanctification or moral development, whether this was seen as desirable for the sake of fellow-creatures or as evidence of the repentance which God required as a condition of salvation. As I have allowed in chapter 3, other-worldliness has sometimes led to a narrowing of Christian social teaching; but it is doubtful if, beyond that, a careless attitude to nature has been engendered.

Further metaphysical options

Yet O'Briant is right in stressing the problems for humans about their own identity which arise from Cartesian dualism, and in holding that beliefs such as the denial of our kinship with creatures of other species are prone to vitiate our practice. In the last century it has been the Darwinian theory of evolution by natural selection which has undermined this denial; but it is important to realize that not all Christians have endorsed Descartes' radical dualism, and that its rejection is not the rejection of our religious tradition as a whole. Thus John Locke held that, for all we know, that which thinks in us may be material, and that God may add to matter the power of thought, just as he adds that of vegetation to peach-trees, and of sense and spontaneous motion to elephants.[25] Indeed Locke employed the status of animals as an argument against dualism. For it seems arbitrary either to hold that animals are bare machines without sensation or to hold that, despite their lack of intellectual and moral capacities, they have immaterial substantial souls, the solution preferred by Cudworth.[26] But if the remaining alternative, that matter can feel, is adopted, then it is arbitrary to deny that matter can think.[27]

A few years later, the scientist, philosopher and theologian, Joseph Priestley put forward the view that humans are systems of matter. Like Locke, Priestley was aware that the Bible teaches the resurrection of the body rather than the immortality of the soul, and Priestley added the claim that belief in an immaterial soul was a perversion of Christianity introduced from Greek philosophy.[28] Price replied that belief in an immaterial soul was indispensable for Christianity and for any account of consciousness; and he subjected Priestley's theory to searching objections, as had Clarke the somewhat cruder theory of Locke's materialist follower, Anthony Collins.[29] Nevertheless it does not seem impossible to reconcile Priestley's position with ordinary understandings of personal identity, or with the belief in the resurrection of a former person with identity intact. Thus the Christian tradition itself includes at least two alternatives to the dualism of mind and matter which O'Briant and Blackstone see as harmful, Priestleian materialism, and also the older view of Aquinas.

Blackstone, indeed, suggests that 'a metaphysic suitable as a companion to a genuine environmental ethic' may be found in Aristotle, Spinoza or Aquinas;[30] while the alternatives considered by O'Briant are the metaphysical systems of Spinoza and Leibniz. But Spinoza's necessitarianism and belief that there is only one substance, all truths about which follow from its nature, seem to underrate the activity and spontaneity both of people and of animals; and in fact, as Passmore points out in 'The Treatment of Animals', Spinoza held attitudes to nonhuman creatures which were exploitative in no small measure. 'I do not deny that beasts feel,' he wrote, 'but I deny that on that account we should not consult our necessity and use them as much as we wish and treat them as we will, since they do not agree with us in nature, and their emotions are in nature different from human emotions.'[31] Even if Spinoza's system were purged of these attitudes, its necessities are too rigid for the metaphysical counterpart of an environmental ethic, and, as we shall see, its treatment of individuals as mere modes of one substance is ethically hazardous, even if the problems about its intelligibility are waived.

O'Briant's preferred alternative is the system of Leibniz, who held that no metaphysics based on inert matter can explain activity or consciousness, and maintained instead that the fundamental units of reality (the monads) are themselves active and possessed of (unconscious) perception. Leibniz's monadology enabled him to stress the similarities as well as the differences between humans and other animals, and to admire their diverse perfections. Though his system has seldom been accepted as a whole, his belief that the organic underlies the mechanical has been revived this century in A. N. Whitehead's doctrine of 'organic mechanism'.[32] Indeed L. Charles Birch has summarized this position in a form O'Briant would be likely to applaud: 'Man is not separate from nature, but a part of nature.'[33] There are in fact considerable difficulties in the way of the acceptance of Leibniz's unextended monads as the basis of everyday physical objects, though there may be less in the way of accepting the view that the capacity for life and consciousness is proper to the elementary particles of matter (a view which Leibniz himself rejected).[34]

While radical Cartesian dualism can be rejected on grounds such as its failure to make action or perception possible, whether in humans or in other animals, and also on evolutionary grounds yet to be presented, it is perhaps unnecessary for present purposes to adjudicate between the remaining metaphysical possibilities. For it is possible to recognize both the kinship of mankind and the other animals and the characteristic rational, cultural and moral capacities of humans on a variety of theories, including Priestleian materialism, Leibnitian monadology, Whitehead's organic mechanism and the Thomist view of man and other animals as ensouled bodies. None of these theories, I suggest, requires the undervaluation of nonhuman creatures (even though Thomism has at times been so interpreted);[35] and, though not all can be equal to reality, it would be superfluous here to attempt to decide between their relative merits. For present purposes, at any rate, a Lockean agnosticism about the nature of that in us (and in the other animals) which feels and thinks will suffice.

Requirements for a satisfactory metaphysics

It is nevertheless worth asking what are the requirements for a metaphysics which encourages sensitiveness towards the natural environment as well as towards human nature. In this connection Mary Midgley makes the point that if human nature is to be understood against the background of the kindred nature of other animals (and it is certainly unlikely to be well understood otherwise), then theories on which human nature as it is could never 'have evolved without celestial interference'[36] are to be rejected. But the theories of Plato and of Descartes can only be squared with belief in evolution if at some stage a wholly alien element was supernaturally added to existing organisms. On their theories, after all, the loss of the body makes little difference to the real person, who continues to exist as a soul. Such a soul is therefore discontinuous with all other characteristics of living organisms, and could not evolve from them. But, as Midgley remarks, such 'celestial interference . . . does not make sense in a nonreligious context . . . [or] in a Christian one either. Christianity is not Platonism. If God created through evolution, he surely designed it and used it properly.' And in fact she goes on to suggest that 'a far more coherent view of human wholeness' is supplied by Bishop Butler, with his contrasting accounts of behaviour which fits the balance of our natural desires, and behaviour disproportionate to their integration.[37] Indeed Midgley's evolutionary requirement is plausibly satisfied by the metaphysical views, presented above, of Aquinas, Leibniz, Priestley and Whitehead alike.

Midgley has another requirement for a satisfactory metaphysics, namely that we must not only refrain from holding, with Kant, that animals and the rest of creation exist for man and that man is nature's ultimate end,[38] but that we need to hold that other creatures either have no point or value or have a point which is quite alien to human purposes. Only thus can we escape from the narrowness of human concerns, and take pleasure in what exists independently of ourselves, and only thus can we benefit from the study of the adaptedness of different creatures each to its peculiar niche and role.[39]

A parallel requirement for a satisfactory metaphysics is suggested in Passmore's contention that 'the philosopher has to learn to live with the "strangeness" of nature, with the fact that natural processes are entirely indifferent to our existence and welfare — not *positively* indifferent, of course, but *incapable* of caring about us — and are complex in a way that rules out the possibility of our wholly mastering and transforming them'.[40] Passmore is partly rejecting here two forms of anthropocentric metaphysics. Cartesianism, he holds, encourages the exploitation of nature as 'the rightful manipulation of a nature which is wax in man's hands'.[41] He grants that Descartes rejected the view that everything else in creation exists for man, but ascribes to him the attitude that everything that man finds on earth may and should be transformed for his use,[42] like the wax which was Descartes' favourite example of variability. (This kind of account may not be altogether fair to Descartes.) Passmore is also rejecting the Hegelian metaphysics of nature on which its exploitation is held to constitute 'the humanising of it in a manner which somehow accords with nature's real interests',[43] and on which nature becomes of value only through the taming of its initial state by man.

That some of Descartes' followers adopted the views attributed to Descartes, or that Marx and others (see chapter 5) in large measure took over those attributed to Hegel can scarcely be doubted. Passmore finds them defective not in rejecting the pre-Christian view that natural objects are sacred; for natural objects cannot be swayed by arguments, can be scientifically understood, and may rightly be in some measure transformed for the sake of 'civilization' and human interests. Rather he finds them defective in neglecting facts such as that 'natural processes go on in their own way, in a manner indifferent to human interests and by no means incompatible with man's total disappearance from the face of the earth', and that human interventions in these processes set off a chain of interactions, some of them unforseeable. If these facts are granted, then we neglect the autonomous nature of natural objects and processes at our peril, and should not construe them either as wax in our hands or as requiring our efforts to realize themselves. I suspect that Passmore is additionally holding that such attitudes to the exploitation of nature are morally wrong, as well as misconceived: certainly this is suggested by his beliefs that the wilful destruction of natural objects is blameable even when human interests are unaffected,[44] and that a more realistic philosophy of nature can promote respect for natural processes.[45] If so he needs to hold some such premise as that some of these objects and processes have an intrinsic value of their own (though, as I shall contend in chapter 8, the importance of understanding natural systems does not require locating intrinsic value in such systems, as holists sometimes require).

Now this rejection of anthropocentrism and the related refusal to undervalue nature are, as we have seen, required by the Old and New Testaments alike. We have also seen how these attitudes clash with Stoic (and, as Passmore points out, with Aristotelian[46]) tenets adopted by Origen, Aquinas and in some places by Kant, and accordingly how some elements in these thinkers' ideas need to be discarded. In chapter 3, moreover, it was argued that the Judaeo-Christian tradition can consistently accommodate the kind of nonanthropocentric metaphysics which is now commended by Passmore. Can it also accommodate the acceptance of nature's 'strangeness' required by Midgley and Passmore?

Satisfying the requirements

It is clearly essential at the very least that nonhuman living creatures should not be regarded as nothing but chattels, property or resources. Val and Richard Routley now hold that the Stewardship tradition involves regarding the world as either human or super-human property,[47] the tenants of which should treat it as resources belonging to the owner. Peter Singer seems to adopt a similar interpretation;[48] and Henryk Skolimowski likewise holds that in the Christian cosmology 'everything is God's personal property' and that for this metaphysics an ethic of reverence for life is an 'anomaly'.[49] But this theory makes the Stewardship tradition adopt an instrumentalist view of nonhuman creatures, which in actual fact its adherents have usually rejected. The suggestion may be that stewards are essentially managers who act on behalf of owners; if so, it should be replied that stewards can be curators, trustees, guardians and wardens, and that in any case the point of the metaphor is the steward's responsibility and answerability, not the devaluation of the world which is their trust, and which is regarded as a reflection of the divine glory, and judged by its creator to be 'very good'. Even if the tradition is secularized and adopts a nontheistic form, people do not forfeit their responsibilities, but remain answerable to the community of moral agents for the fostering and the preservation of all that is intrinsically valuable.

Nevertheless Passmore expresses strong reservations about people's ability to 'face their ecological problems in their full implications' unless they see themselves as left to their own devices, without metaphysical guarantees of survival.[50] Natural processes must not be seen as 'so constructed as to guarantee the continued survival of human beings and their civilisation'.[51] Hence a sufficiently naturalistic understanding of man is needed to guarantee that people are dependent on natural processes. This much, I should contend, can be accepted by anyone, whether a theistic believer or not, who accepts a sufficient kinship between humans and other species to recognize the essentially physical nature of both. Certainly theism does not entail that the earthly survival of our species is supernaturally guaranteed; and, as we have seen, belief in the survival of death need not impair conscientiousness about this-worldly obligations. Further, to affirm the naturalness of humanity commits us neither to the devaluation of nature feared by Skolimowski as a concomitant of some forms of the scientific world-view,[52] nor on the other hand to 'radical biotic egalitarianism',[53] the theory which makes all living creatures have the same intrinsic value, and which Blackstone shows good reason to reject on the count of its unacceptable implications.

Yet for Passmore nature's strangeness consists not only in its less-than-total conformity to human purposes, but also in the gulf between the human and the nonhuman.[54] In part Passmore is here reminding us of nature's otherness, rather as Rodman insists on the inappropriateness of applying to alien creatures, with distinctive ways of life of their own, standards which relate solely to humans.[55] But he is also stressing, to an unusual degree among writers on ecological subjects, the peculiar value of humans and what they create. This far, I suggest, we can follow him: our metaphysics should not so 'naturalize' man as to obscure the difference between characteristic human capacities and relations and the capacities (and in some cases relations) characteristic of other species. To do so is to disown the very responsibilities for future people and for the natural environment which it is essential for normative ethics to stress (see chapters 6—9). Indeed much more is distinctive about mankind than the relative absence of body hair: in fact the importance of stressing the powers of commission and omission which these responsibilities presuppose is a central reason for upholding the belief (so easily misinterpreted) in man's dominion. Yet the peculiar value of the fulfilment of characteristic human capacities can be granted without denying the possibility of rights on the part of nonhuman animals, as Passmore frequently does. Nor can it be necessary for an environmental ethic to be committed to treating species-boundaries *in themselves* as a proper basis for discrimination and differential treatment.

Awareness of our dependence on natural processes and cycles is sometimes thought, particularly by adherents of what Naess calls the 'deep' ecology movement, to require a shift at the level of metaphysics away from an atomistic view of society and the world to an acceptance of systems and wholes as the fundamental units of reality and the ultimate focuses of loyalty. Such seems to be the view of a number of ecological writers, including Leopold, Clark and Rodman.[56] A virtue of this view is its resistance to attempts to construe all morality as concerned with individual rights and interests and to project Western property systems onto the universe as a whole. But the egoistic pitfalls of moral individualism can be avoided without denying the reality of individuals, and the scientific discovery of our interdependence with the other constituents of natural ecosystems does not show these systems to have value in themselves.[57] Though Passmore is mistaken in objecting to Leopold's 'land ethic' that obligations arise only within those communities where they are recognized,[58] he is right to hold that interdependence need not imply a moral relationship. As the Routleys remind us, we need to be able to see ourselves as belonging to societies and systems, and can take pride in communal as well as in individual fortunes;[59] yet there are manifest dangers in any such metaphysical monism as that presented by John King-Farlow,[60] on which the perfection of the one Substance is vastly more important than the well-being of the persons who are among its constituents. Real as social systems and ecosystems are, we should not forget that their value turns on the flourishing of the no less real individual organisms which make them up.

A metaphysics, then, which is suited to our ecological problems needs to treat humans alongside the rest of the natural order in a naturalistic way, without being reductionist about their irreducible characteristics. It must not deny the reality of the natural systems on which we depend, yet must allow the reality of their individual members, and uphold the responsibilities which as individuals and groups people have for the care of the natural environment. For man is neither 'apart from nature' nor simply 'a part of nature', whether nature is regarded as a collection of atoms or organisms or as a single organic system. It must further renounce anthropocentrism, recognize nature's autonomy and otherness and the value of nonhuman creatures, and take full account of evolution. Thus, as Skolimowski points out, since mankind is the outcome of evolution, 'the universe is to be conceived of as the home for man';[61] and, though Skolimowski may be too ready to ascribe value to whatever emerges from the evolutionary process, he is nevertheless right to point out that 'we are the custodians of the whole of evolution'.[62]

Platonism and Cartesianism do not, as we have seen, satisfy these criteria; nor do the anthropocentric aspects of Aristotelianism and of Thomism. But the systems of Aquinas, Leibniz, Priestley and Whitehead are, I should claim, equal to these requirements, or can be reconciled with them. Indeed a new metaphysics is needed only insofar as these longstanding systems need to be made more explicitly consistent with the criteria which have been supplied. Thus the Judaeo-Christian tradition, of which at least the first three of these systems are recognizably variants, is not essentially productive of metaphysical arrogance, despite the fact that such arrogance has often besmirched it. Nor is it committed to regarding man as 'apart from nature'. Indeed it embodies indispensable insights about human capacities and obligations, such as that people are the custodians and stewards of a precious natural order, and have a creative role in actively enhancing it, as well as being among its participants — insights which we cannot afford to disregard.

NOTES

1 John Passmore, 'Attitudes to Nature', in Royal Institute of Philosophy (ed.) *Nature and Conduct*, London and Basingstoke: Macmillan Press, 1975, 251—64, p. 261; *MRN*, (2nd edn) p. 215.

2 John Rodman, 'The Liberation of Nature', *Inquiry*, 20, 1977, 83—145, p. 95.

3 Henryk Skolimowski, 'Ecological Humanism', in *Eco-Philosophy*, Boston and London, Marion Boyars, 1981, pp. 53—89.

4 Walter H. O'Briant, 'Man, Nature and the History of Philosophy', in William T. Blackstone (ed.), *Philosophy and Environmental Crisis,* Athens: University of Georgia Press, 1974, 79—89.

5 Ibid. p. 80.

6 Ibid. pp. 82f.

7 Ibid. pp. 85f.

8 Ibid. pp. 86—8.

9 See Robin Attfield, *God and The Secular,* Cardiff, University College Cardiff Press, 1978, chapter 1.

10 Wisdom 3:4 and 5:15 are apparent exceptions, but even there immortality is not natural to man's soul, but a supernatural gift.

11 Ecclesiastes 3:19f.

12 John Black, *Man's Dominion,* Edinburgh: Edinburgh University Press, 1970, pp. 39f.

13 Cf. J. A. T. Robinson, *The Body,* London: SCM Press, 1952, chapters 1 and 3.

14 Cf. Alan Richardson (ed.), *A Theological Wordbook of the Bible,* London: SCM Press, 1957, under 'Spirit', I(c), p. 234.

15 Aristotle, *De Anima* II, 412a, 20f.

16 Cf. J. N. D. Kelly, *Early Christian Doctrines,* London: Adam & Charles Black, (4th edn) 1968, pp. 280f.

17 See chapter 3 (above), nn. 30, 2 and 8.

18 *Summa Theologiae* 1, q75, articles 2—6. See also Herbert McCabe, 'The Immortality of the Soul', in Anthony Kenny (ed.), *Aquinas: A Collection of Critical Essays,* London: Macmillan Press, 1969, pp. 297—306.

19 *Summa Theologiae* 2:1, q10, a4.

20 Kelly, *Early Christian Doctrines,* pp. 180—8.

21 O'Briant, 'Man, Nature and the History of Philosophy', pp. 83f.

22 Samuel Clarke, *Letter to Dodwell, Etc.,* (1706), (6th edn) London, 1731; Richard Price, *A Free Discussion of Materialism and Philosophical Necessity, in a Correspondence between Dr Price and Dr Priestley, Etc.,* London, 1778.

23 Price, 'The Nature and Dignity of the Human Soul', *Sermons,* London, *c.* 1790.

24 William T. Blackstone, 'The Search for an Environmental Ethic', in Tom Regan (ed.), *Matters of Life and Death,* Philadelphia: Temple University Press, 1980, 299—335, p. 312.

25 John Locke, *Second Reply* to the Bishop of Worcester, *Works,* London, 1823, Vol. IV, pp. 460f. The reference is derived from Michael Ayers, 'Mechanism, Superaddition and the Proof of God's Existence in Locke's *Essay*', *Philosophical Review,* 90, 1981, 210—51, p. 238. Ayers there contests the view of Margaret Wilson that the possible addition of these powers was regarded by Locke as an exercise of the divine *fiat* and contrary to the nature of the things affected. Ayers maintains that

Locke's main position was agnosticism about the nature both of matter and of that which thinks.

26 Ralph Cudworth, *The True Intellectual System of the Universe*, (2nd edn) London: 1743, p. 745; cited by Ayers (see above) at n. 64, p. 239.

27 This account of Locke's position is derived from Ayers (see above), pp. 237—9.

28 In *A Free Discussion*; see n. 22. His materialism is expounded there at pp. 112f.

29 The correspondence of Clarke and Collins is published in Clarke, *Letter to Dodwell, Etc.*

30 Blackstone, 'The Search for an Environmental Ethic', p. 312.

31 Spinoza, *Ethics*, Part IV, Prop. XXXVII, Note 1. From *Spinoza's Ethics*, trans. Andrew Boyle, London: Dent, Everyman's Library, 1910.

32 A. N. Whitehead, *Science and the Modern World*, Cambridge: Cambridge University Press, 1926; see also his later works.

33 L. Charles Birch, *Nature and God*, London: SCM Press, 1965, p. 69.

34 See H. G. Alexander (ed.), *The Clarke—Leibniz Correspondence*, Manchester: Manchester University Press, 1956.

35 See Turner, *All Heaven in a Rage*, pp. 162—6.

36 Mary Midgley, *Beast and Man: The Roots of Human Nature*, Hassocks. Harvester Press, 1979, p. 254.

37 Ibid. pp. 266—71.

38 Kant, however, seems later to have abandoned this view: see Glacken, *Traces on the Rhodian Shore*, pp. 540f.

39 Midgley, *Beast and Man*, pp. 357—9.

40 'Attitudes to Nature', p. 260; *MRN*, (2nd edn) p. 214.

41 'Attitudes to Nature', p. 259; *MRN*, (2nd edn) p. 213.

42 'Attitudes to Nature', p. 256; *MRN*, (2nd edn) p. 210.

43 'Attitudes to Nature', p. 259; *MRN*, (2nd edn) P. 213. Cf. *MRN*, pp. 32—5.

44 'Attitudes to Nature', p. 263; *MRN*, (2nd edn) p. 217.

45 'Attitudes to Nature', pp. 263f; *MRN*, (2nd edn) pp. 217f.

46 *MRN*, p. 14.

47 Val and Richard Routley, 'Social Theories, Self Management and Environmental Problems', in Don Mannison, Michael McRobbie and Richard Routley (eds), *Environmental Philosophy*, Canberra: Australian National University, 1980, 217—332, p. 324.

48 Peter Singer, 'Animals and the Value of Life', in Tom Regan (ed.), *Matters of Life and Death*, 218—59, p. 231.

49 Skolimowski, *Eco-Philosophy*, p. 83.

50 *MRN*, p. 184.

51 'Attitudes to Nature', p. 260; *MRN*, (2nd edn) p. 214.

52 Skolimowski, *Eco-Philosophy*, pp. 8—13.

53 Blackstone, *Philosophy and Environmental Crisis*, p. 303.

54 'Attitudes to Nature', p. 261; *MRN,* (2nd edn) p. 215.
55 'The Liberation of Nature', pp. 94, 118.
56 Leopold, *A Sand County Almanac and Sketches Here and There,*
    New York: Oxford University Press, 1949, pp. 224f; Clark, *The Moral
    Status of Animals,* Oxford: Clarendon Press, 1977, pp. 114 and 171;
    see also his review of Goodpaster and Sayre, *Philosophical Books,* 21,
    1980, 237—40; Rodman, 'The Liberation of Nature', p. 89. See also
    Holmes Rolston III, 'Is There an Ecological Ethic?' *Ethics,* 85, 1975,
    93—109, p. 106; Kenneth Goodpaster, 'From Egoism to Environ-
    mentalism', in K. E. Goodpaster and K. M. Sayre (eds), *Ethics and
    Problems of the 21st Century,* 21—35, pp. 29f; and J. Baird Callicott,
    'Animal Liberation: A Triangular Affair', *Environmental Ethics,* 2,
    1980, 311—38, pp. 327ff.
57 See chapter 8 (below); also Robin Attfield, 'Methods of Ecological
    Ethics' (unpublished).
58 *MRN,* p. 116.
59 See 'Social Theories, Self Management and Environmental Problems',
    passim.
60 John King-Farlow, *Self-Knowledge and Social Relations,* New York:
    Science History Publications, 1978, pp. 216—19.
61 Skolimowski, *Eco-Philosophy,* p. 74.
62 Ibid.

5

Belief in Progress

Why are the societies of both Western and Eastern Europe, and those which descend from them, so expectant of perpetual growth and perpetual increases in human power and happiness? The Judaeo-Christian tradition does not seem to explain these deep-rooted attitudes, despite the views of White to the contrary;[1] yet they do appear to prevail wherever Western (or Soviet) science, technology and institutions are to be found.

This suggests the importance of discussing a more recent idea from the common background of these societies, the idea of progress, a widespread presupposition in one version or another, in both capitalist and Marxist social systems. I shall not argue that this idea as such is at the root of our problems or that it should be rejected; indeed I believe it to be of great value in some of its forms. Yet in other forms it does, I shall argue, underlie our problems. I shall therefore be considering its nature and origins, the extent to which it is tenable, and whether it is compatible with attitudes appropriate to our current dilemmas.

The modern belief in progress

The hope that the passage of time would convey benefits to human well-being, material benefits included, through the application of knowledge about nature originated significantly in the seventeenth century with Francis Bacon and René Descartes. The view which I am here adopting of the idea of progress as a distinctively modern one was put forward by the rationalist historian J. B. Bury,[2] and was not challenged by a writer with a very different standpoint, the theologian John Baillie, for all that he regarded belief in progress as a Christian heresy.[3] John Passmore, certainly, has shown that the

belief that progress comes about by a process of natural development, inherent in human history, can be traced back to Joachim of
Flora in the twelfth century, and that for Joachim the guarantee of
progress was divine providence;[4] but he also holds that belief in the
inevitability of progress, providence or no providence, did not
become part of a systematic social doctrine till the time of
philosophes such as Turgot in France and of Leibniz's eighteenth-
century followers in Germany.[5]

As against all this Robert Nisbet has recently contended that the
belief in progress is not a distinctively modern belief, but originated
with the Greeks, was fostered by Christian millennarianism and is
characteristically sustained by religious faith.[6] Nisbet succeeds in
showing that some of the Greeks believed in periods of improvement, that Augustine prepared the way for millennarian and secular
concepts of progress, and that there is more continuity between
ancient, medieval and modern attitudes to progress than Auguste
Comte and his followers have allowed. Yet he does not succeed in
overthrowing the distinctiveness of the modern idea of progress. As
Passmore had already pointed out:

it is one thing to assert that over a limited period of time the human
situation has improved, or will improve, whether in knowledge or in artistic
achievement, quite another thing to assert that mankind as a whole is
gradually perfecting itself — not only in some particular respect but
universally — and that it will continue to do so throughout the course of
human history.[7]

Indeed for all the encouragement that Judaeo-Christian beliefs give
to scientific enquiry and to the related hope of the amelioration of
the human condition, belief in perpetual progress is no part of
orthodox Judaism or Christianity, nor, as we shall see, have the
various bases, sought over three hundred years to guarantee the
perpetuation of progress, usually been religious ones.

The hope which Bacon and Descartes cherished for earthly
advancement and the alleviation of the human lot was grounded, as
John Baillie says,[8] in the prospect of the growth of scientific
knowledge. Contrary to the impression which Joseph Priestley gave
and which Carl Becker reinforces,[9] Bacon did not quite identify
knowledge with power, but he did hold that the former is necessary
for the latter: 'Human knowledge and human power meet in one;
for where the cause is not known the effect cannot be produced.'[10]
So long as unintended achievements are left out of account, we can

agree; indeed Morris Ginsberg has given Bacon's claim a wider, yet still plausible application: 'It remains that if knowledge is not a sufficient, it is a necessary condition of progress.'[11] Since, further, both Bacon and Descartes supplied grounds for hope of scientific advance, they both prepared the way for the belief in the inevitability of progress: yet neither of them shared this belief. As Baillie relates, they were each content to demonstrate that the kind of progress in which they were interested was possible and to 'argue against the assumption of its impossibility'.[12] Indeed there was no inconsistency between this position and the Christianity which both professed.

With Baillie I accept Bury's view that 'Fontenelle was the first to formulate the idea of the progress of knowledge as a complete doctrine.'[13] In this doctrine, the progress of knowledge was presented as certain and as continuing indefinitely. Fontenelle based his claim on the constancy of nature and of human nature: each generation is therefore able to benefit from the discoveries of the previous one, and to avoid their mistakes. As against Fontenelle, we might fear that in some disciplines errors, ancient and modern, would be perpetuated and discoveries disregarded: but the reply is a cogent one that the critical methods of empirical science make this likely in only a minority of cases within its domain. Nor is the proneness of humans to mould their ideas and institutions an insuperable objection to Fontenelle's conclusion. The real problem lies in the possibility that technological discoveries, supposed to be progressive, will undermine the conditions in which science or other forms of civilized life can be practised at all: to this extent the doctrine that technological progress will continue indefinitely is capable of proving self-destructive.

Accordingly assertions of indefinite progress of any kind are insecure; yet if human nature allows of social improvements, their possibility should not be underestimated. John Passmore has recounted how a succession of social theorists in the eighteenth and nineteenth centuries explored this possibility.[14] This is not the place to enter into the detail of their theories; but it is important to note that they all depend on the rejection, made explicit by John Locke, of the Augustinian doctrine of original sin. In *The Reasonableness of Christianity* Locke denied that people are born with an innate inclination towards depravity.[15] Any innate bias to evil with which a man is born can, he held, be removed, or at least counter-balanced, by education. Locke did not accept, as many contemporary Latitudinarian theologians did, that people are born with benevolent propensities: but he did reject the doctrine that everyone is beset with an innate maleficent bias which supernatural grace alone can remedy.

Locke's claims for education concern in effect the possibility of individual moral improvement, and underlie most secular theories of social or moral reform. Doubtless Locke was prone to exaggerate, as he at one point admitted,[16] the extent to which people are born without instincts or natural inclinations, and may 'be moulded or fashioned as one pleases'; but the orthodox Augustinian doctrine, if consistently applied, could suggest the futility of all efforts at social reform which in any way depended on, or were designed to promote, increased cooperation or wisdom, including even the efforts of Benedictine and Cistercian communities to improve the land (efforts which owed much to Augustine's other teaching). The theology of Augustine, indeed, allows so low a place to human self-determination that numerous Christians down the ages have had to qualify it to acknowledge the role of human effort in any consistent scheme of Christian ethics. Thus even if Locke's positive views misconstrue human instincts and inherited capacities, his claim that there is for each generation of new-born humans the possibility of moral development, and that it can be fostered by entirely secular means, was both an influential and a salutary one. It was, indeed, a modification of the Judaeo-Christian tradition vital for all branches of ethics, environmental ethics included. Even if, morally speaking, no generation starts off in a better position than its predecessor, yet later generations can inherit the advantages of an enhanced social and natural environment.

The modern belief in progress, however, as Passmore, Baillie and Bury agree, originates with the Abbé de Saint-Pierre, who moved in some of the same circles as Fontenelle towards the end of the latter's long life. According to Baillie 'what Saint-Pierre did was to combine Bacon's and Descartes' belief that increase in knowledge was the secret of social and moral progress with Fontenelle's belief in the inevitability of the former; so reaching as a conclusion the belief in the inevitability of the latter'.[17] Saint-Pierre, however, contributed more than a simple application of an elementary argument-form; for, as Baillie himself accepts, Bacon and Descartes did not believe that advances in knowledge would guarantee any sort of progress; nor were they concerned, for the most part, with moral progress at all.[18] At most they harboured hopes of more commodious living (Bacon) or improvements in medicine of benefit to future generations (Descartes). But Saint-Pierre maintained that advances in knowledge were as feasible in the social and political spheres as in the physical, and that in each case corresponding and continuous progress would inevitably follow. Here for the first time is a prediction of ever-increasing happiness and steady moral progress, based on gains to knowledge (such as those made by Descartes, Newton and Locke) and on legislation for social reform. Indeed the recent contributions to knowledge were held, by Saint-Pierre and soon by many others, to suggest that just as the present was an improvement on the past, so the future was bound to bring unlimited further progress.

As Becker and Baillie both relate, views such as these fostered a discontent with existing social arrangements and an ardent desire for social reform, which in the France of Louis XV was certainly overdue. More generally, there is no reason to doubt that understanding of human society is possible and can contribute to the introduction of more beneficient arrangements. What is more doubtful is either that the application of such knowledge is bound to succeed in its aims, or that knowledge of man and society is to be expected to be as well-attested, secure or cumulative as knowledge of mathematics or physics, granted the difference in subject-matter. Besides, as Passmore points out, 'there were great difficulties in the purely inductive argument for progress'. On no criterion did the past bear out the theory of steady improvement, even if the extrapolation from the past to the future had been a permissible one. Yet the belief in the irresistibility of progress, which set in at this stage, has nevertheless been an immensely influential one in fostering confidence in deliberate changes intended to assist that process along.

With qualifications, similar views about the past, the present and the future were put forward by Voltaire (though, as Bury remarks, his optimism was always tempered with cynicism),[19] Turgot (who accepted that progress might be accidental, and who took a more favourable view of the Christian Middle Ages than the other philosophes),[20] Chastellux (who concluded that progress began with the Renaissance, before which all ages were ages of misery)[21] and Condorcet (who believed in uninterrupted progress through nine ages, each superior in knowledge and enlightenment, about to culminate in a tenth age of equality and still greater knowledge, health and virtue).[22] These writers argued on the basis of actual historical progress. But unless the argument that greater knowledge promotes wiser actions is successful, it is hard to see how the discovery of progressive historical tendencies could constitute grounds for optimism: unless these tendencies operate through a credible and continuing mechanism, there is no reason to expect the lessons of history to apply to the future. One mechanism, proposed by Turgot and by Adam Smith,[23] was the production of economic growth by private enterprise operating in a framework of laissez-faire liberalism; Nisbet indeed regards belief in economic growth, which was also harboured by Voltaire and Condorcet, as the natural background to belief in progress.[24] To the extent that these beliefs really belong together, the belief in progress must share some of the blame for our ecological problems; certainly far from all the fruits of economic growth can be regarded as social improvements. (Yet, as Mill was later to point out, there can be social progress even if economic growth is curtailed.)

Nevertheless the new emphasis of the *philosophes* on the human future was morally an important one (see chapter 6). People who expect either a continuing decline of man and nature, or the persistence of the social and natural order of their day, can readily believe that there is little they can do for posterity. Such views do not preclude all sense of obligation: but that sense can be heightened when people become aware that the lot of their descendants depends in large measure on themselves. A different perspective on the attitude of the *philosophes* to posterity is supplied in Becker's chapter 'The Uses of Posterity',[25] in which he exhibits the way in which, for many of the *philosophes*, posterity became the focus of religious feelings previously associated with life after death. (Diderot, to cite one among Becker's many examples, declared that 'La postérité pour le philosophe, c'est l'autre monde de l'homme religieux.') But we should beware of applying to them a theory of psychological projection or irrational wish-fulfilment: some of them, indeed, such as the Abbé de Saint-Pierre, Richard Price and Joseph Priestley, continued to believe in the next world as well as looking forward to a better future in this one. Certainly in the case of Robespierre concern for posterity observably diminished concern for the generation of his contemporaries; yet, once there are grounds for holding that our descendants can be benefited by our actions or harmed by our omissions, it is irresponsible to disregard them, and it is to the credit of the *philosophes* that they realized this.

Metaphysical guarantees

Besides arguments for progress taken from science, education and history, there were also metaphysical arguments. Thus the view of Leibniz that every potentiality must at some time be actualized was

capable either of being restricted, as at first it was, to individual
lifetimes as opposed to the career of humanity as a whole (thus
Moses Mendelssohn), or instead, of being applied to the development of the species through time (as in Immanuel Kant's *Idea of a
Universal History*[26]). With Kant the fulfilment of human potentialities
is located in a perfect universal state which will guarantee perpetual
peace, and which will come about precisely through the evil
inclinations, and the consequent struggles, to which humanity is
prone. The evidence of history was, as Kant saw, insufficient to
warrant his conclusion: the basis of his assurance was rather that the
human sense of duty requires us to believe that there can be
conditions in which it is universally enthroned.

Though Kant explicitly rejected the doctrine of original sin, he
eventually relied on divine grace, as Joachim had before him, to
provide for the consummation of his ideal commonwealth.[27] But
appeal to divine interventions is just as unsupportable in theories
about the human future as in explanations in physics:[28] it is one
thing to set up an ethical commonwealth as an ideal, and hope for
its fulfilment, and quite another to assert its inevitability, particularly
where there is no earthly means of enacting it within the envisageable
future. Indeed believers in its inevitability may easily subordinate all
else to its attainment, and cut corners in bringing it in.

Conscious of this very possibility, Kant's former pupil Herder
held that it is rather by performing their duty to the present
generation that people best further the arrival of an ideal society.
Unlike those *philosophes* who had stressed the misery of the past (or
of the present) he held that every age is capable of relative
perfection, and the fulfilment appropriate to its own circumstances.
Impressed as he was by the variety of empirical conditions in which
societies are set, he had no place for those 'final causes' which Kant
had reintroduced into the philosophy of history. But he was enough
of a believer in the progress and the progressive education of
humanity, to which every society can contribute, both to deplore
some episodes in the past (the barbarities of the Roman Empire, and
the persistence of the Roman Church after the Reformation), and to
avoid that historical relativism which precludes the judgement that
one society can constitute an improvement on another. With
Passmore I agree that he needed such a view if he was to retain
belief in the possibility of progress: it is indeed needed for all inter-
societal appraisals, whether concerned with chronological development or not.[29]

As well as being interested in empirical particularities, Herder was a speculative thinker, who laid down laws of history. His principal law was that 'all the destructive Powers in Nature must not only yield in the Course of Time to the maintaining Powers, but must ultimately be subservient to the Consummation of the Whole'.[30] Evils, Herder believed, serve as a stimulant to progress; his law guarantees that after the stimulated changes have occurred, their stimulants wither away. His laws were supposed to be laws of nature, but turn out to be just as metaphysical as the factors taken to guarantee progress by Kant.

Among Herder's successors in Germany as philosophers of history, Fichte, Schelling and Hegel, his empirical emphasis was disparaged and suppressed, and attention was further concentrated on the discovery of laws of development. With Fichte, all history tends unendingly yet necessarily towards the realization of freedom.[31] Nature too is involved in the process: earthquakes, volcanoes and hurricanes are nothing more than 'the last struggles of the rude mass against the law of regular, progressive, living and systematic activity to which it is compelled to submit'.[32] Thus nature has not yet become subject to regular laws or to human efforts, but it is destined eventually to become controlled, regularized and humanized. (Indeed progress has often been defined in terms of the increasing power of man over nature.[33]) Schelling regarded society as an organism, the growth of which is deducible from biological laws;[34] for his part Hegel regarded history as a developing revelation of divine reason, the emergence of 'consciousness of its own freedom on the part of Spirit',[35] but a process which was already complete in his own day. For these idealists, empirical history at best served to illustrate processes which are deducible by *a priori* reasoning. Their stress was on the inevitability of development rather than of scientific or moral progress; but their influence was considerable on later French as well as German thought, so much so that the idea of historical development became a commonplace even among people who execrated the memory of the pre-revolutionary *philosophes*.[36]

In post-revolutionary France a new generation of thinkers attempted to explain how to organize for progress and to delineate its sociological laws — first Saint-Simon and then Comte. With Saint-Simon the close cohesion of religious, political and social systems was stressed, and a law supplied of the alternation of epochs of organization or construction and of criticism or revolution.[37] Saint-Simon's emphasis on the role of religion in historical development supplemented that accorded to knowledge by Condorcet (and would doubtless have been approved by White). He accordingly predicted that on the road to social happiness a new physicist religion would replace Christianity and Deism. His theories also allowed him to advocate a more immediate and practical condition of social progress, the amelioration of the lot of the working classes. With Comte the fundamental law of history consisted 'in the growing power of altruism over egoism brought about by a fusion of intelligence and sympathy'.[38] Like Condorcet and Fichte, Comte divided history into stages: every branch of knowledge passes in his account through first a theological state, next a metaphysical and finally a positive or scientific one. The dynamic of history is largely supplied by ideas, which in all disciplines need to be raised to the third stage. Political, moral and intellectual progress are so closely related that material and social development proceed in step with that of the intellect. In the third stage, society will be organized along the principles of scientific sociology.[39] Comte did not believe that progress would be indefinite, but he was convinced that it would be continuous. It is entirely predictable that mankind will arrive at a science-based harmony with its environment, and equally clear what people in the interim should do and may rightly be coerced into doing.[40] It is unlikely that the adherents of such an ethic would be willing to adjust their practice in the light of new ecological or other insights, or would be allowed to do so.

Progress popularized

The French thinkers of the early nineteenth century put the idea of progress firmly on the map, not least by blending the German belief in inevitable temporal development with the historically based confidence of the French enlightenment that intellectual and moral improvements would continue in the future. A sign of the times was the definition of civilization advanced by François Guizot in terms of both progress and development. The very word 'civilisation', he claimed, 'awakens, when it is pronounced, the idea of a people which is in motion, not to change its place but to change its state, a people whose condition is expanding and improving. The idea of progress, development, seems to me the fundamental idea contained in the word *civilisation*.'[41] (Guizot's notion of civilization included not only social movement towards prosperity and justice but also intellectual development in individuals of cultivated ideas and sentiments.)

Strictly, as Bury remarks, Guizot's definition implies that there is no such thing as a civilization in a state of equilibrium; such an assumption would, of course, have to be revised before a sustainable society, able to live in harmony with its natural environment, could come about. But significantly, and without further demur, Bury in 1920 wrote of Guizot that 'his view of history was effective in helping to establish the association of the two ideas of civilisation and progress, *which today is taken for granted as evidently true*' (my italics).[42] In this form the idea of progress was soon popularized both in Britain and America:[43] it is accordingly unsurprising that many in the twentieth century have regarded a society which lacks growth as retrogressive and intolerable.

It should also be acknowledged that in this period the idea of progress became associated with that of equality, both by Robert Owen in Britain and by Pierre Leroux in France, and that belief in the possibility of each strengthened belief in that of the other. Also in the writings of William Godwin and, now, of Proudhon, it was seen to be possible to give progress an anti-authoritarian interpretation, far removed from that of Comte. Much more influential than the ideas of either the first socialists or the first anarchists were the distinctive doctrines of Marx and Engels (indeed any assessment of the idea of progress of this or succeeding periods must depend on which of the various conceptions of social advance is in question). A much more immediate influence, however, in the widespread adoption in Western Europe and America of belief in progress was exercised by the writings of Herbert Spencer, whose understanding of progress was of a very different complexion again.

Spencer had already adopted a theory of the evolution of society in his *Social Statics* of 1851,[44] well before the publication of Charles Darwin's *The Origin of Species* in 1859; but Darwin's theories served to give a widespread credibility to his claim, publicized in a sequence of further works, that the whole universe, organic and inorganic, is in process of evolution. As has been seen in chapter 4, acceptance of Darwinism can also give rise to an enhanced sense of kinship to the natural order: and, as T. H. Huxley pointed out, it certainly need not lead to an ethical belief in the survival of the fittest. But Huxley, in order to arrive at this conclusion, had to stress the discontinuity between biological evolution and social progress;[45] whereas Spencer, in asserting their continuity, had an easier task. How, he could ask, can man reverse the law of life?

Spencer's own law of evolution was no improvement on the proposed laws of history of Condorcet, Herder, Fichte or Comte.[46] But if life-forms survive by adaptation, then there is a superficial cogency to his belief that evils, being manifestations of maladaptedness, will wither away as better adapted forms emerge and thrive. Spencer believed that adaptive characteristics can be transmitted down the generations, and therefore expected continuing, and eventually perfect, adaptation to come about.

Spencer's derivation of an ethic from the theory of evolution becomes all the more suspect when he argues from a final cause, and claims that 'the ultimate purpose of creation is to produce the greatest amount of happiness, and to fulfil this aim it is necessary that each member of the race should possess faculties enabling him to experience the highest enjoyment of life, yet in such a way as not to diminish the power of others to receive like satisfaction.'[47] To follow Bury's expression of the implications, 'Beings thus constituted cannot multiply in a world tenanted by inferior creatures; these, therefore, must be dispossessed to make room; and to dispossess them aboriginal man must have an inferior constitution to begin with; he must be predatory, he must have the desire to kill. In general, given an unsubdued earth, and the human being "appointed" to overspread and occupy it, then, the laws of life being what they are, no other series of changes than that which has actually occurred could have occurred.'[48]

Admittedly Spencer holds that to retain these predatory characteristics is to be unfit for man's present social state.[49] Nevertheless Spencer here endorses all depredations past, and might easily be construed as authorizing, in the name of the ultimate purpose of creation, ruthlessness on the part of anyone finding himself confronted by wild nature or by primitive peoples. Moreover even in future ages, to which more altruistic codes will, on his views, be appropriate, the idea of preserving or protecting vulnerable species, habitats or human cultures would be futile and misguided. Spencer may have considered that he was expounding Genesis, but, as Bury points out, the role of Providence in his earlier writings is just to set in motion immutable forces, a role which in later writings was occupied by 'the Unknowable, existing behind all phenomena'.[50] Indeed this transition was a tacit acknowledgement that Spencer's views were entirely alien to those of the Old Testament about God, man and nature.

Spencer's conflation of the notions of evolution by natural selection and of progress was widely accepted, so that evolution in society came to be regarded as desirable, and progress as a natural necessity. Not everyone would have allowed that the survival of the fittest was the criterion of such progress; but it was all too often assumed to be so in the ethics of business, while in society in general 'social Darwinism' made it all the harder for critics of exploitative attitudes, whether towards mankind or nature, to carry conviction. Similarly Spencer's laissez-faire liberalism has been so widely adopted as often to rule out the prevention of exploitation by law. The climate of opinion could in theory have been tempered by the extension of Mill's criterion of right action, the promotion of the greatest happiness of the greatest number, to include the members of future generations, as commended by Kidd;[51] but at a time of technological, commercial and imperial expansion, the very belief in progress seemed to guarantee that fresh ideas or resources would always turn up to meet future contingencies, which could therefore be left to themselves.

Marxist ambivalence

Hegel's belief in the inevitability of historical development was inherited not only by the French founders of sociology but also by Karl Marx and Friedrich Engels. Marx and Engels accepted Feuerbach's view that Hegel's critique of Christianity needed to be inverted, so that talk about God is seen as a confused way of talking about humans and their relationships. They also rejected Hegel's view that the theses, antitheses and syntheses of history were stages in the self-realization of Spirit, in favour of the doctrine that they were 'historical phases in the development of production'[52] and of the corresponding relations to the means of production of different economic classes, and that they would inevitably culminate by means of revolution in a society where all class-divisions had been abolished.

According to Marx, man is alienated under the conditions of capitalism from his own essence, and his alienation can only be overcome when capitalism is overthrown: only then will a truly free and human society emerge. I have elsewhere endeavoured to elucidate the sense of 'alienation';[53] here it should be remarked that their Soviet followers credit the founders of Marxism with having discovered the laws of history, and with them grounds for confidence in irresistible future progress. Thus Academician Innokenty Gerasimov writes, 'Only Marxist-Leninist theory and methodology of scientific analysis were able to reveal the objective laws of the multifarious processes of interaction between nature and society in the general evolution of mankind and the change of the basic social formations.'[54]

Two strands are to be discerned in the attitudes of Marx and

Engels to nature. One is the belief derived from Fichte, that nature must be humanized, and will only then itself be fulfilled. Though the language used often concerns, in Engel's phrase, 'the reconciliation of mankind with nature', the idea is explicated in terms of rational control. Thus Gerasimov writes:

In *Anti-Dühring* Engels points out that until the scientific control of the forces of nature is subordinated to the rational control of productive relations between people, these forces '. . . are at work in spite of us, in opposition to us, so long they master us . . .' The position changes fundamentally in planned socialist and communist societies.[55]

Similarly another contribution to the same collection of essays, by Academician Yevgeny Fyodorov and Ilya Novik, ascribes parallel views to Marx, who 'wrote that socialised man . . . rationally regulated their [*sic*] interchange with Nature, "bringing it under their common control, instead of being ruled by the blind forces of Nature . . ."'.[56] And in the same spirit these writers object to the posture of some Western ecological writers opposed to economic growth as 'a rejection of the humane ideal of social progress'. They prefer 'the rationally understood program of the optimisation of the biosphere'.[57] In this they are true to Marx; 'whenever Marx writes of the "slumbering potentialities" of nature, he is always referring to the objective possibility, inherent in nature, of its transfer into definite use-values,'[58] i.e. use-values for man. Howard L. Parsons, indeed, rejects the accusation that Marx denied the value of the external, non-human world of nature, but unconvincingly.[59] Indeed, as Parsons allows,[60]

Marx and Engels shared the attitude toward nature held by contemporary men of industry and commerce and by the millions of settlers migrating to new lands to struggle with the hardships of the frontier. Whereas eighteenth-century Europeans, for example, viewed America as a utopian garden of abundance, freedom and harmony, the nineteenth-century immigrants saw the wilderness as an obstacle to be conquered[61] and as a reservoir of potential wealth to be subdued and transformed by the labours of man.[62]

The other relevant strand in Marx and (much more emphatically) in Engels is a rejection of the kind of predatory exploitation of nature characteristic of capitalism and of much science-based technology, an advocacy of the recycling of the waste products of industry, and a surprisingly modern stress on the need to take account of side-effects and long-term consequences. Thus Marx holds that 'all progress in capitalistic agriculture is a progress in the art, not only of robbing the labourer, but of robbing the soil; all progress in increasing the fertility of the soil for a given time, is a progress towards ruining the lasting sources of that fertility.'[63] Capitalism, by concentrating people in large towns, prevents the return to the soil of human waste products, and thus further 'violates the conditions necessary to lasting fertility of the soil' and 'disturbs the circulation of matter between man and soil'. The wool and silk industries are commended for utilizing their own worn or defective products, and the chemical industry for utilizing not only its own waste but also that of many other industries.[64] In the same spirit Fyodorov and Novik advocate 'new wasteless production based on closed-cycle technology' as one of the long-term methods of production without pollution.[65]

There again, a fellow essayist is able to cite Engels, who was undoubtedly a pioneer of ecological consciousness, as a critic of technological optimism. 'Let us not, however,' wrote Engels, 'flatter ourselves on account of our human victories over nature. For each such victory takes its revenge on us. Each victory, it is true, in the first place brings about the results we expected, but in the second and third places it has quite different unforeseen effects which only too often cancel the first.'[66] Engels' examples include the devastation resulting from the deforestation of Southern Europe by primitive peoples, the introduction into Europe of the disease of scrofula together with the potato, and the loss of the soil of the Cuban uplands when Spanish planters burned the forests for the sake of fertilizer for *one* generation of coffee bushes and quick profits. Much the same happens, he holds, when manufacturers aim at immediate profit and disregard results which are other than immediate: bourgeois economics is, he holds, predominantly beset with the same flaws (a claim which, as was pointed out in chapter 1, it is hard to gainsay).[67] Engels' sentiments, indeed, assist Oldak in arguing in his turn for closed-cycle technology, as also for a reformed system of economics, and for planning which takes account of the needs of both present and future generations.

The representatives, then, of modern Soviet orthodoxy are enabled by Marx and Engels, as well as by the revelations of recent scientific research, both to criticize careless technology (and not only in capitalist societies[68]) and to encourage the recycling of waste products and pollution-free production. At the same time they reject the ideal of the cessation of growth,[69] insisting that 'Mankind is capable of developing progressively, provided that it takes account

in its activity of the tasks of *optimising the biosphere*' (my italics).[70]
For 'Mankind can not only predict and avert a future degradation of
the environment, but even ensure its purposeful improvement,'[71]
(One of the means suggested by another contributor, Academician
Nicolai Semenov, is to discover how to replicate the natural process
of photosynthesis artificially, and then to occupy the greater part of
the deserts of the entire planet with industrial plant to reap the
proceeds.[72]) It is difficult to avoid the conclusion that the confidence
of Soviet scientists that improved technology can and will solve all
ecological problems is also derived from the predictions of Marx
and Engels that the eventual overcoming of the tensions between
man and nature, and the development of a fully humanized nature
and society, are each inevitable.

Belief in progress assessed

Nevertheless much can be granted to the prophets of progress.
Bacon and Descartes were correct to hold that scientific progress is
not impossible, Locke to hold that individuals can develop morally
without supernatural assistance, and Fontenelle in holding that
scientific and technological knowledge are (at least normally)
cumulative. For, despite disavowals by some philosophers of
science,[73] natural science has progressed wherever extra phenomena
can be explained alongside familiar ones, and new ones predicted,[74]
and technology has advanced wherever new techniques, and hence
new human powers, for the control of natural processes or the
production of goods have become available. Indeed there has even
been some advance in the understanding of human society (e.g. in
the matter of trends in population growth); and there has been a
widespread increase, partially due to the *philosophes*, to Kant and
to the founders of Marxism, in awareness of our obligations to
future generations and of the possibility of equipping them with an
improved natural and social environment. There is no need to
concede to the intellectual or the moral relativist that such talk is
incoherent, nor to the pessimist that all effort is doomed to futility.

But this is not to accept, with Saint-Pierre, that knowledge of
society must advance in step with knowledge of nature, or that
intellectual progress guarantees progress in happiness or in virtue;
nor with the *philosophes* that the evidence of history entitles us to
expect perpetual progress, however well theorists such as Herder,
Saint-Simon and Spencer have attempted to deal with the counter-
evidence. Nor is it to accept, with the German idealists, that in the

course of history the full potential of either man or nature is certain to be realized, nor with Condorcet, Herder, Saint-Simon, Comte, Marx or Spencer that there are laws of history at all, let alone ones ensuring progress. Indeed it is surely a misconception to hold that any natural law, such as that of evolution by adaptation and selection, governs human history: for (as Soviet Academicians frequently assert) mankind moulds its own future, not least by deliberate action and other choices formed under the influence of ideas, and is free, as T. H. Huxley pointed out, to protect the weak and vulnerable, who might in the ordinary course of nature have perished, and, we might add, to falsify laws of history and make the unimaginable come true.

Understanding human society involves, as Saint-Simon says, an understanding of the interconnectedness of many aspects of life, the political, moral and religious among them: even if economic forces were unduly neglected before the time of Marx, the significance of ideas, though doubtless exaggerated by Comte, should not be underplayed. For this very reason it is important to see that some ideas are dangerous. Such, as we have seen, is the idea of perpetual progress in both East and West; such was the evolutionary ethic of Spencer, which forewent for at least some times and places the inhibitions inherent in received morality against predatory attitudes; such was Guizot's notion that civilization must be progressive, both culturally and materially, and that without these tendencies any society is uncivilized; and such, I suggest, are the Marxist ideas that 'nature must be humanised' and that 'the biosphere must be optimised' for human benefit.

Engels too readily assumed a conflict between man and nature, and that where man does not control nature, its unsubdued forces control him. Despite his understanding of the way that human 'conquests' of nature can recoil on the conqueror's head, he continued to insist on conquest, even though he used, to describe it, the language of unity with nature and of overcoming the 'contradiction' between man and nature which he found in Christianity.[75] But, even if human needs often have moral precedence over those of other species (see chapter 9), it is mistaken to regard nature as *either* hostile *or* subdued. For this is nearly as anthropocentric as holding that everything exists for mankind, or that nothing is indifferent to the interests of humanity. Yet life in an optimized biosphere, where nothing on the earth's surface was wild, might easily not be worth living.

Thus Engels' valuable ecological insights fall short of their promise when conjoined with belief in the inevitability of material and technological progress. But much more harmful still has been the prevalent belief in progress in Western society, which has been (until recently) too little influenced by any such insights. Certainly the moralizing of the idea of progress, under the influence of advocates of equality and of freedom, has allowed it to be used as a valuable weapon of social criticism; and advances in the understanding of nature and society have facilitated and enhanced this effect.[76] But the uncritical notion which the same idea has often sponsored, that whatever can be done must be done, that modernization is improvement, and that to oppose the exploitation of opportunities for profit is to fight against the tide of history has served as a rationale for graspingness and has underlain many of the disruptions of nature, both home-grown in the West and exported by the West worldwide. Rather than the beliefs of Judaism and Christianity, the attitude in large measure responsible for environmental degradation in East and West has been the belief in perennial material progress inherited from the Enlightenment and the German metaphysicians, as modified in the West by the classical economists and sociologists, by liberal individualism[77] and by social Darwinism, and in Eastern Europe by the unquestioned deference accorded to Marx and to Engels.

Accordingly there is reason to reject belief that progress is irresistible, that nature should without limit be humanized, or that technological and social planning is bound to solve all our problems. Yet there is no reason to reject belief in the desirability or the possibility of many of the strands in the notion of progress. We can in some measure mould our own future, and to do so we need whatever understanding of nature and society we can come by, combined with a moral vision of states of society and of the world which would count as better than the present ones, and such grounds as there are for hope that we can move towards them. These indeed are prerequisites for the conservation of resources and the preservation of endangered species and vulnerable habitats, as well as for human well-being and social and international justice. But to accept this is to adopt a form of belief in progress; thus, far from all of the humane, secular tradition of the Enlightenment philosophers, of Kant, Marx, Engels and the others needs to be rejected. Indeed the combined resources of this and the older Judaeo-Christian tradition, suitably refined, are capable of allowing us to cope with our ecological problems without devising a new metaphysics or a new ethic. In Part Two an attempt will be made to reason from accepted judgements to a satisfactory environmental ethic, and to observe a few of its social implications.

NOTES

1 John Barr (ed.), *The Environmental Handbook*, London: Ballantine and Friends of the Earth, 1971, p. 10.
2 J. B. Bury, *The Idea of Progress*, London: Macmillan Press, 1920.
3 John Baillie, *The Belief in Progress*, London, Glasgow and Toronto: Oxford University Press, 1950.
4 John Passmore, *The Perfectibility of Man*, London: Duckworth, 1970 (hereinafter *PM*), 212—15.
5 *PM*, pp. 195, 216.
6 Robert Nisbet, *History of the Idea of Progress*, London: Heinemann, 1980.
7 *PM*, p. 196.
8 Baillie, *The Belief in Progress*, p. 103.
9 Joseph Priestley, *An Essay on the First Principles of Government and on Political, Civil and Religious Liberty*, London: (2nd edn) 1771, pp. 4f, cited by Carl Becker, *The Heavenly City of the Eighteenth-Century Philosophers*, New Haven and London: Yale University Press, 1932, pp. 144f.
10 *Aphorisms*, Book One, III: *The New Organon*, ed. Fulton H. Anderson, Indianapolis and New York: Bobbs-Merrill, 1960, p. 39.
11 Morris Ginsberg, *The Idea of Progress: A Revaluation*, Westport, Conn.: Greenwood Press, 1953, p. 77.
12 *The Belief in Progress*, p. 104.
13 Bury, *The Idea of Progress*, p. 110.
14 *PM*, chapter 8, 'Perfecting by Social Action: The Presuppositions'.
15 *PM*, p. 159.
16 At the end of his *Concerning Education*, cited at *PM*, p. 159. For a sustained critique of the Lockean view that the new-born infant is a *tabula rasa*, see Mary Midgley, *Beast and Man: The Roots of Human Nature*, Hassocks: Harvester Press, 1979.
17 *The Belief in Progress*, p. 108.
18 Ibid. pp. 102—4; see also chapter 4 (above).
19 Bury, *The Idea of Progress*, p. 150.
20 Ibid. pp. 156f.
21 Ibid. pp. 186—8.
22 Ibid. pp. 208—10; Baillie, *The Belief in Progress*, pp. 115f.
23 Nisbet, *History of the Idea of Progress*, pp. 185, 189.
24 Ibid. pp. 334f.
25 Becker, *The Heavenly City of the Eighteenth-Century Philosophers*, pp. 119—68.
26 *PM*, pp. 215—19.

27 *PM*, p. 220.
28 Cf. chapter 2, 'Physical Theology', of Robin Attfield, *God and The Secular,* Cardiff: University College Cardiff Press, 1978.
29 I have discussed these matters further in 'Against Incomparabilism', *Philosophy*, 50, 1975, 230—4, and in 'How Not to be a Moral Relativist', *The Monist*, 62, 1979, 510—21.
30 Cited at *PM*, p. 226.
31 Bury, *The Idea of Progress,* p. 251.
32 Cited at *PM*, p. 233.
33 Black, *Man's Dominion,* Edinburgh: Edinburgh University Press, 1970, p. 105.
34 Bury, *The Idea of Progress*, p. 251.
35 Cited at *PM*, p. 233.
36 Bury, *The Idea of Progress,* pp. 260—77.
37 Ibid. pp. 282—5.
38 Ginsberg, *The Idea of Progress: A Revaluation,* p. 24.
39 Bury, *The Idea of Progress*, pp. 291—4, 299—301.
40 Ibid. pp. 304—6.
41 Cited ibid. p. 274.
42 Ibid. p. 276.
43 Ibid. pp. 309—12.
44 Ihid. pp. 336f, *PM*, p. 241.
45 Ibid. pp. 344f; *PM*, pp. 244f.
46 'Evolution is an integration of matter and concomitant dissipation of motion; during which the matter passes from a relatively indefinite, incoherent homogeneity to a relatively definite coherent heterogeneity; and during which the retained motion undergoes a parallel transformation.' Presented at p. 47 of F. Howard Collins, *Epitome of the Synthetic Philosophy of Herbert Spencer*, London: Williams & Northgate, 1889. (Collins' *Epitome* ran to multiple editions in Britain, America, France, Germany and Russia.)
47 Bury's paraphrase, *The Idea of Progress*, pp. 338f.
48 Ibid. p. 339.
49 *PM*, p. 241.
50 Bury, *The Idea of Progress,* p. 339.
51 Ibid. p. 347.
52 Karl Marx, *Selected Works*, 2 Vols., Moscow, 1949 and London, 1950, Vol. II, p. 410, cited in *PM*, p. 236.
53 In 'On Being Human', *Inquiry*, 17, 1974, 175—92.
54 Innokenty Gerasimov, 'Man, Society and the Geographical Environment', in *Society and the Environment: a Soviet View* (ed. anon.), Moscow: Progress Publishers, 1977, 25—36, p. 25.
55 Ibid. p. 26. His quotation is from F. Engels, *Anti-Dühring,* Moscow, 1975, p. 320.
56 Yevgeny Fyodorov and Ilya Novik, 'Ecological Aspects of Social

Progress', in *Society and the Environment*, 37—55, p. 43. Their quotation is from K. Marx, *Capital*, Vol. III, Moscow, 1974, p. 820. See also Richard and Val Routley, 'Social Theories, Self Management, and Environmental Problems', in Don Mannison, Michael McRobbie and Richard Routley (eds), *Environmental Philosophy*, Canberra: Australian National University, 1980, 217—332, p. 318.

57   Fyodorov and Novik, 'Ecological Aspects of Social Progress', p. 47.
58   Alfred Schmidt, *The Concept of Nature in Marx*, New York: Humanities Press, 1972, p. 162, cited by Howard L. Parsons, *Marx and Engels on Ecology*, Westport, Conn. and London: Greenwood Press, 1977, p. 49.
59   Parsons, *Marx and Engels on Ecology*, pp. 43f, 49—51.
60   Ibid. p. 37.
61   At this point Parsons refers, as his source, to Leo Marx, *The Machine in the Garden: Technology and the Pastoral Ideal*, New York: Oxford University Press, 1964.
62   Here Parsons cites Roderick Nash, *Wilderness and the American Mind*, New Haven: Yale University Press, 1967, chapter 2.
63   Karl Marx, *Capital*, Vol. I, trans. Samuel Moore and Edward Aveling, ed. F. Engels, New York: International Publishers, 1967, pp. 505—7; cited by Parsons, *Marx and Engels on Ecology*, p. 174. Cf. his pp. 183f.
64   Karl Marx, *Capital*, Vol. III, trans. Ernest Unterman, ed. F. Engels, New York: International Publishers, 1967, pp. 101—3; cited by Parsons, *Marx and Engels on Ecology*, pp. 177f.
65   Fyodorov and Novik, 'Ecological Aspects of Social Progress', p. 53.
66   F. Engels, *Dialectics of Nature*, Moscow, 1974, p. 180, cited by Pavel Oldak, 'The Environment and Social Production', *Society and the Environment*, 56—68, p. 56.
67   F. Engels, *Dialectics of Nature*, New York: International Publishers, 1954, p. 246; Parsons, *Marx and Engels on Ecology*, p. 182.
68   Fyodorov and Novik, 'Ecological Aspects of Social Progress', pp. 43f; Oldak, 'The Environment and Social Production', p. 61.
69   Fyodorov and Novik, 'Ecological Aspects of Social Progress', pp. 37—41; Oldak, 'The Environment and Social Production', p. 64.
70   Fyodorov and Novik, 'Ecological Aspects of Social Progress', p. 48.
71   Gerasimov, 'Man, Society and the Geographical Environment', p. 34.
72   Nicolai Semenov, 'Energetics for the Future', *Society and the Environment*, 69—98, pp. 93f.
73   Thus Mary Hesse, 'On the Alleged Incompatibility between Christianity and Science', in Hugh Montefiore (ed.), *Man and Nature*, London: Collins, 1975, pp. 121—31.
74   Cf. Ginsberg, p. 51.
75   In *Dialectics of Nature*; Parsons, *Marx and Engels on Ecology*, p. 180.
76   Thus Ginsberg, *The Idea of Progress: A Revaluation*, p. 71.
77   See Mary Midgley's strictures on individualism in 'The Limits of

Individualism' (forthcoming paper), and those of Val and Richard
Routley on conventional liberalism in 'Human Chauvinism and
Environmental Ethics' in *Environmental Philosophy*, 96—189, pp.
97—120.

PART TWO   APPLIED ETHICS

6

Future Generations

I now turn to ethical considerations, and in this chapter in particular to the nature and grounding of our obligations towards future people. This will require a change of method, away from a historical approach to a more traditionally philosophical one. Thus in order to consider the basis of our obligations, I shall be reviewing various theories of normative ethics, theories about the criteria of right action and of obligation. But I shall also be concerned with particular obligations, ones attested by widespread intuitive judgements or by moral reflection on them, even where they do not tally with the predictions or the yield of the theories.

The issue of obligations to future generations proves to bring out the inadequacy of several such theories, and a method is accordingly in place which allows theories to be revised or even rejected where they fail to account for deeply held reflective moral intuitions, rather than one which requires judgements to be uniformly tailored to fit one or another theory. Reflective judgements are, after all, the principal data from which theories in normative ethics are constructed, with the manifest proviso that judgements which are inconsistent must be revised with the help of theory, rather than being sustained at the expense of inconsistency. One of my aims, then, is to arrive at a 'reflective equilibrium' between judgements and theory, and between normative principles and their application.

In my own view, in fact, there are recognizable limits and a recognizable scope to moral reasoning, discernible from *a priori* considerations such as the meaning of the very concept of morality, as well as from the *a posteriori* study of particular judgements; but I shall not be arguing the matter here, and mention it mainly to avoid giving the misleading impression that the methodology of reasoning in ethics is limited to a consideration of the interplay of intuitions and normative theories, the kind of interplay presented just now.

Nevertheless the present chapter is a study of just such an interplay.

Readers, however, may well feel entitled to know what view is here assumed of the status of moral talk and moral claims. My view, argued elsewhere,[1] is that moral discourse is not concerned merely with prescriptions or expressions of attitude or commitment; it aspires to truth and actually admits of knowledge. This view has recently been ably defended by Renford Bambrough,[2] though I should add that I am more sympathetic than he is to naturalism, the view that moral judgements can be validly derived exclusively from facts (e.g. facts about harms or benefits) and conceptual truths. But my naturalism does not prevent me from finding common ground with anti-naturalist writers such as K. S. Shrader-Frechette,[3] at any rate in the area of applied ethics. The current enterprise, then, is aimed at discovering the truth about some of our obligations: and to this enterprise writers of various meta-ethical persuasions seem to have contributed, even if they do not acknowledge that there is such a truth.[4] But as I am not defending moral objectivism here, I cannot complain if some readers treat the chapters which follow as simply a search for the best available consistent and defensible ethical position.

The issue of obligations to future generations is a good starting-point for a discussion of ecological ethics. There are other distinct issues, important examples of which (the status of animals; the value of life) will be discussed in subsequent chapters. The current issue has been chosen because it allows (and indeed requires) normative theories to be assessed, because of its key role in ecological issues, and because it can be tackled without a comprehensive value-theory being elaborated. To keep the present chapter within reasonable limits, I have as far as possible postponed the issues of the obligation to perpetuate the human population and of the intrinsic value of future people, though it has not been possible at all points to avoid related matters, particularly where the question arises of the representation of the interests of possible people who on some plans will exist and on others will not. For the most part, however, I shall be concerned with obligations to people who, for one reason or another, *will* exist, irrespective of whether there should have been less (or more) of them, and whether earlier generations should have acted earlier to modify their numbers.

The importance of posterity in the beliefs of Enlightenment thinkers has already been discussed in chapter 5; indeed their recognition that it is increasingly within the power of those alive to affect the interests of those who are to follow belies the frequent claim in recent literature that there is nothing about the current issue to learn from the philosophical tradition. Yet the extent and the basis of our obligations in the matter are yet to seek. There again the ethic of stewardship, presented in chapters 2 and 3 as immune to the objections of which some other interpretations of the Judaeo-Christian tradition fall foul, might be thought equal to the need to cater for the interests of our successors. Indeed Brian Barry at one point seems, however inadvertently, to regard a recognizable version of it as suiting this need, in preference to all the traditional theories of normative ethics.[5] But to discover whether it really has implications which transcend concern for the interests of humans and other organisms, as he seems to think, it is most convenient to work out first the bearing of some of these theories, and then see whether, as Barry seems to suggest, it is in conflict with them.

Genuine obligations

On the assumption, then, that there will be people in the future, what obligations do we have in their regard? Here there is, as Gregory Kavka has pointed out,[6] an analogy with the case of the obligations of rich individuals and groups to offer aid to strangers in desperate need. If there are such obligations, then where the needs of future people compare with those of contemporary strangers, the same obligations would seem to exist to make sacrifices to alleviate needs which would otherwise be desperate. But future people will need clean air and water, fertile land, and the same natural ecosystems as those on which we ourselves depend, and we can sustain or mar all these things, and conserve or exhaust resources (some renewable, some non-renewable) which they will also require. Since they are in no way relevantly different from contemporary strangers, we have corresponding obligations in the two cases.

That rich societies do have obligations to contemporary strangers in desperate need is a proposition answering to a widespread intuitive judgement, and also a proposition which has been well argued for elsewhere.[7] Once it is accepted that we, the affluent, are morally responsible, in cases where we could prevent it, for the avoidable suffering or misery of a stranger, it is implausible to hold that distance in space makes any difference. (The ability to prevent suffering is certainly a matter of degree, but the degree does not vary with spatial distance.) And the same reasoning which suggests that we have obligations wherever we can prevent suffering or misery to contemporary strangers, however distant in space, suggests that we have similar obligations to future strangers, however distant in time: for distance in time is just as irrelevant as distance in space. Since a whole variety of plausible principles give rise to the same conclusion, it is not necessary to explore its grounds in more detail at this stage.

Richard and Val Routley reach a conclusion about the wrongness of exposing future people to one particular danger, the danger of radiation from nuclear wastes, by means of a graphic analogy. If someone consigns a container full of highly toxic and explosive gas to an overcrowded bus belonging to a poorly managed Third World bus-line, a bus with a long journey to make over hazardous roads, we should regard their action as morally appalling, even if they themselves stand to lose a great deal if they do not thus despatch it. Excuses such as that the worst *may* not happen, or that the passengers *may* be killed by a road accident first, would not be tolerated. 'To create serious risks and costs, especially risks to life and health for . . . others, simply to avoid having to make some changes to a comfortable life-style, or even for a somewhat better reason, is usually thought deserving of moral condemnation, and sometimes considered a crime.'[8] Yet in many respects, the Routleys claim, such an act is analogous to acts with effects on future people like producing and storing toxic nuclear wastes which will be radioactive for over a million years, initiated when no safe way of packaging them is known.

Whether or not they are right (and some reasons for endorsing their view emerge in the course of the current chapter), the bus analogy certainly does mirror any case where we inflict risks and dangers on future people without a good reason, such as the need to overcome a comparable evil threatening millions of people in the present. And even where present costs are at stake, there is no excuse for ignoring costs and risks to future people; present costs may be included in our moral deliberations, but we must not disregard all considerations besides. If so, then it must be acknowledged that we have obligations with regard to future people.

Discounting

But do the needs of future people merit *equal* consideration to that due to present people's needs? Kavka considers three reasons for giving less consideration to the future than to the present, and rejects them all, and others including the Routleys go through some parallel reasoning.

Kavka first considers the view that the very temporal location of future people entitles us to downgrade their interests. The fact that they do not even exist at present has certainly raised problems about whether we can speak of them as having rights; yet, granted that 'in the normal course of events' they will exist, and will be in no relevant way unlike current holders of rights, and that we have it in our power seriously to undermine their interests, there is little reason to cavil at Feinberg's conclusion that they have rights now which can be claimed on their behalf, unless 'right' is so narrowly defined as to make this conclusion false.[9] (We can either construe Feinberg's conclusion as meaning that there are rights which, when they are alive, they will have against our generation, or allow, with the Routleys, that nonexistent entities may even so have properties — bearing rights in the present included.) Kavka's reply to those who discount the needs of future people just on grounds of their temporal location is that as it is recognized that rational prudence treats an individual's future desires as being on a par with present ones, it should also be recognized that a rational morality would attach no intrinsic importance to the temporal location of people's welfare. (Kavka is here setting on one side for the moment *uncertain* future desires, and in this I follow him.)

There is, however, an apparently more plausible ground for discriminating purely on the basis of time, a ground which is seldom remarked. The present generation is the last one which can help those now alive, whereas people in the distant future can be assisted by a number of succeeding generations as well as by the present one. Thus the responsibility of saving for future generations can be shared between the various earlier ones. So in matters where there is reason to think that other generations will be able and willing to play a part, the current generation does not bear the entire burden, and its obligation to provide for some future needs is therefore lesser than its obligation in cases of some contemporary needs, which will be catered for now or never.

The immediate rejoinder to this is the observation that some present actions engender risks or harms to future generations whatever anyone else does henceforth, and that in those cases the opportunities open to our immediate successors to help their own successors are irrelevant. The more general point is perhaps as follows. Where action is needed, but others are likely to do what is necessary (in whole or in part), the difference that we make, and at the same time the extent of our obligation, is less than when, by action or inaction, we make a crucial difference to the future course of events. But in fact we have it in our power irreversibly to mar the distant future; so the general point just made has no bearing on a great many possible present actions with distant effects, and thus does not show the temporal location of the effects of our actions to be of any moral significance in itself. Indeed the general point applies indifferently whether the effects are close or distant, while at the same time explaining the fact that our responsibility to distant generations is in many cases a shared one.

Kavka next considers ignorance and uncertainty. It may be alleged, he remarks, that we cannot know what future people will want, so we cannot rate their interests on a par with those of contemporaries. But, as he says in reply, we can be confident about much that they will need whatever they want — good health, food, shelter and security; and there is much that we can do to facilitate these needs. The same reply is offered by Robert E. Goodin to another form of uncertainty argument, the argument that the costs to future people of present deeds are uncertain, as they are risks, not certainties, as future technology may dispel them, and as everyone may be dead before they have any effect; so we can discount future interests.[10] But the possibility that everyone will be dead before our deeds can harm anyone is, as the Routleys point out, an unacceptable excuse, as is also putting on others the burden of finding means to avert dangers devised by ourselves; and though, as Goodin allows, merely probable risks are less bad than certain ones, much current action is subversive of interests and desires which future people are certain to have. (And if so, Shrader-Frechette is all the more clearly right to point out that the uncertainty of costs does not entitle us to disregard them altogether.[11])

Kavka finds a variant of the argument from ignorance in the claim of Martin Golding that we should regard future people as members of our moral community only if we know what to desire for them, but that we cannot know this for distant generations, as we cannot know what their conception of the good life for man will be.[12] In reply, Kavka denies that holding any particular substantive conception of the good life is necessary for membership of the human moral community. So long as there are people with our vulnerabilities and our general capacities, they will be entitled to our moral concern whatever their beliefs and desires; though doubtless, for one reason or another — their genetic endowment and the general circumstances of social life may be suggested — their conception of the good life will be importantly similar, at least in form, to our own. Thus our ignorance as to their substantive conceptions is no reason for limiting our obligations, as Golding would do, to at most the immediate generations of our successors. Indeed, as the Routleys point out, if we can affect future people by storing nuclear wastes for a million years, we have obligations to at least some 30,000 generations.[13]

Kavka considers, thirdly, the relevance of the contingency of future people, the fact that they may not exist at all, and that how many there are depends in large measure upon ourselves. Feinberg presents a related problem: we do not know who these future people will be, and so, it could be held, we can scarcely owe them obligations.[14] But as he remarks, our nearly certain knowledge that there will be a human future is what matters: we do not need to know people's identity before we can have obligations in their regard. The Routleys present another version of this problem: our ignorance of the numbers of future people, and of most other statistics about them, might be thought to suggest that we cannot weigh their claims alongside those of present people. But as they observe, our ignorance of numbers does not permit us to ignore these claims, even if in some cases the resulting conflicts would be difficult to resolve: for determinacy of numbers is not a pre-condition of moral relevance, and any theory which makes it so is not to be taken seriously in this respect.[15]

But if we can affect the number of future consumers, do we not have a prior obligation to current ones, who exist anyway? As to future ones, perhaps what we ought to do is to curtail their numbers, and thus resolve the possible conflict of interests. This is the version of the contingency problem raised by Kavka himself. I cannot pursue all the implications here, since it raises the complex issues of whether we ought to limit the human population, and whether we should do anything wrong if we allowed it to die out. (To these issues I shall return in the next chapter.) For the present, suffice it to say that the problem concerns possible people only in the sense of 'ones whom we and the groups to which we belong could bring into existence if we chose' (ones called by Trudy Govier 'volitionally possible people'[16]), but not ones who will probably exist anyway, and over whose existence we have no control. In actual fact we can be very nearly certain that there will be a very great many future people, and, once we accept their future existence as given, the present problem ceases to supply a ground for subordinating their interests to those of existing contemporaries.

Goodin mentions two other possible grounds for discounting future interests: the prospect that future people will be better off than ourselves, and the supposed diminished value of benefits which are enjoyed later rather than earlier. His reply on the first count is that future people may for all we know be worse off, and that we should need to know that they will be a good deal richer than ourselves before we could justifiably burden them with the risks of leaking radioactive waste storage dumps. He might have added, had he not been restricting himself to energy policies, that actions of ours which imperil life-support systems could undermine the vital interests of our successors, however rich, and so the effect of discounting could be one of irretrievable disaster for them in exchange for much lesser welfare gains to our contemporaries.

The second count depends on an analogy between costs, benefits and monetary values. The value of money depreciates over time with inflation, so a dollar now is worth much more now than it will be in ten years' time. Something similar is also often true of both benefits and costs: delaying either often involves some of the other. But as Goodin points out, this is no argument for a social discount rate. Interest rates are unstable and unpredictable, and many damages which may be suffered in future as a result of present actions cannot be compensated for in money, even if funds are now invested with a view to the interest providing for predicted costs. Besides, as Derek Parfit points out, benefits are often not reinvested but consumed, and are thus of no greater benefit to anyone than similar benefits received later; while in other cases there is no gain involved in delayed costs, as for example if a genetic defect is suffered by one person in 20 years rather than by another next year. Hence the costs and benefits of deferment should be reckoned only where they will exist; they do not justify a diminished weighting of future interests in general.[17] It should be added that even quite low rates of discounting the future have the effect of attaching a quite negligible value to any at all distant future interests, and are thus, as the Routleys point out, open to the same moral objections as policies which write off future people entirely.[18]

Indeed I can best summarize the conclusion so far reached by endorsing theirs: *'there is the same obligation to future people as to the present.'*[19] Future people count, to speak morally, as much as present ones. Our obligations in their regard are only lessened where special known factors supervene, for example, cases where efforts on their behalf are likely to miscarry. Our obligations to people are not lessened at all by the mere fact of their futurity.

Superseded theories

This conclusion, however, based as it is on reflection on widespread moral intuitions, is, as Brian Barry has pointed out,[20] in conflict with several classical theories of the circumstances which give rise to obligations, and of the scope and limits of our duties. Barry stresses the asymmetry of power between generations which do not overlap; earlier ones can help or hurt later ones, but later ones cannot affect earlier ones (except over their members' reputations). On no less than three classical theories this asymmetry disqualifies the later generations from being the beneficiaries of obligations owed by the earlier ones. The discussion of these theories, which now follows, prepares the way for a search for a more adequate normative theory, one which as well as coping with other departments of morality can also account for our very real obligations towards future people.

According to one theory, that of David Hume, justice and moral obligations have their point because they are in the general interest of partially self-interested persons, persons of approximately equal strength and vulnerable to each other. As Barry points out elsewhere,[21] Hume held that justice arises and has a point in conditions of moderate scarcity, but that there are no obligations where scarcity is extreme; and that it has force among parties who are vulnerable to one another, but would have none in relations between humans and a weaker species, however rational and intelligent its members. Now granted the asymmetry of power between present and future generations, the latter must be regarded by a Humean as in the same position as such a weaker species, and so obligations to them (or even in their regard) would have to be denied. Nor is this surprising, if morality is construed as an artifice of self-defence which at normal times benefits all participants.

Should we then hold to Hume's theory, despite its failure to uphold obligations towards future people? Barry is, I suggest, right to reject it. Hume succeeds in portraying circumstances in which justice might arise and be accepted as advantageous, and then confuses and conflates these circumstances and the limits of justice. In fact his theory is in several ways in violation of our moral intuitions. Thus we do not hold that the right to life holds only in conditions of moderate scarcity, but lapses in circumstances of famine. Nor do we hold that there can be no obligations owed to the defenceless. Indeed, as Barry observes, even Hume does not manage consistently to maintain otherwise.[22]

The second longstanding view discussed by Barry is that obligations arise through people living beside others in a community with its reciprocal relationships. Such a view clearly has no place for obligations to those of our successors who are born after we die. Barry finds such a view in Golding,[23] though Golding does allow there to be possible obligations to those future people with whose conception of the good life ours has enough in common. But, as we have seen, this is too restrictive: and if Golding's community theory is to be rejected on this count, so *a fortiori* must any theory be which does not make provision for non-members of the community to which the agent happens to belong.

Thirdly Barry considers the view on which obligations are grounded in entitlements to property, a view which he ascribes to John Locke and to Robert Nozick's book *Anarchy, State and Utopia*.[24] On this view those who come by a good justly may do what they like with it, and owe no obligations with respect of it to anyone. (Locke in fact accepted such property rights only if there were comparable gifts of nature left over and to spare for others,[25] but seems too readily to have assumed that the condition would always be satisfied.[26]) But if no obligations are owed to contemporaries (except over property rights of theirs), no more, to say the least, will be owed to the people of the future, who never hold property rights at the same time as any of their predecessors.

But once again the theory under consideration conflicts with widely held moral intuitions besides the ones about future people. Thus we do not hold that there is no obligation to give material assistance to a person in desperate need whom we can help, whether a member of our community or a stranger; and, there again, justice may require a redistribution of property (as, plausibly, in several Latin American countries), however justly it was arrived at.

Accordingly I accept Barry's rejection of all these theories of normative ethics. Barry next discusses the theory of John Passmore, which yields the conclusion that our obligations are to immediate posterity only.[27] Passmore draws on the presumed support of the diverse normative theories of Jeremy Bentham, Henry Sidgwick, John Rawls and Martin Golding; but the Routleys cast serious doubt on whether any of them afford it.[28] Passmore's own basic theory is that our obligations depend on what we love. Accordingly, as our loves do not stretch into the distant future, neither do our obligations. To this theory it may be replied that obligations can exist irrespective of feelings, that we have obligations to many distant people about whom we have no feelings; and that the claim that an obligation lapses just because a love has lapsed would be too easy a way of disowning an obligation. Passmore also appeals sometimes to the view that obligations depend on membership of a community, a view which has already been rejected. He also makes great play with the uncertainty of future people's interests. But, as Barry retorts, 'Of course, we don't know what the precise tastes of our remote descendants will be, but they are unlikely to include a desire for skin cancer, soil erosion, or the inundation of low-lying areas as a result of the melting of the ice-caps.'[29]

Towards a better theory

What theory of normative ethics, then, is equal to giving a coherent treatment of obligations to future generations? This question is now pursued with the help of Jere Paul Surber's survey.[30] Surber, like Barry, concludes that no existing type of theory is satisfactory. Surber considers in turn deontic theories, utilitarian theories and the position of Golding. He does not find anyone in the literature even attempting to apply a deontic theory to the issue of obligations to the future, though strictly John Rawls' theory (to which I shall return) is such, for Rawls holds that it is not exclusively their consequences that justify actions or rules,[31] and he certainly discusses what he himself calls 'The Problem of Justice between Generations'.[32] But Surber seems to mean by 'deontic theories' rather theories on which agents possess rights which cannot be abridged, whatever the circumstances, or on which some actions are wrong, whatever the consequences. Some of his criticisms of such theories are less than convincing, but I accept his central criticism that if such a theory accepted obligations to the future alongside ones to the present, it would lack the resources to decide the priorities between these various obligations, just as in general such theories characteristically offer no solution when obligations conflict; and we should lack just the sort of guidance which we might reasonably expect from a theory whose role is to disclose which act is morally right. (I shall later consider whether Rawls surmounts this objection by supplying acceptable principles and rules of priority.)

But Surber does not, in the end, find the position of Golding a satisfactory one, and is quite unimpressed with utilitarianism. He grants that, being a future-orientated, consequentialist type of theory, utilitarianism is apparently well-suited to dealing with obligations towards future people. But he holds that the 'classical formula' on which 'that action (or rule) is the most desirable which will maximize the average utility' is inapplicable when applied to any generation of future people, as we cannot deal in averages when the number of the population is not fixed.

Though I shall be criticizing in chapter 7 some of the deliverances of this, the Average theory version of utilitarianism, the theory is often regarded as being better able to cope with examples where populations are not fixed than its counterpart, the Total theory. And I do not think that Surber's objection suffices to overthrow this assessment. According to the Total theory, it is desirable (or, on other interpretations, obligatory) to maximize total utility. As Surber points out, where populations are fixed, the two theories commend exactly the same acts (or rules), for total and average vary together. They diverge only where the average and the total part company, i.e. in cases where the denominator (the number of people involved) is itself at issue. And here it is often supposed that the Total theory requires the population to be maximized, and that it is an advantage of the Average theory that it does not.

Surber derives his criticism of the Average theory from J. Brenton Stearns,[33] who persuades himself that the indeterminacy of the number of future people makes the Average theory collapse. But upholders of this theory need only maintain instead that the average utility is the average of that of however many people there will be. On their view if an increase in numbers raises this average it should be preferred, but if it lowers the average it should be rejected. The only issue on which it is not equipped to deliver a judgement one way or the other is that of which to prefer of two different populations with the same average utility. But, this issue aside, the theory is not open to Surber's and Stearns' objection, nor therefore to that of the Routleys to theories which require determinacy as a condition of supplying a moral judgement. (Indeed we could in many cases know that total or average welfare would rise or fall without having any particular quantitative level in mind: so utilitarianism in general is immune to this objection.)

Much more than Surber, Stearns is impressed with the fact that the arguments used by conservationists are almost always utilitarian, and naturally so. Concern to conserve resources, ecosystems and gene-pools, or to prevent pollution and ugliness, is most readily grounded in benevolence towards the interests of our contemporaries and successors. (Some conservationists hold that arguments from human interests are insufficient, but I shall postpone arguments concerning other interests to later chapters.) So despite some misgivings, Stearns operates within the utilitarian tradition, and adopts a variant of the Total theory. We have an obligation, he holds, to maximize intrinsic goods and to minimize intrinsic evils, irrespective of which people they befall. Our obligation then is not to definite people, but 'to see to it that human existence continues at a fairly high level of intrinsic value'.

These distinctions, and the rival merits of the Total theory and the Average theory, will be more fully discussed in the next chapter, where their relations with the population issue and with the value of life will be explored. For present purposes it is worth noticing that either of these two versions of utilitarianism could defensibly be held to underpin obligations to future generations, at least as far as we have seen. The only unanswered objection to either so far is the standard criticism of the Total theory that it requires too high a level of population. But as it does not require us to bring into existence people who will not lead lives worth living, or people whose addition to the population diminishes the total happiness, this objection is by no means obviously fatal. This is far from the end of the matter, but the Total theory is obviously not indefensible.

Surber in fact rejects Stearns' own version of the Total theory because Stearns combines it with belief in duties to definite (existent or 'contracted for') people, and believes that this duality of principles gives rise to incommensurable obligations within utilitarianism; and this, it will be recalled, is the weakness over which Surber rejected deontic theories earlier. But it is not clear that benevolence to known persons is incommensurable with benevolence to future persons of indefinite identity: there seems nothing incoherent in asking whether cheap energy for some of the former outweighs the risks of radiation leaks for rather more of the latter. Stearns gets into the position of accepting irreducible duties to assignable persons as well as the duty of benevolence through his less-than-total rejection of Jan Narveson's form of utilitarianism, on which our duties are limited to assignable persons (plus duties of non-maleficence),[34] a theory also to be discussed in the next chapter. Believing that our duties extend beyond this, he takes our duties in the connection of indefinite future people to be incommensurable with some of the duties which Narveson acknowledges: but this concession is, as far as I can see, unnecessary.

Surber, however, has another objection to utilitarian theories in general. Some of the benefits which obligations to future generations secure are, he holds, incalculable. His examples are the *possibility* of encountering a natural environment, and the *experience* of deciding for themselves how to manage it. But utilitarianism, he holds, can only treat with calculable goods.

I, too, doubt whether these goods derive their value solely from the amounts of happiness which they facilitate, and therefore reject any purely hedonistic form of utilitarianism. But I believe that other forms of consequentialism (to which the term 'utilitarianism' is sometimes applied by extension), which count the ability to exercise essential human powers as an intrinsic good alongside happiness, can cope with the examples just mentioned. For, as long as terms like 'more' and 'less' can intelligibly be applied, consequentialists do not need to calculate the value of, say, experiences in terms of units of intrinsic value of their own devising. The use of numerical examples in discussions of utilitarian theory misleads us if we assume that it can only deal with given quantities. The same point applies, so far as their effect on humans is concerned, to Surber's other examples — the loss of an animal species or of the beauty of an unspoiled forest. And even though other interests or considerations plausibly enter into these examples (e.g. animal interests), that is no reason for taking them to involve evils with which utilitarianism cannot deal.

Barry too has an objection to utilitarianism, or at least to the Total theory, an objection which it is important to consider. Having rejected as spurious the claim that ignorance of the future exonerates us of obligations concerning its more distant generations, Barry nevertheless expresses sympathy for the conclusion of John Passmore that what utilitarianism requires of us is too rigorous.[35] I propose to take this view not as a refusal to undertake acknowledged obligations, but as a rejection of the belief that they exist. What, then, is implausible or extreme about the obligations involved in the Total theory? At times Barry implies that consequentialism might conflict with justice, a claim which I have contested elsewhere.[36] But the present context suggests that Barry's objection is rather along the following lines: the Total theory requires us to give equal consideration, as far as we can make any difference, to all generations, present and future; but this extends the duties of the present generation up to, and possibly beyond, the limits of our capacities.

It is not at all clear, however, that this conclusion follows. I do not just have in mind the fact that we cannot have duties beyond our capacities. The main way in which we can serve the people of the distant future is by *refraining* from various actions which would imperil their environment or their health, and these omissions are well within our powers. Besides this, the renewable resources which they will need can be provided for, as far as it is up to us, by conserving them in a self-renewing (or at least renewable) condition:

and the same applies to those institutions the bequeathing of which to our successors constitutes our main obligation to them in Passmore's view.

As to savings, two points are significant. As we may learn from Kenneth Boulding,[37] future people will have most call for a stock of unexhausted natural resources (and of knowledge in the arts and the sciences), rather than for the means to a high level of consumption. Again the likelihood that some of our more immediate successors will provide for some of the needs in question diminishes the difference which can be made by ourselves. Problems certainly remain over the use of some non-renewable resources (e.g. ores and fossil fuels), but, all things considered, the obligations which the Total theory generates do not seem to be unrealistically exacting, extensive though they are. (It is interesting to note that Barry's objection here presupposes the falsity of Surber's objection about calculating benefits.)

The contractarian approach

Barry, however, prefers to investigate the possibility of grounding obligations to future people in a contractarian approach, such as that of John Rawls' *A Theory of Justice*, even though he is not eventually satisfied with this approach. The Total theory, Barry holds, requires too many sacrifices for the sake of actualizing extra people, the Average theory too few; while the Total theory is also accused (but surely mistakenly) of allowing a policy of producing a massive population for the next two centuries, leading to the extinction of the species.[38] (But it is surely implausible that this would even be the best way of maximizing the number of future humans, let alone their happiness.) The Routleys, also, are hostile to utilitarianism, and attempt to reconstruct a Rawlsian basis for our obligations to future people,[39] while Shrader-Frechette, who is so hostile to utilitarianism as to conclude that policies which are inegalitarian are *therefore* utilitarian(!), clearly also favours a Rawlsian approach.[40] So I shall now investigate the adequacy of the Rawlsian theory as the basis of our obligations.

Rawls' basic assumption is that those rules are just which would be chosen by rational contractors, parties about to embark on life with a good understanding of human affairs in general but no knowledge of their own future setting or distinctive beliefs. Their ignorance guarantees that they do not devise rules so as to benefit themselves; and it also has to be assumed that they are rationally self-interested and never sacrifice self-interest either for the sake of others' good or for their harm. But Rawls has a problem about future generations. He considers it too far-fetched to imagine the contracting parties being members of the different generations which will be spread out through history; and, adopting as he does the interpretation of his 'original position' in which the parties know that they are of the same generation as each other, he has to change his assumptions about motivation in order to generate a just savings principle from their choices. Each party is therefore assumed to care for his own immediate descendants, and sees to it that rules are chosen which provide for them.[41]

Rawls' modification of the motivations of the parties in the original position is properly attacked by Barry on grounds of method: it is an *ad hoc* device, guaranteed to derive obligations which correspond with the author's intuitions. It is also arbitrary and implausible: if the parties care for their descendants, why should they not also care for their families and their friends? Besides, the derived principle of just savings has no bearing on the question of obligations to *distant* future generations.[42]

Barry accordingly concludes that instead of this motivational device, Rawls should have dropped the postulate that the parties in the original position are contemporaries. This view is considered (but not endorsed) by D. Clayton Hubin,[43] and accepted by the Routleys.[44] Instead Rawls should have assumed that all generations are represented (Barry), or better, that some are (the Routleys). Hubin in fact raises the difficulty for such a move that the circumstances of justice, as depicted by Hume and largely echoed by Rawls,[45] do not exist between generations. But, as we have seen, Barry has well criticized the view that where Hume's circumstances of justice are absent, no obligations of justice exist between the parties. (Hubin's own view is that injustice towards future generations is possible, but only where it issues from injustice to an agent's contemporaries, with their natural concern for their children and grandchildren.[46] This, however, is to assume that we only have obligations to people as a result of voluntary agreements, communal ties, or the like: it has been argued above that in fact the basis of obligation is much broader than this.)

The original position as revised by Barry and the Routleys will clearly yield unsuitable results if the parties are required to believe that justice only arises in the kind of circumstances portrayed by Hume: so this belief must be discarded. So also should be the belief that all generations are represented, for the parties could deduce from this belief and some simple arithmetic how many generations there will be; but this is one of the issues which in some measure is supposed to depend on their deliberations.[47] The scenario provided by the Routleys, however, goes some way towards resolving this problem, as the parties know only that some (not all) generations are represented, and do not know which ones.

From this interpretation of Rawls' original position the Routleys are able to show that there would be chosen not only, as Rawls allows, a just savings principle but also a principle governing the just distribution and rate of usage of material resources over the generations. This principle would severely restrict the consumption of non-renewable resources, since their depletion threatens the interests of later generations, except where substitutes can be found. At the same time, as the Routleys plausibly claim, these interests would preclude the development of energy from nuclear fission at any time before safe storage methods for waste products had been discovered. F. Patrick Hubbard, working with approximately the same interpretation,[48] similarly derives both a principle guaranteeing a minimum of resources to all generations and also one setting a ceiling or maximum on consumption, which would prevent exponential increases in production and pollution and facilitate a sustainable form of society. As he recognizes, the minimum and the maximum would in some circumstances be far apart, and in others coincide. He also considers the possibility that liberty might need to be restricted to ensure compliance with the ceiling principle.

Similarly Victor D. Lippit and Koichi Hamada 'extend' Rawls' original position to supply principles of intergenerational distribution: their requirement that 'people do not know into which generation they will be born,'[49] taken in the context of their claim that no one can effectively represent future generations, suggests that the parties are not drawn from the same generation as each other. They point out that later generations, though advantaged in respect of technology and capital stock, are not advantaged as to the state of the natural environment: 'if current trends are not reversed future generations will live by making grotesque adaptations to a polluted environment or not live at all.'[50]

Accordingly the principles which would be chosen in their extended original position include one enjoining absolute limitations on polluting activities (the 'polluters-stop principle') — but this is surely too drastic — and one requiring 'each generation to leave the earth's environment no more polluted than it was at the time of that generation's arrival on the scene'.[51] The only permitted exceptions would be granted to prevent the current generation becoming the most disadvantaged; for the sake of its food supplies, some environmental disruption could be allowed, but not, for example, for the sake of every family having a car. Altogether the effect of the application of these principles would be the curtailment, though not a total prohibition, of further economic growth.

Such principles could readily be supplemented, for example, by ones governing the preservation of species and of wilderness. Indeed many of them could readily be derived from other normative theories, such as either the Average or the Total theories within the utilitarian tradition. The Rawlsian framework is proving to be a valuable one in allowing economists as well as philosophers to review long-cherished assumptions about efficiency and discounting. But it also has serious defects, not all of which can be remedied by modifications of the original position.

Not by contract alone

One problem, raised by both Leon H. Craig and by Barry,[52] is that as the number of generations or of future people who will eventually live is not settled prior to the decisions made in the original position, anything there agreed will be prejudicial to the interests of generations which *might* exist, unless they are somehow represented. Otherwise many possible generations may be prevented from existing. Whether possible people have interests is, of course, disputed: but it is clear that if there is no representation of possible people the outcome could easily be the extinction of humanity in a few centuries' time — a very great evil on most views.

The solution to this difficulty seems to be the inclusion of representatives of possible people in the original position. But this solution (which Barry seems to envisage in a parenthesis probably intended as whimsical) is surely an illusory one: for as they are infinite in number, their total presence is out of the question; and, for the same reason, no delegation representing them could fairly be assigned any particular number of votes to counterbalance the votes of the representatives of actual people. Perhaps their representatives could be assigned a veto (likely to be applied to *any* proposal involving the consumption of resources in our period of history). Or perhaps no one should be allowed to know that they themselves are going to be actual. But it then becomes difficult to tell what principles would be arrived at in such an assembly, and even harder to see why we should accept them as just ones.

It will be readily allowed, of course, that possible persons are a problem for any normative theory. But the present point is that for Rawls' theory the problem seems to be insuperable. Possible people will appear again in the next chapter. For the present I turn to a different problem for Rawls and his followers.

The problem is that there is reason to doubt Rawls' most basic assumption, that all and only those rules chosen in some suitably depicted original position would be just. The reason consists in the fact that the contracting parties are self-interested humans: there is nothing to ensure that they see justice done to all the other candidate holders of rights. Certainly they will provide for all the kinds and conditions of human life of their own generation, as they each know that such might be their own kind and condition. But they will not devise rules which accord rights to members of nonhuman species, which thus must fall outside the domain of justice. Now certainly Rawls holds that duties to animals fall under a quite separate province of morality, that of compassion; but if, as Feinberg holds, animals can have moral rights,[53] or if obligations are in some other way due to them, and if the same holds good of the rational denizens of other planets whom we may some day encounter, then this is not enough. Besides, if Barry is right about Hume, then Rawls is mistaken in following Hume's account of the circumstances of justice, and accordingly the rules of justice will not be confined to those which Rawls' more or less equal contracting parties, selected to satisfy these conditions, would choose. The present point is not just that the beliefs of the contracting parties should be varied (as above): it is rather that they are unsuitable as parties fit to decide what shall be just.

Accordingly in order to discover principles of obligation and of justice, there is reason to doubt whether our method should be to ask what rational people would choose or bargain for, and all the more reason to doubt whether Rawls' principles, either of substance or of priority, are the correct ones, since (apart from whatever intuitive appeal they may happen to have) they rest upon his dubious basic assumption. It is open to us to reason direct from the needs of people (including, perhaps, possible people) and of members of species with similar capacities and vulnerabilities; indeed this is what is done by those variants of consequentialism which allow prominence to needs (and not just to happiness).[54] Such a position, unlike its rivals, is so far unscathed, and will be explored further in the chapters following.

But it by no means follows that the principles governing

obligations to future generations which have been arrived at on a Rawlsian basis must be abandoned. Certainly they need to be supplemented, but in most cases it turns out that a plausible consequentialist theory will supply suitable foundations for the principles put forward on a Rawlsian basis by the Routleys, Hubbard, and Lippit and Hamada. So it is worth discovering what principles such a form of consequentialism sustains.

Implications of consequentialism

Now the form of consequentialism which I shall further expound and defend in chapter 7 is a version of the Total theory. On this version the maximization of intrinsic value is always morally desirable and, where a significant difference can be made, it is also morally obligatory. Intrinsic value is best maximized, I shall further be claiming, by provision for everyone's basic needs; and this clearly involves equal provision for the needs of each generation, once population has stabilized.

It has been suggested by Kavka that just this kind of equal provision could be implemented by applying across the generations a form of the condition which John Locke laid down for (as it so happens) the acceptability of private property, namely that each should leave enough and as good for others. Thus each generation may 'use the earth's physical resources only to the extent that technology allows for the recycling or depletion of such resources without net loss in their output capacity'.[55] Non-renewable resources may be used, so long as they are not wasted, but only on condition that renewable resources are conserved and technology so applied that the remaining resources (non-renewable ones included) can sustain the same levels of population as earlier. A generation which more than replaces its own numbers would be required to leave proportionately more total resources, so that equal provision could be made for each member of the next generation. Increases in resources would take the form of improved technology; as we have seen, even though it cannot be assumed that every problem has a technological solution, there is reason to believe that technology can continue to solve problems in its own proper sphere by building on achievements and knowledge attained in the past. Kavka's 'Lockean standard' thus involves the conservation of reneewable resources, and technological improvements which match depletions in non-renewable ones. As he says, 'If all succeeding generations abided by it, mankind could go on living on earth indefinitely' (or could if the environment too were suitably conserved).

It may be objected to what I am suggesting that consequentialist theories need not be committed to equal provision for the needs of different people, whether in one generation or in more; and doubtless some variants of consequentialism are vulnerable to this objection. But, as proponents of the law of diminishing marginal utility have long since been claiming, provision for basic needs does much more good than provision for what is less needed or not needed at all: and so the best way to bring about states of the world with the greatest intrinsic value is to provide equally for the needs of all, with priority being accorded to needs which are basic. If so, consequentialist theory can furnish a grounding for a good number of our intuitive beliefs about obligations of justice (e.g. obligations towards future people), and about such rights as they either will have or do have already. Thus Kavka's 'Lockean standard' exactly fits the requirements of a plausible consequentialist theory.

Kavka is also concerned, in fact, about the distribution of burdens between the generations, and solves it in the first instance by holding that each generation is obliged to provide for the availability to each future generation of benefits equal to those enjoyed by itself. But when he confronts the problem of inaugurating this overall intergenerational arrangement, he remarks that the current generation would be overburdened, granted the investments needed to bring about the sort of development in poor countries which alone is likely to stabilize world population at a level at which it can be sustained.[56] From this he concludes that our generation would be justified in using up more than would otherwise be its fair share of resources, if by doing so it could create the conditions in which the Lockean standard would become possible for future generations without excessive sacrifice. This is a salutary way of relating solutions of developmental and ecological problems, and serves to draw attention to the fact that world society can only be sustainable if it is also just. If, then, the claim about the need for investment for development and the stabilization of the human population is accepted, this distribution of burdens and exemptions is also supportable in the name of maximizing the satisfaction of needs.

Kavka's 'Lockean standard' is all of a piece with Surber's concern that the current generation should provide for equivalent possibilities and opportunities for experience and choice for future people to those enjoyed by itself.[57] As argued above, this concern will readily fit into a consequentialist framework; it seems also to call for the kind of equal provision principle which Kavka favours. So too does

Boulding's stress on the importance of conserving the stock of natural resources and on minimizing pollution.[58] (Kavka's programme does not seem to outlaw pollution, as Lippit and Hamada would, but requires its containment and the prevention of its escalation. Thus waste heat would be minimized to avert the eventual overheating of the atmosphere or of the more industrialized zones.) Similarly Barry maintains that the overall range of opportunities available to successor generations should not be narrowed: if some are closed off — for example, by the depletion of resources — others should be opened up, even at the cost of some sacrifice.[59] And Mary Williams argues that instead of the discounting of the interests of future people, utilitarianism enjoins a policy of 'maximum sustainable yield', on which renewable resources are harvested at a level which can be maintained indefinitely.[60] (This conclusion, however, needs to be modified when the interests of nonhumans are taken into account.[61])

The 'Lockean standard' also accommodates several proposals put forward by followers of Rawls. This applies to the restriction advocated by the Routleys on any one generation's use of material resources, and similarly to Hubbard's principle of a consumption maximum, though as we have seen, the maximum might in fact need to be varied, and the principle of equal provision for each generation is best expressed in a positive way, rather than in the form of an absolute restriction on growth, which might too greatly narrow future opportunities, especially for the poor. The Routleys' conclusion that nuclear power programmes ought to be avoided, at least until safe storage techniques exist, is also upheld, as otherwise the risks to future people are too great. Indeed, as Goodin points out, almost any serious decision procedure for the assessment of risks supports the anti-nuclear case.[62] Finally Lippit and Hamada's principle requiring each generation to leave the earth no more polluted than it received it is for all practical purposes congruous with Kavka's programme.

That programme, it must be allowed, could well be chosen as an intergenerational rule by a gathering of representatives randomly selected from the different generations. But, granted the defects mentioned above in contract theories of justice (and indeed in the other nonconsequentialist theories considered), it is important that it can also be supported from within the consequentialist tradition. This, I should claim, is its true basis: the 'Lockean standard' is right because it maximizes the satisfaction of human need throughout the generations without undue harm to nonhuman species. This claim is further vindicated in chapter 7 and in the chapters following.

But what is this claim if not an interpretation and a defence of the ideology of stewardship? Stewardship can after all be described and defended in terms of human interests (alongside the interests of other creatures),[63] even though, for the religious believer, it continues to constitute an expression of responsibility before God, and before the moral community of which God is the principal member. No new ethic is needed to cater for our treatment of our successors: what is needed is the detailed application of some very ancient traditions.

NOTES

1   Robin Attfield, 'The Logical Status of Moral Utterances', *Journal of Critical Analysis,* 4 (2), 1972, 70—84.
2   Renford Bambrough, *Moral Scepticism and Moral Knowledge,* London and Henley: Routledge & Kegan Paul, 1979. See especially chapters 2—3. My reservations are expressed in a review in *The Philosophical Quarterly,* 31, 1981, 177—8.
3   K. S. Shrader-Frechette, *Nuclear Power and Public Policy,* Dordrecht, Boston and London: Reidel, 1980. My disagreement over meta-ethics concerns her remarks on the so-called 'naturalistic fallacy' in chapter 6.
4   An example is Jonathan Glover's book, *Causing Death and Saving Lives,* Harmondsworth: Penguin Books, 1977. Glover waives all claims to moral objectivity at p. 35, but supplies an admirable example of the search for it throughout his book.
5   Brian Barry, 'Justice Between Generations', in P. M. S. Hacker and J. Raz (eds), *Law, Morality and Society,* Oxford: Clarendon Press, 1977, 268—84. See in particular p. 284.
6   Gregory Kavka, 'The Futurity Problem', in R. I. Sikora and Brian Barry (eds), *Obligations to Future Generations,* Philadelphia: Temple University Press, 1978, 186—203, p. 187. (Kavka's article is reprinted in Ernest Partridge, *Responsibilities to Future Generations,* New York: Prometheus Books, 1981, 109—22.)
7   See Peter Singer: 'Famine, Affluence and Morality', *Philosophy and Public Affairs,* 1, 1971—72, 229—43; 'Reconsidering the Famine Relief Argument', in P. G. Brown and H. Shue (eds), *Food Policy,* New York: Free Press, 1977, 36—53. Several of Singer's fellow-contributors argue to this effect in William Aiken and Hugh La Follette (eds), *World Hunger and Moral Obligation,* Englewood Cliffs, NJ: Prentice-Hall, 1977, in which 'Famine, Affluence and Morality' is reprinted. Onora Nell argues to the same conclusion from a different premise in 'Lifeboat Earth', *Philosophy and Public Affairs,* 4, 1974—75, 273—92. I have

presented some considerations in support of Singer's stance in 'Supererogation and Double Standards', *Mind*, 88, 1979, 481—99.

8   R. and V. Routley, 'Nuclear Energy and Obligations to the Future', *Inquiry*, 21, 1978, 133—79, p. 135.

9   See Joel Feinberg, 'The Rights of Animals and Unborn Generations', in William T. Blackstone (ed.), *Philosophy and Environmental Crisis,* Athens: University of Georgia Press, 1974, 43—68; also in Richard A. Wasserstrom (ed.), *Today's Moral Problems* (2nd edn), New York: Macmillan Co. and London: Collier-Macmillan, 1979, 581—601; and in Ernest Partridge (ed.), *Responsibilities to Future Generations*, 139—50. See also the papers there by Ruth Macklin, Richard T. de George, Galen K. Pletcher and Annette Baier. All these writers accept obligations to future generations. Whether we speak of future people's rights depends on the sense of 'right', and as Baier says, is a subordinate issue. As is argued in chapter 7, not all morality turns on rights.

10   Robert E. Goodin, 'No Moral Nukes', *Ethics*, 90, 1980, 417—49, at p. 429.

11   Shrader-Frechette, *Nuclear Power and Public Policy,* chapter 3. Though there is insufficient space to launch into a full assessment of the risks of nuclear energy, the conclusions reached in this paragraph will stand independently of such a study.

12   Martin Golding, 'Obligations to Future Generations', *The Monist*, 56, 1972, 85—99, p. 97f., reprinted in Partridge (ed.) *Responsibilities to Future Generations*, 61—72. Daniel Callahan's reply to Golding embodies points parallel to Kavka's; thus he insists that 'our moral community' be construed as the human community and not some subsection of it. See Callahan's paper 'What Obligations do we have to Future Generations?' in *American Ecclesiastical Review,* 164, 1971, 265—80, reprinted in *Responsibilities to Future Generations,* 73—85.

13   R. and V. Routley, 'Nuclear Energy and Obligations to the Future', p. 137. I have argued in 'On Being Human', *Inquiry,* 17, 1974, 175—92, that human nature and needs set limits to defensible substantive conceptions of the good life for a human.

14   Feinberg, 'The Rights of Animals and Unborn Generations', p. 65.

15   R. and V. Routley, 'Nuclear Energy and Obligations to the Future', pp. 158—60.

16   Trudy Govier, 'What Should We Do About Future People?' *American Philosophical Quarterly,* 16, 1979, 105—13.

17   Derek Parfit, 'Energy Policy and the Further Future', forthcoming in Peter Brown and Douglas MacLean (eds), *Energy Policy and Future Generations,* Tottowa, NJ: Rowman & Littlefield.

18   R. and V. Routley, 'Nuclear Energy and Obligations to the Future', p. 150. A similar point is made by Kenneth Boulding in 'The Economics of the Coming Spaceship Earth', in John Barr (ed.), *The Environmental Handbook,* 77—82, p. 81.

19   'Nuclear Energy and Obligations to the Future', p. 161.

20   Barry, 'Justice Between Generations', at pp. 270—6.
21   Barry, 'Circumstances of Justice and Future Generations', in R. I.
     Sikora and Brian Barry (eds) *Obligations to Future Generations,*
     204—48: also David Hume, *A Treatise of Human Nature* and *An
     Enquiry Concerning the Principles of Morals,* in T. H. Green and T.
     H. Grose (eds), *The Philosophical Works* (4 Vols.), London: Longmans,
     Green, 1874—75.
22   'Circumstances of Justice and Future Generations', p. 221. See further
     Mary Midgley, 'Duties Concerning Islands', forthcoming in Elliot and
     Gair (eds), *Environmental Philosophy: A Collection of Readings,*
     Brisbane: University of Queensland Press.
23   'Justice Between Generations', p. 272.
24   Robert Nozick, *Anarchy, State and Utopia,* Oxford: Blackwell and
     New York: Basic Books, 1974.
25   See Kavka, 'The Futurity Problem', p. 200.
26   See F. Patrick Hubbard, 'Justice, Limits to Growth, and an Equilibrium
     State', *Philosophy and Public Affairs,* 7, 1977—78, 326—45, p. 345,
     n. 12.
27   John Passmore, *MRN,* p. 91. A similar view is held by Peter Laslett in
     'The Conversation Between the Generations', in Royal Institute of
     Philosophy (ed.), *The Proper Study,* London and Basingstoke:
     Macmillan Press, 1971, 172—89, and is open to parallel objections.
28   R. and V. Routley, 'Nuclear Energy and Obligations to the Future',
     pp. 144—9, 166—73, and 176, n. 14.
29   'Justice Between Generations', p. 274.
30   Jere Paul Surber, 'Obligations to Future Generations: Explorations
     and Problemata', *Journal of Value Inquiry,* 11, 1977, 104—16.
31   See Robin Attfield, 'Toward a Defence of Teleology', *Ethics,* 85, 1975,
     123—35, pp. 128—31.
32   John Rawls, *A Theory of Justice,* London, Oxford, New York: Oxford
     University Press, 1972, Section 44, pp. 284—93.
33   J. Brenton Stearns, 'Ecology and the Indefinite Unborn', *The Monist,*
     56, 1972, 612—25. Reprinted in Richard A. Wasserstrom (ed.), *Today's
     Moral Problems,* 602—13.
34   Jan Narveson, 'Utilitarianism and New Generations', *Mind,* 76, 1967,
     62—72.
35   Barry, 'Justice Between Generations', p. 275.
36   See 'Circumstances of Justice and Future Generations', p. 219: Robin
     Attfield, 'Toward a Defence of Teleology'; also 'Racialism, Justice and
     Teleology', *Ethics,* 87, 1977, 186—8.
37   Boulding, 'The Economics of the Coming Spaceship Earth', p. 78.
38   These objections are to be found in 'Justice Between Generations',
     pp. 283f.
39   See R. and V. Routley, 'Nuclear Energy and Obligations to the Future',
     pp. 151f, and 167—73, respectively.

40 See Shrader-Frechette, *Nuclear Power and Public Policy,* pp. 94 and 149, and 122f, respectively.
41 Rawls, *A Theory of Justice,* Sections 4, 24, 25, 44 and 45.
42 'Justice Between Generations', pp. 279f. Also D. Clayton Hubin, 'Justice and Future Generations', *Philosophy and Public Affairs,* 6, 1976—77, 70—83 (see p. 75, n. 4).
43 Hubin, 'Justice and Future Generations', pp. 72—81.
44 R. and V. Routley, 'Nuclear Energy and Obligation to the Future', pp. 167f.
45 *A Theory of Justice,* p. 127.
46 Hubin agrees with Edwin Delattre that obligations regarding future persons should not be analysed as obligations owed to those persons. See Delattre, 'Rights, Responsibilities and Future Persons', *Ethics,* 82, 1972, 254—8.
47 Thus Barry, 'Justice Between Generations', p. 281.
48 F. Patrick Hubbard, 'Justice, Limits to Growth, and an Equilibrium State'. For his interpretation of the original position, see p. 330, n. 4. Cf. the principles of maximal and minimal provision for future generations derived by Michael Bayles in 'Famine or Food: Sacrificing for Future or Present Generations' in Partridge (ed.) *Responsibilities to Future Generations,* 239—45.
49 Victor D. Lippit and Koichi Hamada, 'Efficiency and Equity in Intergenerational Distribution', in Dennis Clark Pirages (ed.), *The Sustainable Society,* New York and London: Praeger Publishers, 1977, 285—99. The requirement here quoted is from p. 293.
50 Ibid. p. 295.
51 Ibid. p. 297.
52 Leon H. Craig, 'Contra Contract: A Brief Against Rawls' Theory of Justice', *Canadian Journal of Political Science,* 8, 1975, 63—81; Barry, 'Justice Between Generations', pp. 280—3.
53 Feinberg, 'The Rights of Animals and Unborn Generations'. This criticism of Rawls has been made by Michael S. Pritchard and Wade L. Robison, 'Justice and the Treatment of Animals: A Critique of Rawls', *Environmental Ethics,* 3, 1981, 55—61, and by Mary Midgley in 'Duties Concerning Islands'.
54 Stephen Bickham, in 'Future Generations and Contemporary Ethical Theory', *Journal of Value Inquiry,* 15, 1981, 169—77, holds that no current normative theory can cope with the objections to it until our metaphysical presuppositions are revised. This I believe to be too pessimistic a view.
55 Kavka, 'The Futurity Problem', p. 201.
56 Like Kavka, I reject the view of Garrett Hardin in *The Limits of Altruism,* Bloomington: Indiana University Press, 1977, that famine relief and improved nutrition in poor countries in the present diminish the quality of life there in the future. But space is lacking for any

ampler discussion of international politics, or of the nature or levels of whatever authorities would be called for to implement the policies here advocated. Indeed the conclusions arrived at in the present book preclude neither world government, nor anarchism, nor intermediate arrangements.

57   Surber, 'Obligations to Future Generations', p. 115.
58   Boulding, 'The Economics of the Coming Spaceship Earth', pp. 78 and 81f. I take the conservation of renewable resources such as trees to be compatible with the planned use of non-renewable resources such as coal.
59   'Circumstances of Justice and Future Generations', p. 243.
60   Mary B. Williams, 'Discounting Versus Maximum Sustainable Yield', in Sikora and Barry, *Obligations to Future Generations,* 169—85.
61   The need for an ampler utilitarian position is well argued by Peter Singer in 'Not for Humans Only: The Place of Nonhumans in Environmental Issues', in K. E. Goodpaster and K. M. Sayre (eds), *Ethics and Problems of the 21st Century*, Notre Dame and London: University of Notre Dame Press, 1979, 191—206.
62   Goodin, 'No Moral Nukes', pp. 435—43.
63   *Pace* Barry, 'Justice Between Generations', p. 284.

7

Multiplication and the Value of Life

The increasing size of the human population is widely regarded as an ecological problem. A social problem it certainly is, at least in some places; and it results in some measure from people's transactions with other species, since advances in the control of disease must be part of its explanation. Indeed this is already enough to make it an ecological problem. But it also results, plausibly, from poverty in places where life-expectancy is short, and to this extent is to be seen as one facet of the many-sided problem of development and underdevelopment, rather than as primarily an ecological issue. There is another ground, however, for regarding it as an ecological problem: its role in causing squalor, pollution, erosion, the loss of forests and the growth of deserts. As remarked in chapter 1, it is probably not the main cause of these problems; but if it even exacerbates them, as it surely does, then its ecological significance is considerable. The growth in human numbers also seems to endanger numerous nonhuman species, and thus contributes to yet another ecological problem.

But before anyone can designate the problem one of 'overpopulation' (manifestly a normative expression), let alone talk of 'the population bomb',[1] some idea is needed of what an optimum human population would be like, or at any rate of what population changes would count as improvements, and thus of what level of population we ought to aim at. This, as Michael Bayles points out,[2] is an issue prior to such other population issues as the rate at which change is due and the methods of control to be employed; and it is also an issue which at once takes us to basic principles of normative ethics. It also takes us to basic question about value, such as whether all life is valuable, or only certain kinds and qualities of life, and, if only certain kinds, then which. To dwell on these issues may seem to risk losing sight of the practical problems; yet to leave them unexamined, or to take for granted the answers to them, involves lacking a clear view about what the problems are and what makes them problems. On such a basis as this, even if satisfactory solutions are found, their discovery can at best be an accident, and we stand to overlook ways in which, through provision for a quite different population, we might have made the world a much better place.

Principles of obligation and of value in population matters are also required to supplement the discussion of obligations to future generations in chapter 6. It was there claimed that we have far-reaching obligations to whatever people there will be. But it was necessary to postpone the question of how many people we should cause to exist or allow there to be; and without some answer to that question the answers so far arrived at are plainly deficient.

The points so far made may supply some kind of explanation of the fact that most of the writings of philosophers on population issues concern the bearing of basic principles on human numbers rather than issues such as which forms of population control are allowable, and which forms, if any, of political pressure may be employed to foster it. Most of the writers concerned have a vivid awareness of the urgency of population issues, yet their concern to be right over matters of principle must surely be applauded. By contrast, where a philosopher deals only with the more immediate problems, the resulting discussion is prone to appear somewhat superficial,[3] and this even though the problems are on a worldwide scale.

Yet the layman who turns to philosophers for help over matters of principle may here be beset with perplexity. Thus only some theories of normative ethics, those which make obligations and justifications turn on an action's consequences, seem to have anything relevant to say on the level of the human population at future times. As we have already seen in chapter 6, other theories either have nothing to offer, or fail to give a satisfactory account of the extent to which principles relating to anything other than consequences override principles of a consequentialist character. Among consequentialist theories, however, negative theories, enjoining the diminution of suffering and misery, would best be satisfied by the painless elimination of humanity altogether, an ideal which clashes with most people's most deeply felt intuitions; while positive theories at least seem to run the risk, by enjoining the maximization of happiness or of years of worthwhile life, of encouraging yet further increase in the growth of population.

In due course I shall argue that this perplexity would be premature. But first I shall present the main positive consequentialist theories, and also the various difficulties with which they are confronted. The examination may also serve to bring to light widespread values which people are prone to forget that they hold once they are confronted with the quite genuine problems associated with population growth.

The Total theory and the Average theory

As was mentioned in chapter 6, both the Total theory (which, despite Surber, must be regarded as the classical form of utilitarianism) and the Average theory commend or enjoin the maximization of utility. Utility is most usually construed as happiness or the means to happiness, and the two Theories require respectively the maximization of the total happiness level of a population and of the average happiness level. Alternatively these theories can require the maximization not of the level of happiness but of some other (or some more inclusive) state of people which may be regarded as intrinsically valuable, such as well-being or periods of worthwhile life. As I have rejected in chapter 6 the belief that nothing but happiness is of intrinsic value, and accepted the view that the satisfaction of people's basic needs does much more good than the provision of other goods, my own commitment is clearly to one of the alternatives. But this said, it is simpler to follow for the present the practice of most writers in treating the Total and the Average theories as concerned with levels of happiness.

The main objections to the Total theory were prefigured in chapter 6. It seems to require population to be maximized; and (though this has not till now been treated as an objection) it seems to require us to make happy people rather than to make people happy, and thus to be more concerned with happiness than with people. More precisely, it implies that it would be better, with respect to a population of any given size enjoying distinctly worthwhile lives, for there to be a larger population so long as life remained a little more than barely worth living. For each extra just-about-happy person would, up to this point, add to the total of happiness. This conclusion is widely regarded with horror, and it has become customary for philosophers to refer to it as the

'Repugnant conclusion'. There again the other objection arises
because the Total theory seems to be impersonal, and seems to
advocate the procreation of extra people simply as bearers of
happiness, as if happiness were a product like milk.

The Average theory is often supposed to overcome these
difficulties, and to provide for the maintenance of a high level of
happiness rather than for the enjoyment of a relatively low level on
the part of large numbers. But the Average theory has implications
of its own which are altogether counter-intuitive.[4] Thus where there
is a high average level of happiness the theory prohibits the addition
of any children whose happiness level would be even a little lower
than the previous average (unless the addition further increases the
already high happiness level of existing people). Indeed in this
connection the Average theory appears to discriminate in favour of
present people against future ones. But this would not always be the
case: for where a population lives in extreme misery, the theory
requires the conception of any number of people whatever, as long
as the average happiness can be raised thereby, even if the extra
people are miserable themselves and wish they had never been
born. There is no discrimination here, but the upshot is a most
dubious social policy. Again, if a happy population can only
reproduce itself at the expense of a slight but continuous deterioration in resources and happiness-levels, then the theory forbids any
reproduction and requires the extinction of humanity.

It has also been suggested that the Average theory requires the
elimination of the miserable from among an otherwise happy
population. But it need not require this, as the miserable could
instead be provided with the means to happiness; and as the
provision of basic needs makes a great deal of difference to people's
happiness and brings about a great deal of good (on all accounts), it
is likely that the average would be better raised in this way. For
similar reasons the Total theory, which is sometimes subjected to a
parallel objection, also survives it.

Nevertheless the Average theory is vulnerable to the other
objections just given: most strikingly it could require the production
of extra people so as to maximize happiness (rather as the Total
theory is accused of doing), and it could involve the extinction of
the species. Also, as it can require the calling of extra people into
existence for the sake of levels of happiness, it is open to the charge
of impersonality; and so (as Anglin points out), if it is ever an
objection that a theory is more concerned with happiness than with

people, then the objection applies to the Average theory as much as to any other.

The Person-affecting principle

Now in the view of a number of philosophers, what is wrong with both the Total and the Average theories is that they involve concern for possible people. The true appeal of consequentialist theories such as utilitarianism, on these philosophers' view, is that they call upon us to make actual people happy, leaving possible people out of account. Accordingly they urge that utilitarianism be understood to concern promoting the happiness either of existing people only or, more cogently, of existing people plus people who are likely to exist whatever any particular agent may do. In the course of attempts to state this interpretation of utilitarianism in a form immune to objections, various forms of it have been put forward.[5] They have in common what Derek Parfit has called the Person-affecting principle: the better of two outcomes is the one which affects people for the better, and the worse is the one which affects them for the worse. Merely possible people are not in this connection regarded as people.

But, despite its intuitive plausibility, the Person-affecting principle has been subjected to searching criticisms, in particular from R. I. Sikora and Derek Parfit.[6] Thus Sikora remarks that it can yield a conclusion similar to the Repugnant conclusion mentioned above. Imagine a population of fairly unhappy people (e.g. the survivors of a nuclear war), able, at some sacrifice to themselves, to raise both the average and the total happiness and repopulate the world by producing and rearing some test-tube babies who would predictably be very happy. The principle forbids them to enter upon this policy of making happier people; and thus, by giving priority to actual people, ensures in at least these circumstances a low level of happiness, even though humanity might have had a brighter future. Yet it is the contrivance of avoidably low levels of happiness which is supposed (in part) to give the Repugnant conclusion its repugnant character. Sikora's argument occurs in the course of a survey of all the possible kinds of 'ontological preference theories' — theories which prefer the interests of actual persons, and take it to be wrong to require them to make sacrifices to bring about the existence of possible persons — a survey which shows that they all embrace a form of 'Repugnant conclusion'.

There again, the Person-affecting principle cannot be taken to construe the likely people, whose interests are to be heeded, as people likely to exist whatever anyone does; for of these there are very few, and all other future people could be disregarded. It must concern people likely to exist whatever a particular agent or other subgroup of humanity may do; but the people likely to exist whatever any *one* group does will be different in identity and number from the people likely to exist whatever any second or third group may do. This being so, the principle exhorts different population policies for each different group of agents. Besides, there would be no co-ordination between these policies: for each group would have to take account of the likely offspring of other groups, but not the potential offspring of their own group, which it is within their power to prevent from coming into existence at all.

Another group of difficulties for the Person-affecting principle cluster around the issue of the identity of future people, and have been raised by Derek Parfit. Thus the adoption of different social policies very considerably affects which people are born, granted that even the postponement of conception issues in the birth of a different child. Consider a policy of consumption, which yields a higher standard of living for a hundred years than a policy of conservation would, but a lower standard of living thereafter. Such a policy does not harm any actual or likely people, nor, if it is carried out, is anyone worse off in a hundred years' time than they would have been on the other policy: for on the other policy they would not have existed, and different people would have existed in their place. Thus the Person-affecting principle cannot criticize this objectionable, consumption-orientated policy, as it affects no one, likely or otherwise, for the worse.

A parallel point can be made about individual mothers. A mother who bears a handicapped child, but had the opportunity to bear a healthy and happy one by postponing becoming pregnant, might well, in fact, be subject to moral criticism; yet no child has been affected for the worse. But on the Person-affecting principle she is above criticism. Moreover social planners who could advise such mothers to postpone conception but fail to do so can only be blamed to the extent that the mother and other actual persons are made miserable as a result of their omission.

Thus the Person-affecting principle is satisfactory until it is applied to the issues for the sake of which it was introduced — cases of decisions about the existence of future people. Where populations are constant it fares well enough, but yields exactly the same results as the Total and Average theories, and thus has no advantage over either of them. But in the area of morality with which I am at present concerned, its failure is a disastrous one. Indeed, since as time goes on the proportion of people alive whose individual existence is at present actually likely is a proportion which decreases progressively, the principle authorizes us to disregard most (at least) of the people of a century from now, and almost all their successors. But the wrongness of such disregard has been amply exhibited in chapter 6.

Narveson in fact holds the view which most people could endorse, that there is an obligation not to bring into existence people whose lives would be miserable. He attempts to reconcile this view with the Person-affecting principle on the basis that such people would otherwise be actual, and would experience misery which can actually be prevented. But this is to allow the moral significance of at least some possible lives. Proponents, for example, of the Total theory are concerned about possible lives on just the same basis, i.e. that they could be made actual, and that the quality of these lives thus forms an element in one or more of the options open to actual agents. At the same time Narveson denies any obligation to bring into existence people whose lives would be worthwhile, and adds that new additions to the population 'ought to be made if the benefit to all, *excluding* the newcomer, would exceed the cost to all, *including* him or her, as compared with the net benefit of any alternatives which don't add to population'.[7]

But this position is no more plausible than the basic Person-affecting principle. Thus it fails to explain why the mother of the handicapped child was wrong not to delay and conceive the happy child instead. Further, it takes into account the misery which unhappy people would complain of if they became actual, but disregards the blessings which people enjoying a worthwhile life would prize if they became actual, as Timothy Sprigge has pointed out,[8] and this without any defensible rationale. (Thus it will not do to say that our only obligations are to prevent bad future states of affairs, for reasons already pointed out.) Again, granted that we have obligations to promote the welfare of actual people, and are willing to produce extra people to do so, it is hard to justify ignoring their welfare, and thus treating them, as Narveson effectively does, as second-class citizens. Finally, the asymmetrical position would in some circumstances actually require the extinction of the human species.[9]

One of Narveson's more emphatic claims is that 'duties which are

not owed to anybody stick in the conceptual throat.'[10] But despite
his belief that all duties are owed to someone (surely a generalization
which does not hold once duties are construed as whatever it is
wrong not to do), and to actual persons at that, he himself deviates
from the Person-affecting principle by allowing (negative) duties
with regard to possible (unhappy) people. Thus possible people
sometimes count, and further reflection is required to discover
when they count and in what ways.

Efforts at salvage

Trudy Govier has attempted to defend Narveson's basic position by
holding that we should pay some heed to the interests of
'epistemically possible people' (those who are likely to exist for
reasons independent of our choices) but less to those of 'volitionally
possible people' (those whose existence would depend on our
choices). Govier attempts to meet Parfit's objections over identity
by acknowledging that different people will exist on different social
policies but maintaining that we ought to consider *'those people
who will likely exist at a future time'.*[11] These I take to be any
members of the variable class of likely future people: if on any
policy there will be *n* people, then even though their identity would
differ as between policies, the *n* people who there will be are the
ones we should care about.

But this revision merely diminishes the size of the population of
second-class citizens. For Govier remains committed to Narveson's
asymmetry with respect to volitionally possible people. Yet wherever
families are planned, all the future offspring are, seen from the
present, volitionally possible. Indeed despite Govier's attempts to
justify the asymmetry, most of the objections to Narveson's position
are objections to hers also. Nevertheless as she accepts positive
obligations with regard to epistemically possible people, whatever
their identity, her position marks an advance on that of Narveson.

Another philosopher who has attempted a consistent position
which implies the kind of asymmetry favoured by Narveson is Peter
Singer. Singer has contended that the appealing ingredient in
utilitarianism is the following axiom: 'Given that people exist, or
will exist independently of our actions, it is better that they be
happy than that they be miserable, and the happier they are, the
better it is.'[12] Like Narveson and Govier, Singer was unwilling to
recognize value in any additional lives. But to cope with Parfit's
identity objections, he devised a population policy which did not

require the interests of any fixed group to be given priority, but did require that there be always a group of the population of the size of the least population possible, enjoying at least the average (and thus also the total) happiness which the least population would have.

Now as Parfit and Sikora have pointed out,[13] the spirit of Singer's remarks involves also an obligation to maximize the happiness of such a group (hereinafter the 'core'), even if this requires procreating extra people. But this would be done for the sake of the core, not of the extra people, unless some of them happened to belong to it. Singer, however, believed that wherever extra people would be miserable his principle implied an obligation not to produce them, because of the side-effects arising for others from the fact that the extra people in question would be better off dead. No corresponding positive obligation existed, in Singer's belief, where extra people would be happy.

But Singer's principle does not even guarantee the asymmetrical view which he favoured, for, as Parfit points out, the side-effects of the existence of miserable people could be beneficial to the core group. Besides this, it labours under serious difficulties itself. Thus it can require a succession of additions to the initial population, so long as a subset of the new total is on average as happy at each stage as the population at the previous stage had on average been, until a large, barely happy population is attained, as in the 'Repugnant conclusion'. Thus Singer's principle fails to fare any better than the Total theory. Further, as Sikora remarks, it can prefer a smaller addition of barely happy people to a larger addition of moderately happy people, so long as the core is better off. Again, if the minimum number (the core) is small, but happiest in a very large population of otherwise barely happy people, this population is preferred to one where the core is only slightly less happy, and everyone else is as happy as the core. Again, it could require parents not to make sacrifices in the timing of conception so as to increase the happiness of a resulting child. Moreover it could require the present generation to use up and benefit by a scarce resource of which, as they might be aware, future people would have more need to cure an inherited disease. But each of these preferences of the theory is, at least apparently, wrong; and in some cases there is no need of the qualification.

There is also a technical difficulty inherent in Singer's principle. As previously mentioned, it can require successive increases in population with a diminishing overall average happiness, so long as after each increase there is a core at least as happy as the population had been on average up to that stage. Accordingly the principle can require in two moves a development which it would initially have forbidden, and can thus represent such a development as both forbidden and obligatory. (For the average happiness of the larger population at each stage is allowed to be lower than beforehand, and this lower level is all that the core at the next stage has to be allowed to sustain; so after two transitions there may be no group of the same size and happiness level as the initial population.) Singer's solution to this problem of 'intransitive preferences' (where B is better than A, C better than B, but C is worse than A) consists in holding that as the forbidden outcome can be foreseen, the first application of the principle must be regarded as forbidden. But, as Parfit remarks, this is unacceptable unless some independent ground is supplied for not doing what the principle requires.

The interests of potential people

Now Singer, like Govier, advanced beyond Narveson by accepting the moral relevance of at any rate a minimum predictable number of future people, whatever their identity, but his principle fails where the interests of others who might become actual are disregarded. How can these interests be accommodated? One way might be that of philosophers who defend a principle on which all possible people have interests and rights as such. Thus R. M. Hare holds that it is morally wrong, other things being equal, to prevent potential people from becoming actual.[14] (Among potential people Hare includes foetuses and also pairs of gametes, even ones which are not currently united: indeed in his article 'Survival of the Weakest' he includes people who could be born within the next two years.[15]) Hare defends his position by appealing to the widely accepted basic principle that we ought to treat others as we would wish to be treated, and this Hare applies to the bestowal of life. The obvious difficulty, however, arises over holding that all potential people, whether foetuses or hitherto unconceived potentialities, count as people: for if they do not, then no question of the interests or rights of potential people can arise.

Can conception constitute harm or benefit? The issue is far from clearcut, but has been illuminatingly discussed by Parfit and by T. G. Roupas.[16] In the light of their discussions, perhaps the most cogent view is that for an actual person leading a worthwhile life, to have been conceived was indeed a benefit, but that conception is no benefit to merely potential people, as they are then nonexistent.

There is a sense in which potential people can have rights and interests: the sense in which actual people have interests and rights which can count as reasons for action on the part of others at times prior to their lives, and when they are merely potential. But potential people do not, *as such*, have interests or rights. We do not let them down by allowing them to remain nonexistent. (If I am right, conception cannot constitute harm, as nothing exists beforehand to be harmed,[17] yet to a person leading a wretched life conception will have been a crucial liability, without which none of life's miseries would have arisen.) But if potential people do not, *as such*, have interests, then Hare's principle has already been rejected.

Now if potential people were people who stood to be affected by conception, then, as Parfit has pointed out,[18] the Person-affecting principle could be reinstated in a form which would be free of the deficiencies highlighted above. For its deficiencies lie in its failure to provide for the interests which potential people have, or rather would have if they became actual. But if potential people are themselves people liable to be affected by the course of events, then their interests would be covered already by the principle. If this were so, however, the principle would have lost the reason for which it was introduced, which was precisely to exclude these supposed interests from consideration.

It is surely preferable to allow the Person-affecting principle to have the application intended by its sponsors, who would of course deny that potential people in general have interests. I have already supplied reasons for doubting the view that morality fundamentally consists in duties owed to individuals (or, therefore, in individual rights): accordingly the Person-affecting principle, which presupposes otherwise, may be rejected (as I have claimed it must be in any case), and does not need to be modified so as somehow to include possible people, even if such a modification were plausible. If extra happy or worthwhile lives are valuable and should be provided for, this can be expressed in some more impersonal principle, such as the Total theory or a variant of it. I now present the case for just such a position, step by step.

The value of worthwhile life

That in fact each worthwhile life is intrinsically valuable has been impressively argued by Roupas; by 'worthwhile' Roupas means a life the liver of which is or would be glad to be alive. If his conclusion is right, this may account for the cogency of Hare's claim that there is

at any rate something regrettable about abortions (or most
abortions), in that the further development of something potentially
valuable is forestalled. (Many abortions may still be right, but that is
not the present point.) Each agent who is glad to be alive, Roupas
observes, must prefer a world in which he exists and is glad to be
alive, to one in which he does not exist at all. This granted, it can
further be maintained that the former state of affairs is of greater
value than the latter. For, an observer who is asked to consider the
two states of affairs from the point of view of each individual
present in either will discover this preference, and, so long as the
other individuals concerned are all present in both states of affairs,
will discover no countervailing preference; and if then asked which
state is preferable if he has an equal likelihood of being any of these
individuals, he will still prefer the first, and would actualize it on this
basis if he could. This impersonal and 'objective' procedure for
determining judgements of value is elaborated by Roupas on the
basis of work by J. C. Harsanyi,[19] and is also employed to support
the conclusion that, provided someone continues to be glad that
they are alive as long as they are alive, a longer life is in their case
more valuable than a shorter one, and the further conclusion that a
life's value is unchanged by *whose* life it is.

Not everyone, perhaps, will endorse Roupas' method for arriving
at judgements of value. It might, for example, be held to be weighted
in favour of entities capable of preferences; or it might be contended
that such judgements need not be functions of preferences at all.
Yet there is a striking agreement between Roupas' conclusions and
those of Jonathan Glover, arrived at by the quite distinct method of
examining the presuppositions of widespread reflective moral
beliefs.[20] Glover, indeed, points out that the mere desire to live does
not show that the continuation of life would be either in the interests
of the person concerned or worthwhile; and this is a modification
which Roupas could, perhaps, allow, as long as his impartial observer
could be equipped with the requisite information about which lives
were in the interests of the people (or animals) living them. (Glover,
in fact, does not tell us what a worthwhile life consists in; nor is
there space to discuss the matter further here — though I have
elsewhere discussed some of its key aspects.[21]) But if the notion of a
worthwhile life can for the moment be taken for granted, and it can
be allowed that gladness to be alive is a good indicator, but not an
invariable concomitant of a worthwhile life, then Roupas' conclusions about what is valuable may for present purposes be accepted
as expressing an important part of the truth, whether on the basis of

his own method or on that of reflection on our intuitive judgements. (It should be noted that Roupas' conclusions do not cover the same range of cases as Hare's view, even though both concern possible as well as actual people, for Roupas' position concerns only those lives which would, if made actual, be worthwhile, whereas Hare's position lacks any such restriction.)

Objections to the Total theory assessed

Now as Roupas remarks, his position is congruous with the Total theory of utilitarianism, without entailing it. If further we ought to maximize whatever is of intrinsic value, and we accept Roupas' view, we do seem to be thrust back into accepting a form of the Total theory, complete with the 'Repugnant conclusion'. To many readers this may seem a disastrous idea: I will attempt now to explain why it is not.

To begin with, the Total theory, as Hare, Singer and Sikora have all pointed out,[22] does not require an increase in the human population of our planet. This point needs to be amplified. With 800 million people already living in absolute poverty, additions to the population are very unlikely in most cases to increase the total of happiness, or, to follow Roupas' and Glover's account of value, of years of worthwhile life. If the additional people are not mal-nourished or miserable themselves, their arrival would in any case be likely to lengthen the worldwide food queue; and if they have more purchasing power than those least able to procure food, they will prevent yet more people in poor countries from being able to afford what they need. Just on this count alone, then, the Total theory probably commends a standstill rather than an increase in world population. (For current circumstances, the Average theory may even counsel a drastic reduction: something which is unlikely to commend it, granted the theory of value just accepted. But we have already encountered conclusive objections to the Average theory.)

The next point to note is that it is mistaken to isolate a population policy from among the deliverances of a general theory of normative ethics. Thus, as the current world population could be fed, and a vast amount of difference would be made to the worthwhileness of lives if it were, the Total theory must advocate that it should be. But if suitable measures were to be set afoot, including a development policy enabling people to be properly fed in perpetuity without needing to rely on donations from others, then the Total theory would not advocate for these conditions an overall decrease in population (though it might well prefer a decrease as against maintaining current population levels without such a development policy). Yet it would still probably not advocate an overall increase, for the following reason.

The Total theory, even if it enjoins a larger number of lives than some of its rivals, does not require them to be simultaneous. Much the likeliest way to maximize the number of worthwhile lives is to guarantee a population level sustainable into the indefinite future; and to maximize population in the short term might precisely exclude this outcome, through the exhaustion of resources, the ruination of fertile land, pollution, losses to the natural gene-pool or the breakdown of whole ecosystems on which humans ultimately depend. Thus the theory commends no higher a population than the maximum sustainable, and, for the reasons given above, a somewhat lower one in current conditions.

Further, the requirement of the theory to add worthwhile lives cannot be applied to the planetary population as if there were infinite space to accommodate extra people in the manner to which the more fortunate of existing people have become accustomed. Space and resources are limited, and to ignore these limitations is likely to involve multiplying misery; indeed this would be likely even if there were no problem about the supply of food.

The general moral of these various points is that the horror with which the Repugnant conclusion is received may well be caused by applying it to conditions for which no such conclusion of the theory could imaginably be yielded.

At the more theoretical level, Anglin has isolated three reasons why people find the Repugnant conclusion repugnant.[23] It ignores the quality of individual lives, it allows sheer numbers to make a morally relevant difference, and it advocates the production of people for the sake of utility. In each case Anglin replies that the complaint applies to *any* utilitarian theory, for all such theories allow trade-offs between individuals' happiness for the common good, welcome extra happy lives, and, unlike the theory of Narveson, advocate levels of population solely on the basis of their theory of value, and without importing independent principles.

To some, this may appear a catalogue of reasons for rejecting utilitarianism, or, come to that, any other consequentialist theory. Yet *on any theory* conflicting interests or values must be weighed up against each other. There again, the objection about numbers basically turns on whether each worthwhile life is valuable, and whether, as Parfit has argued, 'more count for more'.[24] Finally the Total theory does not strictly enjoin the production of people so as to be the bearers or locations of the abstraction, utility. It seeks, among other things, to maximize lives of intrinsic value (either happy ones or worthwhile ones) — and to maximize their length — and any such life would necessarily be enjoyed by a person (or other animal), even if not all the persons concerned are currently actual ones. It has already been concluded that duties need not be owed to actual (or even to likely) people, and by expressing this truth the Total theory is in one way impersonal. But it is not impersonal in the way in which a theory might be which required people to be produced not for the sake of the intrinsic value of their own lives but for the sake of some ulterior abstraction like the glory of the nation or the race.

Thus the Total theory does not yield the Repugnant conclusion in the actual world, and even though the Conclusion might be yielded in some possible (ampler) world, that does not seem to be a conclusive reason for rejecting the Total theory. For the alternative theories fare far worse. (In case this is still not clear, see Sikora's *tour de force* in which all the alternative possibilities are reviewed and found wanting.[25]) The Total theory is immune to the main objections and has much to commend it (including considerations in defence of consequentialism which I have put forward elsewhere[26]), and the theory of value which was presented above lends the Total theory further support. Besides all this, arguments have been put forward by Parfit in favour of the Repugnant conclusion, by Anglin in favour of an obligation to bring extra people into existence, and by Sikora in support of the Total theory itself.[27]

Accepting the Repugnant conclusion

Parfit's argument runs as follows. By comparison with there being just a given population with lives very well worth living, it would be at least no worse if there also existed, perhaps somewhere else, a like number of people with a lower quality of life, but with lives still worth living. (There might be no injustice here, if perhaps the two groups did not know of each others' existence.) If we call the state of affairs with the given population 'A', and the second situation 'A Plus', then A Plus is better than A, or at any rate, no worse. We now envisage a state of affairs, B, with the same numbers as A Plus, all parties equally well off (i.e. leading equally worthwhile lives), and an average quality of life slightly higher than the average in A Plus, but markedly lower than in A. It is now hard to deny that state of affairs B is better than state A Plus, and thus that, as A Plus is no worse than A, B is better than A. We thus arrive by two natural stages at a conclusion favoured by the Total theory and incompatible with the Average theory: it is better for the average level to drop from a very high one if the population at the same time doubles. But by parity of reasoning, further reductions of level and doublings of numbers are also desirable, until we reach a very large population with a uniform level of quality of life just above that at which life is barely worth living.

Now Parfit in fact wrestles with this Repugnant conclusion with a view to rejecting it if possible. But the move from A Plus to B cannot be rejected either by Average theorists or by anyone else who accepts the law of diminishing marginal utility. As to the move from A to A Plus, the Average theory was criticized above for rejecting this transition, which is clearly in place on any theory of value remotely similar to that of Roupas and Glover.

The problem, then, is to explain people's reluctance to accept the conclusion. This reluctance, I suggest, stems partly from the presumption that a succession of such doublings of population and lowerings of levels of quality (or worthwhileness) of life could take place on our planet without grave side-effects, and is thus being proposed as an improvement. In fact any additional numbers would issue certainly in famine and probably in epidemics and war, making life worse for all. There again, people reflecting on the two transitions may too readily assume that they themselves are to be included in the population in state of affairs A, and stand to lose much that they enjoy. But to adopt an impartial view, as Roupas points out, they must imagine (instead) that they have an equal likelihood of being one of the extra people in A Plus. The experience of these people would not be of falling standards but, in most cases, the discovery that life is sweet.

One further remark is in place. For some populations, a doubling is readily possible without anyone's life being miserable or not worth living. But actual doublings often fall short of this. Where this would be the case for a significant number of people, the overall balance of good over evil (at any rate on the account of value shortly to be introduced) would cease to rise, and the Total theory would authorize a halt to be called.

The Extra Person Obligation

I now turn to Anglin's Extra Person Obligation argument. Trimmed of its detail Anglin's argument is based on the premise that it is obligatory to bring into existence a happy person at slight cost to oneself rather than to bring into existence at no cost to oneself someone whose happiness would be exactly matched by their unhappiness. But to do the latter is no better or worse than bringing no one into existence. Therefore, in a choice between the first course of action and doing nothing, the former is obligatory. The more problematic premise is the first one, but, as Anglin says, an Average theorist must accept it. But if this premise is accepted, there is an Extra Person Obligation, which could, if conditions allowed it to apply many times over, yield a Repugnant conclusion. But no conclusion can be repugnant which issues from a genuine obligation. More significantly there is sometimes an obligation to bring extra people into existence even at some cost to existing people.

Anglin's argument is an attempt to replace an argument of Sikora which Anglin finds inconclusive. Sikora's argument begins with the premise that it would be permissible to allow the coming into existence of a 'package' of extra people of whom the vast majority would be happy but of whom at least one would be very unhappy (and accordingly there is no obligation not to do so). But there is an obligation not to bring into existence a person who will be very unhappy. Therefore there must be an obligation to bring into existence the happy people, an obligation which overrides the obligation not to bring into existence the very unhappy person.[28] Anglin's reaction is that the obligation might be overridden by the prospect of happy people, even if bringing them about was not obligatory: for it could be an act of supererogation. But it takes an obligation to override an obligation: so Sikora's argument succeeds after all, or so I should contend.

Jonathan Bennett further objects to Sikora's conclusion as follows. The case for continuing the human species (for no less is at stake) could turn on the utilities of actual people, because of the suffering which the phasing out of the species would cause. But this consideration scarcely justifies humanity being continued for millennia, and in any case fails to account for the Extra Person Obligation which Anglin so cogently argues to exist even where there is some cost to existing people. Alternatively the case might lie, according to Bennett, in the importance of projects which matter to us — the living — being continued, on the axiom that unfinished business must be completed. This is only plausible if projects can be given the kind of significance accorded them by Bernard Williams, against which I have argued elsewhere.[29] Bennett's third point boils down to the claim that the factors which outweigh the obligation need not generate another obligation: here I believe that Sikora is right to reply that if they do not generate an obligation, they are too slight to count. Sikora's argument thus stands. It follows that there is a fairly extensive obligation upon existing people to bring into existence people who, as far as can be foreseen, will lead happy or worthwhile lives.

The Total theory defended and modified

Sikora proceeds to develop his argument further so as to produce a new defence of the Total theory.[30] His earlier argument may be taken to suggest that there is at least as much value in increasing happiness by adding extra people as there is negative value in adding unhappy people. But, as he now adds, where equal amounts of unhappiness are in question, adding unhappy people is just as bad as making actual people unhappy. Therefore there is at least as much positive value in increasing the happiness total of the world by adding happy people as there is in preventing an equal amount of suffering (or adding an equal amount of happiness) for those alive.

But the earlier argument, as Sikora acknowledges, may not show that the value of extra happy lives balances the negative value of the same number of unhappy lives. What is really at stake here is whether the misery of either an existing or an extra life is no more important than an extra happy life, and accordingly whether, other things being equal, it is indifferent whether resources are spent on rearing an additional happy person or on preventing someone's misery. It is not in question that many agents should do both (indeed perhaps most should). Nor am I suggesting that the race should not be continued until all existing misery has been relieved, a view which would in any case be ruled out by the earlier argument, an argument which I have accepted. The point is rather that the earlier argument is compatible with the prevention of misery being much more important than the production of happiness.

As Sikora points out, to accept this is to forfeit the simplicity of classical utilitarianism. It certainly involves a modification of that position. But, as I have pointed out earlier, I cannot accept that happiness is the only good; and I further maintain that the satisfaction of people's basic needs does much more good than does increasing the happiness of those whose basic needs are satisfied already. But I can go along with Sikora when he argues that in any case what we ought to do is to maximize the balance of whatever is intrinsically valuable over what is intrinsically bad, and that the obligation to bring into existence people with worthwhile lives is still derivable on this basis.[31]

But the modification of the Total theory just introduced allows me also to agree with James P. Sterba's case for a policy involving a severe restriction on any increase on the current world population.[32] Sterba argues as follows:

Given that the welfare rights of future generations require existing generations to make provision for the basic needs of future generations, existing generations would have to evaluate their ability to provide both for their own basic needs and for the basic needs of future generations. Since existing generations by bringing persons into existence would be determining the membership of future generations, they would have to evaluate whether they are able to provide for that membership. And if existing generations discover that, were the population to increase beyond a certain point, they would lack sufficient resources to make the necessary provision for each person's basic needs, then it would be incumbent upon them to restrict the membership of future generations so as not to exceed their ability to provide for each person's basic needs.

Accordingly, Sterba holds, the welfare rights of future generations justify a compromise position between the policies of the Average and the Total theories. But in fact the position reached (which, incidentally, turns on needs rather than on rights) may be regarded as a modification of the Total theory, on which intrinsic value is most readily maximized by provision for basic needs and prevention of the existence of people whose basic needs would not be satisfied, and these contributions to the worthwhileness of present and future lives, for that very reason, take priority over the fostering of happiness.

Implications of the modified theory

What policy, then, does the modified Total theory sustain? Does it, for example, imply the Repugnant conclusion? It does not imply this conclusion in our actual world, and for the same reasons as those given above about the implications of the unmodified theory. In a possible world with enough space and resources, and with mechanisms to ensure the even distribution of these resources, it would imply something like the Repugnant conclusion (though only if the interests of nonhumans were not undermined thereby). But as basic needs should be taken to include the need to develop essential human capacities, including the capacity for practical reason, at least some provision for education (formal or informal) would be included, and thus a quality of life rather above that of the barely tolerable would be involved. In such a world there might be privations, but life would be distinctly worthwhile for nearly everyone except, perhaps, the incapacitated. But all this is a depiction of the most that the modified theory could imply for a world very different from our own.

Does the modified theory, on the other hand, provide for the continuation of human life at all? The obligation to do so, successfully defended by Sikora, concerns cases where even if some miserable people are produced, many more people are also born who are expected to lead worthwhile lives. Thus, even on Sikora's view, if all or most of our possible successors would be expected to lead miserable lives, we should have no obligation to bring them into existence; indeed we should have an obligation, other things being equal, to refrain from doing so. The area of apparent conflict, however, concerns cases where worthwhile lives cannot be produced without some other people being born who are expected to lead lives of misery. But such cases, it might plausibly be held, are not too dissimilar to the state of the actual world, and do also genuinely raise the question of whether, on the modified theory, it is right to continue the human race under current conditions. Sterba himself seems not to doubt this, but a critic might question his consistency.

The following considerations, however, suggest that the conflict is more apparent than real between the policies yielded by the modified and unmodified theories. Firstly, any population, even one where everyone's basic needs are supplied, is likely to include some miserable people, including some whose lives are not worthwhile. But this is no criticism of that generation's predecessors; nor does Sterba's position imply that such a population should not be brought into existence. Secondly, as the current world population could be fed, and resources exist to satisfy everyone's other basic needs, there is a sense of 'provide for' in which the basic needs of successive generations are provided for, so long as succeeding generations are of the same size as the present one. Thus, as long as Sterba's remarks are taken in this sense (as I suggest that they should be), he can consistently advocate a policy of zero population growth (in which the world population gradually replaces itself), and is not committed to a policy of zero birth rate (in which it is not allowed to do so). Thirdly, though there is another sense of 'provide for' in which basic needs are not provided for unless what is needed is accessible to the person concerned, Sterba cannot be interpreted as advocating provision for basic needs in this sense. For such provision depends on just institutions, and each generation has at least the final say over what its own institutions shall be. The current generation may well have an obligation to provide in the stronger sense for the basic needs of all its members, as Sterba would doubtless agree; but it cannot be obliged in this sense to provide for its successors. It can, of course, facilitate this sort of provision by inaugurating fair institutions, encouraging equitable forms of development in the Third World and by shouldering the obligations mentioned in the last chapter, but it cannot guarantee the provision of future people's needs, whatever their number.

Thus Sterba's position is in keeping with the Extra Person Obligation which (in different forms) both Anglin and Sikora defend. What it adds is a limit to the range of circumstances in which that obligation holds good. Thus if the basic needs of all members of a population could not be provided for, however just its distributive system, then it would be wrong to produce a population of that size rather than to bring into existence a smaller population the needs of which could be provided for. (Since the larger population would be likely to be beset with widespread misery, this is a conclusion which Sikora might accept, but he could not accept it for cases where there was more happiness than unhappiness.)

It follows that increases in the world population should be severely restricted, but that within this restriction as many people as possible who are likely to lead worthwhile lives should be brought into existence, except where their arrival would mean that other people's basic needs could not be met (whether those other people were contemporaries or successors). It does not follow, in theory, that population should be restricted to its current level, as a greater total could be fed and provided for. On the other hand the prospects that social and international arrangements will be so improved that everyone, or even nearly everyone, in an increased population could lead a worthwhile life are minimal; and besides this any increase is likely to lead to severe strain on vital ecosystems and on nonhuman species, at least if the increased population is to be sustained indefinitely. Another consideration militating against a policy of increase is the obligation argued for by Kavka (and implicit, as was remarked in chapter 6, in the obligation to provide for basic needs equally) that each generation should leave the planet in as good a state for its successors as that in which it was received, except in the case of an initial generation which needs to invest resources to make this obligation capable of fulfilment by its successors. For we could well make this obligation impossible to fulfil by increasing the population beyond the minimum by which, as demographers tell us, it is certain to increase whatever we do.

A general population policy is also affected by the consideration that rapid change in population size usually produces undesirable side-effects and suffering. Thus if it is agreed that a sustainable population is to be aimed at, its level depends in part on rates of change of a non-disastrous character as well as on the current population size. In the actual world, population increase itself is proceeding at a rapid rate, with undeniable strains on the social service provisions of many Third World countries, and this constitutes an independent argument for less rapid increases. But any rapid reversal of population trends would also involve acute social strains. Accordingly we need a policy in which sustainability and zero population growth is an eventual aim, and in which these aims are attained by a gradual and progressive diminution of the present rate of increase. It will doubtless follow that each country should have a population policy of its own, and also that a more equitable system of international arrangements should be introduced. But these matters cannot be taken further within the present book.

On not disparaging life

What should here be remarked is that the existence of each extra person is not the curse which some ecological writers purport to believe. Certainly if there are too many simultaneously, the planetary life-support systems may be irreparably damaged, imperilled species may be lost, and even in the short term there may be war, famine and pestilence. Yet all this is tenable only if some lives are of value; and in fact, as we have seen, there is good reason to accept the value of each and every worthwhile human life, and of each person concerned having what they need to live such a life. This theory of value will need to be supplemented when members of other species are taken into account (see chapter 8); but that would not detract from its truth.

Thus the traditional belief of most communities, Judaeo-Christian and otherwise, that children are a blessing and that life (except where special factors make it not worth living) is a gift, is not merely the product of adverse evolutionary conditions and the vagaries of human history, as some philosophers speculatively maintain. It is all of a piece with the theory of value advocated above; and but for some such theory of value little sense could be made of our various obligations in matters of population. I do not wish to enter here into issues such as the morality of abortion, beyond remarks made above over Roupas' theory; but make these concluding remarks rather to point out that, though multiplication has its limits (ecological limits among them), there is nothing intrinsically wrong with it.

NOTES

1   Cf. the title of Paul R. Ehrlich's *The Population Bomb,* London: Pan Books/Ballantine, 1971.
2   In the editor's Introduction to Michael D. Bayles (ed.), *Ethics and Population,* Cambridge, Mass.: Schenkman, 1976.
3   Cf. Robert G. Burton, 'A Philosopher Looks at the Population Bomb', in William T. Blackstone (ed.), *Philosophy and Environmental Crisis,* 105—16.
4   In the passage which follows, I draw on two papers in R. I. Sikora and Brian Barry (eds), *Obligations to Future Generations,* Robert Scott, Jnr, 'Environmental Ethics and Obligations to Future Generations', 74—90, and L. W. Sumner, 'Classical Utilitarianism and the Population Optimum', 91—111; and also on Bill Angin's paper 'The Repugnant Conclusion', *Canadian Journal of Philosophy,* 7, 1977, 745—54.
5   Cf. Jan Narveson, *Morality and Utility,* Baltimore: John Hopkins Press, 1967, pp. 46—50; 'Utilitarianism and New Generations', *Mind,* 76, 1967, 62—72; 'Moral Problems of Population', in Michael D. Bayles (ed.) *Ethics and Population,* 59—80; 'Future People and Us', in Sikora and Barry (eds), *Obligations to Future Generations,* 38—60; Thomas Schwartz, 'Obligations to Posterity', in ibid. 3—13; Mary Warren, 'Do Potential People Have Moral Rights?' in ibid. 14—30; Trudy Govier, 'What Should We Do About Future People?', *American Philosophical Quarterly,* 16, 1979, 105—13. A partially similar position was adopted by Peter Singer in 'A Utilitarian Population Principle', in *Ethics and Population,* 81—99.
6   R. I. Sikora, 'Utilitarianism: The Classical Principle and the Average Principle', *Canadian Journal of Philosophy,* 1975, 409—19; 'Is it Wrong to Prevent the Existence of Future Generations?', in Sikora and Barry (eds), *Obligations to Future Generations,* 112—66; 'Utilitarianism and Future Generations', *Canadian Journal of Philosophy,* 9, 1979, pp. 461—6. (Sikora's argument has been criticized by Jefferson McMahan

in 'Problems of Population Theory', *Ethics*, 92, 1981—82, 96—127; Sikora shows that his case remains substantially intact in 'Classical Utilitarianism and Parfit's Repugnant Conclusion: A Reply to McMahan', ibid. 128—33.) For Derek Parfit's contribution, see 'Rights, Interests and Possible People', in Samuel Gorovitz *et al.* (eds), *Moral Problems in Medicine,* Englewood Cliffs, NJ: Prentice-Hall, 1976, 369—75; 'Energy Policy and the Further Future', forthcoming in Peter Brown and Douglas MacLean (eds), *Energy Policy and Future Generations,* Tottowa, NJ: Rowman & Littlefield; and 'Overpopulation, Part One' (unpublished paper), revised as 'Future Generations: Further Problems', *Philosophy and Public Affairs,* 11, 1981—82, 113—72.

7   'Future People and Us', p. 55.

8   Timothy L. S. Sprigge, 'Professor Narveson's Utilitarianism', *Inquiry,* 11, 1968, 337—41, cited by William Anglin, 'In Defense of the Potentiality Principle', in Sikora and Barry (eds), *Obligations to Future Generations,* 31—7, p. 35.

9   Further trenchant criticisms of such an asymmetrical position are to be found in James P. Sterba, 'Abortion, Distant Peoples and Future Generations', *Journal of Philosophy,* 77, July 1980, 424—40.

10   'Future People and Us', p. 45.

11   Trudy Govier, 'What Should We Do About Future People?' The passage quoted is from p. 111 (Govier's italics). (On page 113a there is a misprint at line 13. If her summary is to fit her text, 'dependent' must be read as 'independent'.)

12   Peter Singer, 'A Utilitarian Population Principle', p. 86. See also his *Practical Ethics,* pp. 87f.

13   Parfit in 'On Doing the Best for Our Children' in Bayles (ed.), *Ethics and Population*; Sikora in 'Is it Wrong to Prevent the Existence of Future Generations?' (see especially pp. 127—32). Singer has acknowledged in the light of Parfit's criticisms that his attempt to defend an asymmetrical theory of obligations failed: see his 'Killing Humans and Killing Animals', *Inquiry*, 22, 1979, 145—56, p. 155, n. 5. But the revised position which he there adopts, a combination of Govier's position where self-conscious beings are concerned and the Total theory where merely conscious ones are in question, is still open to the objection of disregarding the interests of people who will exist if the agent makes them actual.

14   R. M. Hare, 'Abortion and the Golden Rule', *Philosophy and Public Affairs,* 4, 1974—75, 201—22, p. 212.

15   R. M. Hare, 'Survival of the Weakest', in Samuel Gorovitz *et al.* (eds), *Moral Problems in Medicine,* 364—9, p. 366.

16   See Derek Parfit, 'Rights, Interests and Possible People', 'Overpopulation, Part One' and 'Future Generations: Further Problems'; T. G. Roupas, 'The Value of Life', *Philosophy and Public Affairs,* 7, 1977—78, 154—83. See also Jefferson McMahan, 'Problems of Population Theory', pp. 104—7.

17   A somewhat similar view is taken by Michael Bayles in 'Harm to the

Unconceived', *Philosophy and Public Affairs*, 5, 1975—76, 292—304, and by George Sher in 'Hare, Abortion and the Golden Rule', in that same journal, 6, 1976—77, 185—90.

18 In 'Overpopulation, Part One'; an echo of the point remains in 'Future Generations: Further Problems'. See also Jefferson McMahan, 'Problems of Population Theory', pp. 101f.

19 Roupas explains his sources and how he modifies them in n. 12 on p. 127.

20 Glover, *Causing Death and Saving Lives*, pp. 45—57.

21 In 'On Being Human', *Inquiry*, 17, 1974, 175—92.

22 Hare in 'Abortion and the Golden Rule', p. 218; Singer in 'A Utilitarian Population Principle', p. 82; Sikora in 'Is it Wrong to Prevent the Existence of Future Generations?', pp. 118f and p. 158, n. 4.

23 'The Repugnant Conclusion', pp. 748ff. (I add extra reasons below. Taken together, Anglin's reasons and mine supplement Sikora's account of why the conclusion is thought to be a Repugnant one, and our assessments of them suffice to show that, even if, as McMahan holds, the conclusion seems Repugnant for reasons beyond those which Sikora allows, the appearance of repugnancy can be allayed.)

24 Derek Parfit, 'Innumerate Ethics', *Philosophy and Public Affairs*, 7, 1977 78, 285—301, p. 301.

25 Sikora, 'Is it Wrong . . .', pp. 114—16, 119—32, 133—6.

26 In 'Toward a Defence of Consequentialism', *Ethics*, 85, 1975, 123—35.

27 For Anglin, see 'The Repugnant Conclusion', pp. 752—4; Parfit's argument is presented in the 1973 draft of 'Overpopulation, Part One', in 'Future Generations: Further Problems', by McMahan; 'Problems of Population Theory', pp. 122f; and by Singer in 'A Utilitarian Population Principle', p. 94; for Sikora, see 'Is it Wrong . . .', pp. 140—5. It should be remarked that the Extra Person Obligation is obligatory only where the alternatives are to do nothing or to do something of less value than producing a worthwhile life. For many couples there are alternatives of equal or greater value, and so the obligation does not apply.

28 Sikora, 'Utilitarianism: The Classical Principle . . .', pp. 412—16, summarized by Anglin in 'The Repugnant Conclusion', p. 752, and presented afresh by Sikora in 'Is it Wrong . . .', pp. 136—40.

29 Jonathan Bennett, 'On Maximizing Happiness', in Sikora and Barry (eds), *Obligations to Future Generations*, 61—73; Bernard Williams and J. J. C. Smart, *Utilitarianism, For and Against*, London and New York: Cambridge University Press, 1973, pp. 113—17; Robin Attfield, 'Supererogation and Double Standards', *Mind*, 88, 1979, 481—99, pp. 492—4.

30 'Is it Wrong . . .', pp. 140—5. (I have here presented his argument in simplified form. I have also omitted his mention of timeless utilitarianism, as its role in the argument is not clear.)

31 Ibid. pp. 144f.

32 'Abortion, Distant Peoples and Future Generations', pp. 433f.

8

The Moral Standing of Nonhumans

So far I have confined the basis of the argument to human interests. If the interests of future humans, including those whom we could bring into existence, are taken into account, there is already a formidable case for the conservation of natural resources, wildlife, wilderness and ecosystems, as also for population policies allowing people to have what they need if their lives are to be worthwhile. But perhaps not only humans are entitled to moral consideration. Perhaps some nonhumans, or even nonhuman nature in general, are of moral relevance. There again, perhaps some nonhumans, or some states of nonhumans, are of value in their own right. These are the questions to be tackled in the present chapter.

As Kenneth Goodpaster has observed,[1] the question of the scope and limits of moral consideration is not to be confused with that of moral significance. An answer to the first question commits nobody to any particular view about the relative importance of one set of claims or interests over another. The question of moral significance is a subsequent question, and though it surfaces from time to time in the current chapter, a fuller treatment is postponed to the chapter following. Yet the answers to the first question can throw light on the second, particularly if they include a theory of intrinsic value. For, once we know the basis of a thing's value, we can begin to compare that value with the value of other states or beings, and to consider priorities.

The present investigation has a bearing at once on applied ethics, normative ethics and meta-ethics. Thus if some animals' interests are to be taken into account, there is an extra ground for preserving their habitats. Normative theory is also affected, for we should be maximizing the satisfaction not just of human needs but, perhaps, some animals' needs too. But this is only possible if, at the level of meta-ethics, the concept of moral consideration is taken to allow the interests of nonhumans to count. In theory the meta-ethical question, 'Can x be morally considered?' is distinct from the normative question, 'Should x be morally considered?' In a similar spirit Feinberg tries to keep separate the questions, 'Can animals have rights?' and 'Do animals have rights?'[2] But, as Goodpaster points out,[3] they are closely related; and, although he accepts too readily that meta-ethical beliefs may be tailored to normative ones, it is certainly not easy to see how, once it is acknowledged that x is a possible object of beneficence, the claim that x should be taken into account beneficently should be resisted, unless the analogies between it and accepted cases of items having moral standing are very weak.

Though rights have just been mentioned, the current investigation (and, in general, the current volume) does not concern the location of rights. For even if only some humans bore rights, or even if nothing at all bore rights, it would still be possible that humans or other animals or plants deserved moral consideration. Rights are not the only basis of moral concern: something can lack rights, yet still have moral standing. Besides, no consequentialist can treat rights as morally basic; such claims as I make from time to time about rights should be construed as being grounded in the good which accrues, or the evil avoided, when rights are recognized and respected. It is in any case in order to search beyond rights to their moral grounds. Moreover rights-talk is used in a wide range of senses, depending on whether rights are regarded merely as liberties, or are taken always to be matched by corresponding obligations,[4] or are strong grounds against interference,[5] or can only be overridden when very great harm would otherwise result,[6] or are 'side-constraints' not to be overridden at all (except perhaps when they clash with each other).[7] Accordingly rights-talk needs its sense to be elucidated before it can be appraised; the range of application varies with the sense employed, and things could well have value without most (or perhaps any) of the senses of 'rights' applying to them.

Sentience and other capacities

Do only humans, then, deserve moral consideration? Indeed do all humans deserve it? As Richard Routley points out,[8] a social contract theory would lead us to limit consideration to the contracting individuals: but such theories, as was observed in chapter 6, improperly omit even those humans who are not in a position to enter into contracts. Similarly, as Geoffrey Warnock remarks,[9] the Kantian position on which only rational agents can be respected is intolerably narrow: this position, after all, omits infants and imbeciles. But if infants and imbeciles are instead included, as they ordinarily are, then it is extremely hard to justify excluding those animals which can, like them, suffer pain and frustration.

Most infants and many mentally defective people, certainly, share capacities (in the sense of potentials) for rationality, rule-following and self-determination lacked by most, if not all, nonhuman animals; and these are capacities essential to humanity in the sense that the lack of them from most members of a species shows it not to be human, and at the same time inessential to other species. This fact may not be without its significance, as an organism's inherited capacities (essential ones included) are, it is reasonable to maintain, determinative of its good as a member of its kind; and the potentials of a chimpanzee or a dolphin are different from those of humans. Indeed it seems reasonable to hold that a worthwhile life involves the ability to exercise the essential capacities of one's species. If so, then human individuals with the capacities mentioned need to be allowed to develop them or they will be deprived of their good. Yet all this, though important for value-theory, is beside the present point. For some imbeciles, infant ones included, lack these potentials, yet do not for that reason forfeit moral consideration. And if they do not, then those animals which can likewise suffer pain and frustration must also have moral standing, quite apart from the case for it which might be based on their having some capacities in common with most humans and some distinctive ones of their own.

Sentience, then, seems sufficient to qualify an organism for moral consideration. This could be because, as hedonists claim, pleasure is the sole good and pain the sole evil; if the balance of pleasure over pain is to be maximized, all creatures susceptible to either must be taken into account. But it is reasonable to hold that there are other goods, among them the ability to exercise self-determination, and other essential (but not in all cases distinctive) human capacities: for these, sentience is doubtless in most cases necessary, but the value of autonomy, etc., does not seem to depend on the pleasure which it may give rise to. Nevertheless pleasure and pain remain of positive and negative value in themselves, even if they are not the sole good and evil, and accordingly the (current) susceptibility to them is indeed sufficient for being morally considered. Thus most nonhuman animals have moral standing alongside humans, even if, perhaps, there are differences of value in the goods and evils to which they are liable.

Tom Regan's view of the importance of sentience[10] is that it is a logically necessary condition of a being having or leading one form of life that is better or worse for the being in question, one involving pleasure and pain. The mere value of pleasure and pain, he holds, does not explain why it is wrong to treat beings susceptible to them only as a means: intrinsic value really attaches to beings which are the subjects of a life which can be more or less valuable from their point of view. Regan's position presupposes that only individual organisms have intrinsic value, not their experiences or dispositions; and he considers that only the possession of intrinsic value makes it wrong for a being to be treated as a means. (Having intrinsic value is itself suggested as a necessary and sufficient condition of having irreducible moral rights; but, as I have indicated, the question of rights is not one which I shall here be considering.)

But if pleasure is of intrinsic value and pain of intrinsic negative value, the susceptibility to each of them *does* explain the wrongness of being treated solely as a means: or rather does explain it if it is allowed that we are obliged, in nonmarginal cases, to maximize intrinsic value. For if the organism in question were treated solely as a means, its liability to pain or pleasure would be totally disregarded: whereas if it is taken into account, the organism will not be treated as if it were of no moral relevance at all — indeed it will sometimes make a crucial difference — even if its importance is sometimes outweighed by that of other beings. Accordingly there is no need to regard only individual organisms as possessed of intrinsic value, rather than their states and experiences: the moral relevance of these beings can readily be maintained in the absence of this stipulation.

As to the suggestion that the necessary and sufficient condition of being an organism not to be treated only as a means (and thus of being of moral relevance in one's own right) lies in being the subject of a life which can be better or worse from one's point of view, I believe that there is here a sufficient condition of moral relevance but perhaps not a necessary condition. This is certainly so if the proposed criterion is taken in a strong sense and requires the organism to have a concept of its own identity and future. Peter Singer sometimes[11] uses this form of the criterion to mark off most humans and a few animals (beings whose deaths he believes to be intrinsically evil) from infants, some imbeciles and most nonhuman animals (to kill which is wrong, if at all, because of effects on other beings). But he is rightly concerned about the pains and pleasures of many creatures which do not satisfy the criterion in this form as well as about those which do.

The criterion also admits of a weaker sense which requires neither a concept of the self nor a sense of the future: something could be a subject of a life which can be better or worse from its point of view so long as it is conscious and has attitudes of gladness or frustration to what befalls it. All such organisms have a good of their own (to be glad or frustrated about), even perhaps some which do not have pleasant or painful sensations. (This could be true of some insects, fish or molluscs.) Now if whatever is susceptible to satisfaction and frustration merits moral consideration, then the Regan criterion, even in this weaker sense, marks a sufficient condition of moral relevance. But it is far from self-evident that it marks a necessary condition. For it is plausible that many creatures which do not satisfy it have interests and are capable of being benefited, and it is not obviously absurd to hold that whatever has interests falls within the class of 'moral patients'. Accordingly the interests criterion now falls due for consideration.

Regan's view about the scope of interests in one recent paper was that only conscious or potentially conscious beings have interests: thus human foetuses may qualify, but trees are explicitly excluded.[12] But Regan may here be using 'interests' in a special sense — he glosses 'having interests' as 'having desires, needs, etc.' — a sense other than that of 'having a good of one's own': for in subsequent and previous writings he has held that nonconscious beings can have a good of their own, and has criticized Feinberg for claiming to show that they cannot.[13]

At all events this restrictive view of the scope of interests is adopted without qualification by Feinberg,[14] who thus excludes 'mindless creatures' from the class of things with interests, though he is not altogether consistent about this. Feinberg is of the clear view that interests require desires or aims on the one hand, and cognition on the other. He also holds that when we speak of the good or the needs of plants, the functions which they need to discharge 'are assigned by human interests, not their own'. On the other hand, in an earlier passage concerning the conditions for a thing to have a good of its own, he lists as one of the alternative requirements for having a conative life, which may in turn qualify a thing for having a good of its own, 'latent tendencies, direction of growth and natural fulfillments' (sic).[15] But plants manifestly satisfy all the elements of this requirement. Moreover, as Goodpaster observes, it is absurd to hold that humans have assigned to trees the functions of growth and maintenance (or, we might add, many others). Indeed the needs of trees have not altered since long before humans existed on the planet.

I have assessed Feinberg's views elsewhere,[16] and here wish only to reaffirm the obvious truth that trees and other plants have a good of their own (a good which often conflicts with the interests of people). Accordingly neither sentience, consciousness or cognition are necessary for needs and interests. Having a good of their own, trees can be beneficiaries of human action, and are thus at least serious candidates for moral standing. As Goodpaster realizes, their lack of enjoyments, etc., may well make them of less moral significance than are sentient creatures, and we may take it that this is because less that is of value can befall them. But he concludes at this stage that, however slight their moral significance may be, all living things are 'morally considerable'.

But is being a possible beneficiary or having interests a sufficient condition of being deserving of moral consideration? Goodpaster's main argument for holding that it is so, apart from his replies to objections, lies in the necessary connection between beneficence and morality. This connection granted, the range of application of each is likely to be the same. This argument is reaffirmed in stronger form in a reply to W. Murray Hunt.[17] Beneficence and non-maleficence, he there points out, are central in morality. Accordingly as inanimate objects have no interests and cannot be benefited or harmed, they cannot be given moral consideration: but as living creatures do fall within the scope of beneficence, so they do within that of morality. This argument does indeed show this in the weak sense that moral consideration for the good of plants is not a conceptual impossibility, but does not show that the interests of plants ought to be taken into account. If so, an obstacle for the belief that plants merit moral consideration has been removed, but the belief itself, despite beginning to look less eccentric, has not been established.

Goodpaster also has a subsidiary argument, designed to explain reluctance to accept his conclusion. There is probably a noncontingent connection between theories of value and conceptions of 'moral considerability'. In particular the sentience criterion of the latter ties in with a hedonist theory of value. Thus anyone who accepts, as many people do, that only enjoyment is of positive intrinsic value and only pain is of negative intrinsic value is unlikely to accept that items not susceptible to either are morally to be considered. This is, I think, true; but to support his own conclusion further from this angle Goodpaster would need to put forward a cogent view of the value which attaches to nonsentient life or its states. For even if hedonism is rejected, what replaces it need not repose value in plants, or be echoed by a theory which accords them moral consideration. (In fact Goodpaster has more recently located value in the biosphere as a whole;[18] attention will be given later to such holistic theories.)

Environmental concern

Nevertheless the dealings of humans with nonconscious items in their environment do, as Regan points out, have their 'moral dimensions'.[19] (Thus it is widely believed to be wrong to eliminate a species, whether its members are conscious or not, or to destroy trees or forests without good cause; and there are also objections to tampering with some inanimate natural objects, as when mountains are quarried or rivers dammed.) Regan accordingly depicts an 'environmental ethic', and urges in its defence that the most common alternative ways of accounting for moral concern in these matters do not suffice to do so. In the environmental ethic which Regan presents it is acknowledged not only that some nonhumans have moral standing[20] but also that all conscious and some nonconscious beings have too. The same beings would be held to have value independently of any awareness or appreciation of them or interest in them on the part of any conscious being.[21] (Though Regan here employs the phrase 'inherent value', I shall continue to use 'intrinsic value', as 'inherent value' is also used in a contrasting sense, as will be seen below.) This value would be consequential on their other natural properties.

Regan is right to hold that the alternatives which he considers cannot account for environmental concern. Thus the argument that despoliation of nonconscious nature (e.g. unchecked strip-mining) is wrong because it makes its agents ruthless towards humans (or other animals) is as vulnerable as its empirical premise — that these effects do actually ensue. Besides, the objections to such practices would remain even if there were no such effects.

Another argument which Regan considers turns on the ideal of not destroying anything unthinkingly or gratuitously. Plundering the environment, so goes the argument, is wrong because it violates this ideal. Another form of this argument is put forward by Passmore,[22] who holds that our reactions to such deeds are explained by our disapproval of vandalism and wanton destruction, and that accordingly no such environmental ethic as Regan here proposes is required. The answer to this argument is that if vandalism is wrong then either, as I have claimed elsewhere,[23] some evil effect is perpetrated and there is a loss of value to the world, or, as Regan holds, the object which is destroyed must itself have value. Thus the vandalism theory is parasitic on an account of value which it does not supply. It does not follow, as Regan seems to think, that objects which can be vandalized must have intrinsic value,[24] for their value could depend on states of conscious perceivers. But the possibility that some of them or their states have intrinsic value remains an open one.

The next argument is that what makes it wrong to extirpate whole species or destroy forests is the adverse effect of doing so on the balance of pleasure over pain. As Regan acknowledges, this theory is not human-centred, as it can take into account animal pains and pleasures: and if it is sufficiently broadened as to include human interests and the interests of sentient beings in general, it accounts for more of our judgements in environmental matters than Regan allows. Thus it is important to preserve many plants and animals for reasons of scientific research, for recreation, retreat and the enjoyment of natural beauty in their habitats, and to retain as wide a gene-pool as possible for the sake of medicine and agriculture. These reasons are well presented by Passmore[25] and drawn just from human interests. If the interests of nonhuman animals are also taken into account, there are also reasons against practices such as clear-cutting forests, as the Routleys and Singer have contended.[26]

But any such theory is open to a difficulty noticed by Laurence H. Tribe: if these interests only are taken into account, it would often be justified to replace natural trees with plastic ones.[27] Many of the functions of trees can be carried out by alternative plants with greater practical benefits to humans; and though the reasons just given require the preservation of some trees, they may well not be conclusive in all cases. Indeed if we reason from pleasures rather than interests, fashion could lead to plastic trees being preferred and thus dictate their universal installation. The appalling implication that natural environments should be replaced by plastic ones justifies, in Regan's view, rejecting the theory.

A way forward consists in rejecting the hedonism which is the focus of Regan's protests, and adopting a theory in which the development of humans' aesthetic capacities counts among intrinsic goods, and also the development of individual wild animals after their kinds in their natural surroundings. But even such a broadened consequentialist theory seems at risk of allowing too much replacement of the natural by the plastic, and to be in danger of yielding this implication for as long as trees are only considered instrumentally and accorded no value of their own.

The fourth argument considered by Regan is based on the premise that parts of the natural environment symbolize cultural values which cannot satisfactorily be expressed without them, and that the loss of significant scenes and places diminishes ourselves. This consideration is held by Mark Sagoff to override utilitarian considerations.[28] A similar argument has also been presented about historical landmarks by M. P. and N. H. Golding.[29] The symbolic value of natural objects probably does explain a good deal of our concern to preserve them: but the argument is, as the Goldings acknowledge about theirs, grounded in human interests — interests which cannot claim immunity from comparison with other such interests. This, indeed, makes the argument a salutary one, as far as it goes: for it reminds anyone who assesses actions by their consequences that they must not neglect the effects which an action has, both upon the agent and upon others, through its psychological or cultural significance as a symbol.

But the argument is defective for reasons which include those given by Regan. Firstly there are difficulties in identifying which values should be expressed: manifestly our culture embodies diverse valuations of wilderness itself (to cite the conflict of values most immediately relevant to the matter in question), and it is not clear that we should prefer the values of the cultural elite who value it highly to those of the rest. Secondly the argument is powerless where the local culture (or the culture of the time) does not call for the preservation of nature. Indeed the argument could actually in some circumstances enjoin the manufacture and preservation of plastic forests. Besides this, the argument is no stronger than the potency of the symbolism of wild nature: even if for some people a river symbolizes freedom or the hills integrity, it is difficult to believe, except in cases of historical landmarks, that the symbolism will be perennial or persistent. There again, many of the species liable to be extinguished through the unintended side-effects of human activity have not sufficiently obtruded themselves upon human consciousness as to enter into our systems of self-expression at all; but their members can scarcely lack all standing simply because we have failed to notice them.

The four arguments which Regan considers, then, do not seem to account for certain widespread moral judgements, and do further suggest that trees have a value which in some cases is not purely instrumental. But this does not show that they (or their flourishing) have intrinsic value, and thus constitute a wholly independent object of moral concern. Much less does it show that inanimate natural objects have such a value: indeed about objects such as rocks and rivers I follow Goodpaster in holding that things which lack a good of their own cannot be the objects of moral consideration (as opposed to the creatures which live in or around them), or have intrinsic value. Some theory, certainly, is needed to explain the non-instrumental value which we attach to a variety of natural objects. But it is still an open question whether this value lies in the desirability of diversity, or in the value of species, rather than in the value of their individual members, or indeed in the value of the experience of wild things not made or controlled by people. There is also the alternative theory to consider that what is of intrinsic value is not individual organisms but entire ecosystems, each regarded as a community, or the biosphere, or the planet, and that the value of individual natural objects consists in their participation in the value of a greater whole.

The value of diversity

The value of diversity is a longstanding theme in our culture, a theme the history of which has been traced in A. O. Lovejoy's *The Great Chain of Being*.[30] The more diverse a world is, it has often been held, the better. In ecological connections this is an attractive principle: thus it accords a measure of value to those unimposing species which often turn out to play an indispensable role in an ecosystem, and still more to ecosystems which are internally diverse and which often turn out to be more stable for that reason than simpler ones. But this could all be accounted for by the importance of the preservation of a system of interdependent creatures, rather than by the value of diversity itself; and the reason for the importance of such systems being preserved could be the benefit of the sentient beings involved in it (sometimes including humans), or the external benefits to humans of the system remaining intact (e.g. a large gene-pool, recreation, scope for scientific research). Moreover where diversity is valued independently of these grounds, it is plausibly of value because of the enjoyment it affords to those able to experience it. Once it is granted that the enjoyment of sentient creatures is desirable for its own sake, and that it is in general increased by the experience of diversity both in the worlds of nature and of human culture, it may readily be acknowledged also that this, together with the range of worthwhile activities which it facilitates, is why value is attached to diversity.

This account of the value of diversity cannot be accused of being human-centred, as it includes the value of some of the experiences and activities of nonhumans. Moreover it does not follow from it that there is nothing inherently bad about the loss of a species; for there may well be other reasons to think that there is something bad about this, lying either in living species, or in their members, or in states of their members. But diversity extends indifferently to the inanimate as well as to the animate, and I cannot see that there is any reason to accept that the more kinds there are, of whatever nature, the better. I have explored the question of the value of diversity further elsewhere;[31] as to the effects of diversity, Passmore has argued persuasively that they are a mixture of good and bad.[32] So we may accept that diversity is valuable by making our lives, and those of our fellow-creatures, fuller and richer, without being of value in itself; and proceed to the question of the value of living species.

The value of species

Ample reasons why the elimination of a species is usually contrary to human interests have been given above: to these Peter Singer adds that there would often also be consequential harm to members of other nonhuman species.[33] But, as he points out, species are not, as such, conscious entities. Can species be said to have interests? According to Singer it follows that they cannot. Though I reject his reasoning, I believe that the conclusion that species lack interests is correct, at least if it means that a species has no interests over and above those of its members. Viewed abstractly, a species has interests no more than abstract classes have in general; and, though species are often viewed concretely, as the current population of the species, the interests which may then be spoken of reduce to those of the current members without remainder. Where the interests of further species are at stake, it is of course often desirable that there should be, for example, grass or legumes, without it mattering which individual organisms stay alive; but in questions of intrinsic value, the value would have to turn on that of particular individuals, or at least on particular flourishing states being attained by some individuals or other.[34]

But it is important not to forget the future members of a species. In some small measure this consideration is already implicit in the mention of the interests of the current members. For, among sentient organisms, it is often in the interests of those currently alive that their immediate successors should thrive. Yet, as was remarked in chapter 7 about humans, this point on its own hardly justifies preserving a species in perpetuity. The real question concerns whether the future members of nonhuman species will have value and should be considered in the present, in any way analogous to that which was claimed in that chapter for future people. The answer here must be that where the existence or the flourishing of future beings would have value, and we can facilitate or prevent it, we must take it into account. But the elimination of a species guarantees that it will have no future members; and many species are precisely threatened with extinction, either through the direct effects of human action or through reluctance to forestall the effects of pollution, the loss of natural habitats or other harmful trends. Therefore we must take into account the value of the future members of these species.

This is to say nothing about the extent of their moral significance, which might well easily be overridden in many cases. (Nor is it to declare that future nonconscious organisms are of intrinsic value, as the issue of the value of present ones remains unresolved.) But where members of these species (or their states) have value, it is to say that their future members have moral standing, including those possible future members the existence of which we can veto altogether. And in this area, as in that of future people, we could have duties regarding future creatures without owing the duties to particular ones or even knowing their identity. Thus for practical purposes we can speak of the value of the continued life of a species, although this value in fact hangs on that of the several present and future members.

Conscious and nonconscious life

Now to see how far such commitments would extend, we need to resolve the issue of the intrinsic value of nonconscious living organisms. But before that can be done it is necessary to assess a rival theory of Frankena and Singer. William Frankena follows C. I. Lewis in calling 'inherent value' the value which an object has through its ability to contribute to human life by its presence, and contends that this is the kind of value which attaches to things whether alive or not which are interesting to watch or study, or beautiful to contemplate, or which heal us when we are with them. C. I. Lewis' example is a painting. Frankena contrasts such inherent value with instrumental value, and applies the notion to natural as well as cultural items which benefit those who observe or contemplate them.[35] His example is the value which birds have for birdwatchers.) As birds are sentient, he would doubtless allow them intrinsic value too, but he would not say the same for plants or rocks.)

Peter Singer holds a similar view, expressed in different terms. Singer considers the suggestion of Val Routley that the destruction of a species is analogous to that of a great work of art, and that some of the 'immensely complex and inimitable items produced in nature' (Singer's quotation) have a non-instrumental value, just as a great painting has value 'apart from the pleasure and inspiration it brings to human beings'.[36] He replies by asking how it can be shown that a work of art such as Michelangelo's *Pieta* has value 'independently of the appreciation of those who have seen it or will see it'. It is unfortunate that Singer appears to imply that, not being non-instrumental, the value of the *Pieta* is merely instrumental, for his views suggest that he could agree with Frankena in holding its value not to be instrumental either, but inherent. But in any case his view is that its value depends on the possibility of its being perceived and enjoyed, and he sustains this view with a thought experiment not unlike that of Richard Routley, and a variant recently put forward by myself.[37] We imagine the last sentient being on earth making a bonfire of all the paintings in the Louvre. As long as the possibility of a visit from interstellar tourists is excluded, Singer does not hold that anything wrong is done. (He should perhaps exclude the likelier possibility also that the agent would have enjoyed the paintings later, by stipulating that the last sentient being knows that he or she is shortly to die.) If so, the value of works of art is inherent rather than intrinsic. Now if we also rule out the possibility that the interests of the dead, or of God, make a difference, it is hard to conclude that the act is wrong; and this conclusion is fortified by the reflection that inanimate objects have no good of their own. Works of art thus have inherent rather than intrinsic value, and if there really is an analogy between them and species (or their members), as has also been suggested by Stanley Benn,[38] then the analogy, *pace* both Benn and Val Routley, supports no stronger conclusion than this about any of the items concerned.

My agreement with Frankena and Singer applies not only to works of art but also to natural objects like rivers and rocks. Thus both the symbolic significance which they sometimes have and their curious diversity turn out to be facets of their inherent value. Nor should I dispute that very many living species, whether sentient or nonsentient, are possessed of inherent value also: an example is supplied by what Regan pleasantly calls 'pleasures rooted in real redwoods'. This may seem to clash with Mary Midgley's point, mentioned in chapter 4, that wild nonhuman creatures must be held either to have no point or value or to have a point which is quite alien to human purposes.[39] But the conflict is only apparent. As far as any intrinsic value which they may have is concerned, Midgley's view may be accepted; but granted her observation that we can derive pleasure and renewal from that which is wild and alien to our purposes, it follows that in any case the wild and alien creatures concerned have inherent value. What is clear, however, is that it does not follow from their having inherent value that this is the only value which they have. Singer is easily able to arrive at his view that this is the extent of their value, holding as he does that trees only have interests and needs in much the same sense as that in which cars do.[40] But cars lack natural fulfilments and, except in an artificial sense, direction of growth; trees, by contrast, have a good of their own, quite independent of that of people or other purposers.

Accordingly, although Goodpaster's reminder that plants have a good of their own does not establish that they have moral standing, there is some analogy between them and items which are widely agreed to have such standing, consisting precisely in their having interests and in the qualities and capacities which make this true. Thus the capacities for growth, respiration, self-preservation and reproduction are common to plants and sentient organisms (as also to many unicellular organisms). So there is an analogical argument for holding that all the organisms concerned not only can but also do have moral standing. There is, in fact, a qualification to make, as the analogical argument applies only to organisms with interests; and though sentient organisms whose flourishing was in the past clearly still have interests as long as they have any prospect of consciousness, the same cannot be said, in general, of nonsentient beings. For the interests of these beings lie in the fulfilment of their capacities, and once this fulfilment is in the past and decay sets in (often through the flourishing of other organisms) their interests decline and vanish. Only what retains a potential for realizing the generic good of its kind has interests and is valuable, even if the above argument is accepted; and accordingly it may well be that living organisms are not valuable as such, but that what is valuable is their flourishing or their capacity for flourishing after the manner of their kind, for as long as such a capacity can to any extent be sustained.

But can the argument be allowed to proceed even this far? For its implications seem devastating, and there are in any case disanalogies to consider. The implication which Goodpaster considers of respecting all life is that one cannot *live* on these terms, and Passmore actually accepts a corresponding objection to Schweitzer's view that all life merits reverence.[41] This implication is not greatly weakened by the qualification about organisms which are past their prime, as millions of others remain to be considered. The objection may thus be expressed as follows. If plants (or bacteria) have any more-than-negligible moral significance, then in their millions their interests must sometimes outweigh those of individual humans or other sentient beings; but this flies in the face of our reflective moral judgements, and should thus, short of compelling reasons, be rejected.

To this, however, there is a reply. Moral standing should not, as we have seen, be confused with moral significance; and the unacceptable conclusion is implied only by claims about the moral significance of plants and bacteria, not by claims about their moral standing. For they could have a moral standing and yet have an almost infinitesimal moral significance, so that even large aggregations of them did not outweigh the significance of sentient beings in cases of conflict. It could be that their moral significance only makes a difference when all other claims and considerations are equal (or nonexistent). Yet, as Goodpaster says, as long as plants have moral standing, it is worth bearing this standing in mind as a 'regulative consideration' which should at least ideally be taken into account. (In the actual world, the inherent and instrumental value of plants and generally of nonconscious organisms will quite often outweigh other moral considerations, and will constitute the main reasons against, for example, eliminating a species. But the intrinsic value of healthy plants could still add slightly to those considerations.)

The argument thus survives this objection, but it is no stronger than its analogical basis allows, and at this point the disanalogies between conscious and nonconscious organisms become important. The limited nature of the interests of the latter has already been noted. Moreover they cannot be pained or gladdened, satisfied or

frustrated; and, except for the most primitive, they have no prospect
of ever evolving into anything which could bear characteristics of
this kind. There again they are not the subjects of a conscious point
of view, and theories which base value on choices or preferences
between living the life of one creature and the life of another are apt
to accord them no value whatsoever.[42] Besides this, they are not in
any morally interesting sense agents, even though causally their
activity is vital for those beings which are so.

But how much do the disanalogies count for? Doubts were
expressed in chapter 7 about theories which rest values on
preferences; and the disanalogies do not annul the interests which
seem to qualify plants (and the rest) for intrinsic value. The
importance of the disanalogies seems rather to concern moral
significance. Thus if pain and frustration constitute what is centrally
of negative value, but plants and bacteria are susceptible to neither,
then relatively little of negative value can befall them: and this
suggests that relatively little of positive value can befall them either.
If so, their moral significance will indeed be very slight, but this
does not begin to show that they lack moral standing.

Even if plants have only slight moral significance, their moral
standing would account for Benn's remark that 'if the well-being of
persons could not be protected anyway, it would certainly be better
to leave behind a world of living things than a dead world', and also
for what Stephen Clark calls 'our distress at the destruction of a
living tree',[43] a distress which, Clark holds, 'is not merely at our loss
of pleasure in its beauty'. To test whether this is so, we need to
imagine a state of affairs in which there are no sentient organisms,
so that no one is impoverished by the tree's destruction. We thus
imagine that all sentient beings, human and nonhuman, are doomed
to imminent nuclear poisoning, and that this is known to the last
surviving human. In 'The Good of Trees' I asked whether the
survivor does wrong if he chops down with an axe 'the last tree of its
kind, a hitherto healthy elm, which has survived the nuclear
explosions and which could propagate its kind if left unassaulted'.
Most people who consider this question conclude that his act would
be wrong. I still believe that this is a valid test, which survives the
objections about method which I there considered; and, though I
grant that stray intuitions may need to be reined in by a consistent
moral theory, in this case intuitions confirm a theory which already
has some independent support. But it should be acknowledged that
the destruction of the elm is seen in a worse light than might
otherwise prevail because it involves the elimination of a species

and guarantees that there will be no future elms. Destroying without good reason a tree of a plentiful species might be regarded as somewhat less serious, though still, doubtless, as wrong.

Yet even so, the case of the destruction of the last elm, where the existence of future elms is at stake, is still a fair test of whether elms are of intrinsic value: and the judgement that they are helps to explain our objections to the elimination of species (and to letting them die out) as well as our regrets at individual uprootings, as expressed by Clark. Further, though a species does not constitute a moral individual, the case of the last elm shows how the extinction of a species is worse than the killing of individual members. (I am not suggesting that eliminating a species is always wrong, but rather that, whatever the inherent or the instrumental value of the members, it always constitutes a significant intrinsic evil which needs to be weighed up against the benefits which may derive from it. Nor *a fortiori* am I suggesting that it is always wrong to tear a leaf from a tree, but I do consider Frankena to be mistaken when he implies that there is no harm in doing so whatever.[44])

Holism

On the theory which has been advanced, then, the class of things with moral standing does not extend beyond that of individual beings with a good of their own. Thus when species count it is because of their individual members, whether actual present ones or future ones which could live and flourish unless deprived in the present of the necessary ancestors. This type of theory, however, is likely to be criticized by those who see such positions as unduly atomistic, a mere extension of moral standing from moral agents *via* other humans to nonhuman animals and individual plants, rather than to the biotic community, or to nature as a whole. As Frankena remarks, phrases such as 'everything' and 'all life' may be taken either distributively or collectively; and he observes that Holmes Rolston[45] both pleads the intrinsic value of 'every ecobiotic component' and commends the enlargement of the moral focus 'not only from man to other ecosystemic members, but from individuals of whatever kind to the system, . . . (a) community (which) holds values'. Also Goodpaster himself in 'On Being Morally Considerable' takes seriously the possibility of the biosphere having moral standing,[46] and in his later 'From Egoism to Environmentalism' contends that the enlargement of the class of morally considerable beings cannot without arbitrariness be tied to individuals but must extend to systems as well:[47] only thus can we escape an 'individual-istic' model of thought and the 'concentric reasoning' of humanism enlarged. Sympathy for such a move has been expressed too by Clark,[48] and has been encouraged by the claim, made in a scientific journal, that the biosphere may be regarded as an organism.[49]

There are two strands in this accumulating holistic view, one which conceives of the biosphere as a community and the other which conceives of it as an organic whole. Both may be traced to the writings of Aldo Leopold. Leopold advocates a 'land ethic' in which the scope of ethics is enlarged; and sometimes he interprets this as the enlargement of the moral community. 'All ethics so far evolved rest on a single premise: that the individual is a member of a community of interdependent parts . . . The land ethic simply enlarges the boundaries of the community to include soils, waters, plants, and animals, or collectively: the land.'[50] The suggestion here is that whenever two or more natural things are interdependent, they bear mutual obligations, and that this is the case within the community which Leopold calls 'the land'.

This suggestion has been severely criticized by Passmore,[51] even though he accepts that all the elements listed by Leopold form part of an ecological 'life-cycle'. But this sense of 'community', he holds, fails to generate ethical obligation. For obligations to be generated there must be two conditions which are not satisfied in the ecological case: common interests among the members, and the recognition of mutual obligations. But the second requirement begs the question against Leopold, and is in any case too strong; thus people in a community can have obligations without there being recognition of these obligations on all sides, and indeed it cannot be necessary that obligations should be recognized for them to exist. As to the first requirement, the suggestion that common interests are shared, for example, by humans and bacteria cannot be denied unequivocally, and is in some ways quite cogent.

Leopold's suggestion has been elaborated by J. Baird Callicott, who stresses that it is absurd if taken to imply that trees, rocks and rain have duties and are subject to ethical limitations. These limitations apply only to moral agents, but these agents, who are aware of mutual obligations in the human community, should recognize that they are also members of the interdependent biotic community, and accept parallel obligations to its other members.[52] Similarly Clark urges us to recognize the claims of other creatures in 'earth's household', the land community.[53]

But, as Benson has written in reply, 'not every relationship of

mutual dependence automatically carries with it a moral relationship.'[54] This is clearly true where that on which we depend is
inanimate and lacks a good of its own. Clean air should be preserved
not for its own sake but for that of living creatures. Where living
creatures with a good of their own are concerned, there is, as we
have seen, the possibility of a moral relationship (of human to
fellow-creature), but even this need not amount to a matter of
obligations *to* particular plants or animals. We are obligated, I
should grant, to take their interests into account, but this holds
good of creatures whether they and we are interdependent or not.
Conversely interdependence does not proportionately strengthen
our obligations in this regard, but rather strengthens the argument
from human interest to preserve the systems of which they form
part. Thus to represent the biosphere as a moral community serves
as an evocative metaphor of the consilience of self-interest and
morality, but does not add extra grounds for respect to the 'ecobiotic
components'.

Leopold has also written that 'a thing is right when it tends to
preserve the integrity, stability, and beauty of the biotic community.
It is wrong when it tends otherwise'.[55] This passage could be
construed as expressing a concern for all the members of the
biosphere, considered distributively, in accordance with the obligations internal to a community. But it seems to go further and make
the criterion of right conduct the preservation of the biosphere as a
whole. This is unlikely to mean the maximizing of intrinsic value
within it, for talk of its 'integrity, stability and beauty' suggests
otherwise. More probably it concerns upholding its systems and its
diversity. A similar view is taken by Thomas Auxter,[56] who assesses
the rights of individuals and species by their contribution to the
richness of the biosphere, to the greater development of systems,
and to their members' mutual co-adaptation.

Now the stability of ecosystems is clearly crucial for the
maintenance of all life; no new ethical basis is required to support it.
Co-adaptation is desirable for the same reasons. Diversity is, as we
have seen, of inherent value, and this accounts for our preference
for rich natural systems. Neither the preservation of ecosystems,
however, nor diversity are of intrinsic value, and their conjunction
is not guaranteed to foster what is such, or even to cohere with it.
Thus the death of a quarter of the human population would not
prejudice ecosystems or the diversity of species; and though the loss
of individual diversity would be inestimable (and Auxter could
perhaps deplore it as such) I doubt if this would infringe Leopold's

criterion. To put matters in a different way, if the whole biosphere is regarded as having moral standing, then there can be a conflict between maximizing its excellences and maximizing the intrinsic value of its components.

But the biosphere will only have intrinsic value or moral standing if, as Frankena puts it, it has 'a value that is not reducible to the value in or of the lives or beings of the entities which make it up'.[57] Like Frankena, I can see no reason to accept this view. Certainly everything which is of value (and located anywhere near our planet) is located in the biosphere, and the systems of the biosphere are necessary for the preservation of all these creatures. But that does not give the biosphere or its systems intrinsic value. Rather it shows them to have instrumental value, since what is of value in its own right is causally dependent on them. As to the biosphere as a whole, with all its richness and beauty, those features which it has but which its components lack suggest that its value is inherent. Admittedly if all its conscious members expired, it would retain its beauty, but there would be value in this beauty only as an object of contemplation either by further conscious beings or by ourselves as we envisage its lonely grandeur.

I cannot therefore accept the full claims about intrinsic value of the 'deep, long-range' environmental movement;[58] more particularly I do not find intrinsic value in inanimate beings (or in each and every animate one), or again in ecosystems, the biotic community or the biosphere. Nor can I accept the mystical metaphysics which sometimes accompanies these judgements of value, a metaphysics on which the distinctions between individual organisms pale before the unity of the whole, of which moral agents and other apparent individuals are mere manifestations. Such talk is parasitic on belief in the substantiality of the 'ecobiotic components', and neither their reality nor their value can be disregarded at the stage when thought has reached the level of the biosphere as a whole, not at any rate with consistency intact.

Similarly there seem no grounds to accept what Henry Byerly has characterized as the 'Holist Design Principle', which 'tells us not to interfere with natural systems because this would be to act contrary to the general design of nature'.[59] Seriously to hold that 'Nature knows best' (Barry Commoner's Third Law of Ecology[60]) is to abandon the attempt to do what is best in the light of the best evidence about the consequences; and there is no reason to suppose either that nature intends otherwise (or indeed intends anything), or that God prefers the nonrational zones of creation to proceed unaffected by rational creatures. Nor could it be so, since rational creatures are part of nature, and survive by employing their naturally endowed capacities for the purposive modification of their natural surroundings. Nor, *a fortiori*, should we with Leopold make the stability, integrity and beauty of the biosphere the sole criterion of morality. With Byerly I recognize the need for an alternative principle which exhorts caution over random changes to crucial natural systems without prohibiting action to make the world a better, or a tolerable, place.

Values and valuers

Nevertheless by accepting the intrinsic value of some nonconscious entities I am clearly rejecting most forms of the plausible view that what is of value is necessarily valued by some conscious subject. (Not all forms need to be rejected, as this doctrine could concern just those subjects who value what there is good reason to value: but I need to reject any form of it in which what conscious subjects prefer determines what is valuable, rather than *vice versa*.) This doctrine has been termed the 'no detachable values assumption' by Richard and Val Routley,[61] who have effectively criticized the argument that only the interests of valuers, and what promotes those interests, are of value. As they point out, even such an instrumentalist theory of value carries an assumption of its own about what is intrinsically of value: and if such an assumption concerns the interests of a privileged class only and omits other interests, the assumption cannot easily be defended. Doubtless, it may be acknowledged, lines have to be drawn somewhere between what is of value and what is not, and not all delimitations can be 'chauvinist'; but the line which is actually drawn must nevertheless be a defensible one. The Routleys' critique of the 'no detachable values' assumption also serves to show that any theory of value, however instrumentalist in tenor, must recognize intrinsic value somewhere, or there is nothing which gives anything of value its point. Accordingly there is nothing mystical or irrational in talk of intrinsic value, or attempts to locate it. Such attempts must, as we have seen, begin with agreed cases and then proceed outwards through a consideration of analogies and disanalogies, as has been attempted above.

By this method I have arrived at a position at once deeper than the shallow environmental movement and shallower than the mystical depths of the deeper movement of Naess' characterization.

In brief, I have arrived at a position on which whatever has interests of its own has moral standing and on which the realization of those interests has intrinsic value. This view may be accused alike of chauvinism by holists and of irrationality by adherents of the growing consensus view that all and only the sentient have moral standing. It may also be resisted by those who hold that value is too far detached from valuers. But to these positions I have given my responses already.

Finally the position adopted should be related to the Judaeo-Christian theistic tradition. What is asserted coheres well with the Old and New Testaments, and conflicts only with such later adherents of the tradition as Aquinas, Descartes and Kant. Frankena, in fact, gives several positions which a theist might hold in matters of moral standing, some of which would not cohere with the position presented above.[62] On his first alternative all that matters morally is whether we are benefiting or harming God. On this view, strictly interpreted, only states of God are of intrinsic value, whereas states of creatures are only of derivative value, the extent of which depends on their effects on God. This alternative, as Frankena sees, may well be rejected by those who hold that God cannot be harmed or benefited: but his second alternative, on which what matters is obeying God's commands or loving what he loves, has a parallel upshot. For once again only the fulfilment of God's will is of intrinsic value, and the states of creatures have value only insofar as they contribute to it. Frankena's third alternative is that what matters in morality is promoting 'the glory of God' in a sense irreducible to that of the preceding alternatives, a sense which Frankena does not supply. His final alternative splits into two: either the wholehearted love of God is morally basic, and love of one's neighbour is subordinate to it; or the love of God and of neighbour are co-ordinate and each basic in their own right.

Now according to Frankena, only if the second variant of the final alternative is adopted is anything but God or his states or will of intrinsic value. Yet the third alternative, as he describes it, need not be interpreted as excluding this. Thus the glory of God could consist in the flourishing of his creatures, and this could be what counts primarily in morality. At any rate a theist is free to adopt such a view, which coheres with the position of this chapter. It may, of course, be asked why the fulfilment of creatures' interests redounds to God's glory: but if *ex hypothesi* this happens to be his creative purpose, the answer is to hand. Love of God could still supply an extra motive for love of fellow creatures, but it would not be the only route to such a love. The remaining question is whether creatures have an additional, inherent value through the creator's enjoyment of them. This could be so, as long as God's enjoyment is not treated as an episode. But it would not affect the grounds of human action. For whatever has inherent value of this sort also has it because of the possible enjoyment of creatures; and though it could persist when all conscious creatures have perished, no extra reason is provided in the form of preserving things for God to enjoy, as his enjoyment is timeless, and unaffected by change, decay or death. I conclude that the above discussion is fully in line with biblical talk of God's love for his creatures and injunctions to do his will.

NOTES

1 'On Being Morally Considerable', *Journal of Philosophy,* 75, 1978, 308—25.
2 Joel Feinberg, 'The Rights of Animals and Unborn Generations', in William T. Blackstone (ed.), *Philosophy and Environmental Crisis,* 43—68.
3 'On Being Morally Considerable', p. 312.
4 Senses distinguished by Lawrence Haworth, 'Rights, Wrongs and Animals', *Ethics,* 88, 1977—78, 95—105, p. 95.
5 Ibid. p. 102.
6 Thus Tom Regan, 'Animal Rights, Human Wrongs', *Environmental Ethics,* 2, 1980, 99—120, p. 113.
7 Thus Robert Nozick, *Anarchy, State and Utopia,* Oxford: Blackwell, 1974. Nozick applies the notion to animals at pp. 28—42.
8 'Is There a Need for a New, an Environmental Ethic?', *Proceedings of the XVth World Congress of Philosophy,* Varna, 1973, Vol. I, 205—10, p. 210.
9 *The Object of Morality,* New York: Methuen, 1971, pp. 150f. Much the same applies to the egoistic position, with which Narveson has recently found himself in sympathy; for on that position, as Regan has observed, there are no grounds whatever to give consideration to those infants and imbeciles who have no friends or family to care about their fate. See Jan Narveson, 'Animal Rights', *Canadian Journal of Philosophy,* 7, 1977, 161—78, and Tom Regan, 'Narveson on Egoism and the Rights of Animals', ibid. 179—86.
10 'An Examination and Defense of One Argument Concerning Animal Rights', *Inquiry,* 22, 1979, 189—219, section IV, 204—12.
11 In 'Killing Humans and Killing Animals', *Inquiry,* 22, 1979, 145—56, and in 'Not for Humans Only: The Place of Nonhumans in Environmental Issues', in K. E. Goodpaster and K. M. Sayre (eds),

Ethics and Problems of the 21st Century, Notre Dame and London: University of Notre Dame Press, 1979, 191—206.

12 Ibid. p. 205.

13 Regan contends, against Feinberg, that in one ordinary sense of 'interests' it is not impossible for nonconscious beings to have interests, in 'The Nature and Possibility of an Environmental Ethic', *Environmental Ethics,* 3, 1981, 16—31, p. 19, and also in 'Feinberg on What Sorts of Beings Can Have Rights', in *Southern Journal of Philosophy,* 14, 1976, 485—98, pp. 494—7.

14 'The Rights of Animals and Unborn Generations', pp. 51—7.

15 Ibid. p. 49.

16 Robin Attfield, 'The Good of Trees', *Journal of Value Inquiry,* 15, 1981, 35—54. (This paper was in fact accepted for publication some time before Goodpaster's paper was drawn to my attention.)

17 W. Murray Hunt, 'Are *Mere Things* Morally Considerable?', *Environmental Ethics,* 2, 1980, 59—65: Kenneth Goodpaster, 'On Stopping at Everything: A Reply to W. M. Hunt', *Environmental Ethics,* 2, 1980, 281—4.

18 In 'From Egoism to Environmentalism', in Goodpaster and Sayre (eds), *Ethics and Problems of the 21st Century,* 21—35, pp. 28—33; also in 'On Being Morally Considerable', p. 323.

19 'The Nature and Possibility of an Environmental Ethic', p. 21.

20 The phrase 'moral standing' is modelled on the title of Christopher Stone's book *Should Trees Have Standing?,* (Los Altos, Cal.: William Kaufman, 1974), in which Stone argues that some natural objects should be accorded legal rights.

21 Regan, 'The Nature and Possibility of an Environmental Ethic', p. 27.

22 *MRN* p. 124 and p. 217 (in 2nd edn, 1980).

23 'The Good of Trees', section II.

24 Regan, 'The Nature and Possibility of an Environmental Ethic', pp. 22f.

25 *MRN*, pp. 101—10.

26 R. and V. Routley, *The Fight for the Forests,* Canberra: Australian National University Press, 1974; Singer, 'Not for Humans Only', p. 198.

27 Laurence H. Tribe, 'Ways not to Think about Plastic Trees', *Yale Law Journal,* 83, 1974, 1315—48.

28 'On Preserving the Natural Environment', *Yale Law Journal,* 84, 1974, 205—67.

29 'Why Preserve Landmarks? A Preliminary Inquiry', in Goodpaster and Sayre, *Ethics and Problems of the 21st Century,* 175—90.

30 *The Great Chain of Being,* Harvard, Mass., Harvard University Press, 1936.

31 In 'The Good of Trees', section II.

32 *MRN*, 119—21.

33 'Not for Humans Only', p. 203.

34 For another view see Stephen Clark, *The Moral Status of Animals,* Oxford: Clarendon Press, 1977, p. 171.

35 See W. K. Frankena, 'Ethics and the Environment', in Goodpaster and Sayre (eds), *Ethics and Problems of the 21st Century,* 3—20, p. 13. C. I. Lewis' position is cited at p. 20, n. 23.

36 'Not for Humans Only', p. 203. Cf. Val Routley, Critical Notice of John Passmore, *Man's Responsibility for Nature, Australasian Journal of Philosophy,* 53, 1975, 171—85, p. 175.

37 Richard Routley, 'Is There a Need for a New, an Environmental Ethic', p. 107; Robin Attfield, 'The Good of Trees', sections II and III.

38 'Personal Freedom and Environmental Ethics: the Moral Inequality of Species', in Gray Dorsey (ed.), *Equality and Freedom,* New York: Oceana Publications, 1977, Vol. II, 401—24, p. 415.

39 Mary Midgley, *Beast and Man,* pp. 357—9.

40 Singer, 'Not for Humans Only', p. 195.

41 Goodpaster, 'On Being Morally Considerable', p. 322; Passmore, *MRN,* pp. 121—4. Cf. Albert Schweitzer, *Civilisation and Ethics,* 1923; trans. C. T. Campion, 3rd edn, London: Adam and Charles Black, 1946, p. 244.

42 Cf. the theory of Singer, 'Not for Humans Only', p. 199f; also that of Roupas, discussed in chapter 7 (above).

43 Benn, 'Personal Freedom and Environmental Ethics', p. 421; Clark, *The Moral Status of Animals,* p. 172.

44 Frankena, 'Ethics and the Environment', p. 11.

45 Ibid. pp. 11f; and p. 20, nn. 19, 20; Holmes Rolston III, 'Is There an Ecological Ethic?', *Ethics,* 85, 1975, 93—109, pp. 101, 106. My own criticisms of holistic ethics are further developed in 'Methods of Ecological Ethics'.

46 'On Being Morally Considerable', p. 323.

47 'From Egoism to Environmentalism', Goodpaster and Sayre (eds), *Ethics and Problems of the 21st Century,* 21—35, pp. 29f.

48 *The Moral Status of Animals,* p. 170.

49 J. Lovelock and S. Epton, 'The Quest for Gaia', *The New Scientist,* 65, 1975, 304—9, cited by Goodpaster (see above), p. 35, n. 25. See also J. E. Lovelock, *Gaia: A New Look at Life on Earth,* Oxford: Oxford University Press, 1979.

50 *A Sand County Almanac,* New York: Oxford University Press, 1949, pp. 203f, cited by Clark (see above), p. 164.

51 *MRN,* p. 116.

52 J. Baird Callicott, 'Elements of an Environmental Ethic: Moral Considerability and the Biotic Community', *Environmental Ethics,* I, 1979, 71—81, p. 76. Callicott takes matters further in 'Animal Liberation: A Triangular Affair', (see chapter 4, n. 56, above), to which I have replied in 'Methods of Ecological Ethics' (unpublished).

53 *The Moral Status of Animals,* p. 164.

54 John Benson, 'Duty and the Beast', *Philosophy,* 53, 1978, 529—49, p. 542.

55 *A Sand County Almanac,* pp. 224f; cited by Frankena, 'Ethics and the Environment', p. 12 and p. 20, n. 21; and by Goodpaster, 'From Egoism to Environmentalism', p. 21.

56 'The Right not to be Eaten', *Inquiry,* 22, 1979, 221—30, pp. 222f, and p. 228f, n. 2.

57 'Ethics and the Environment', p. 17.

58 Arne Naess, 'The Shallow and the Deep, Long-Range Ecology Movement', *Inquiry,* 16, 1973, 95—100.

59 Henry Byerly, 'Principles of Noninterference with Nature in Ecological Ethics', in *Ethics, Foundations, Problems and Applications, Proceedings of the Fifth International Wittgenstein Symposium,* Vienna: Verlag Hölder-Pichler-Tempsky, 1981, 318—20.

60 *The Closing Circle,* London: Jonathan Cape, 1972, p. 41.

61 'Against the Inevitability of Human Chauvinism', in Goodpaster and Sayre (eds), *Ethics and Problems of the 21st Century,* 36—59; see p. 42, and the discussion at pp. 42—52, and p. 58f, n. 13. For a contrary view, see Robert Elliot, 'Why Preserve Species?', in *Environmental Philosophy,* (see chapter 4, n. 47, above), 8—29, pp. 18—21. I favour a more objectivist view than the Routleys or Elliot.

62 Frankena, 'Ethics and the Environment', p. 8. See also my criticism in chapter 4 (above) of the Routleys' understanding of theistic ethics.

9

Inter-species Morality:
Principles and Priorities

Granted that nonhuman animals and most plants have moral standing, what principles of inter-species morality should we recognize? What, indeed, is the relative moral significance of the various species and their members, and what bearing does their moral significance have on our practice? These are the questions to be addressed in the course of the present chapter.

I have argued that each of a wide range of organisms has moral standing. But no particular conclusion follows about their relative moral significance. Some, such as Arne Naess, favour, insofar as it is possible, the equality of species,[1] while others, such as Philip Devine, hold that humans may be preferred to nonhumans simply as such.[2] The latter view is stigmatized by Peter Singer (following Richard Ryder) as speciesism,[3] and in its stead Singer has proposed the principle that 'the interests of every being affected by an action are to be taken into account and given the same weight as the like interests of any other being.'[4] I shall begin by examining this Equality of Interests principle, but shall bear in mind at the same time the views of those who, for various reasons, reject discussions of interests and rights as irrelevant in ecological matters, whether because they are based on an unduly individualist, atomistic and man-centred method[5] or because they hold that nonhumans lack interests and rights altogether.[6]

Equal consideration

Singer's principle is clearly less radical than that of Naess, for some organisms lack interests possessed by others, and will thus not receive as much consideration if this principle is accepted. It is indeed intended as a merely formal principle, which through settling which creatures' pains and pleasures count and how much they count allows the calculation of costs and benefits to begin. As such it might be regarded as entirely nonarbitrary, since entities lacking interests are discounted solely on the grounds that they cannot be benefited. Singer, a utilitarian, favours maximizing the balance of intrinsic good over evil, and this will be accomplished only if like interests are given nothing but the same weighting as each other. Accordingly the principle is devised so as to debar either nonsentient organisms being treated on a par with sentient ones (as deep ecological radicals sometimes urge) or the suffering of nonhumans not being considered equally with the like suffering of humans (in the manner of speciesism).

Now if the argument of chapter 7 is accepted — that there are obligations with respect to possible people (an argument extended in chapter 8 to apply to some possible nonhumans), then this Equality of Interests principle cannot supply the sole basis for deciding which of an action's effects to take into account. But insofar as items already in existence are concerned, the principle must be a sound one, once it is duly interpreted. For what has interests, it has been concluded, has moral standing, and the principle ensures that nothing with moral standing is disregarded. Moreover as long as intrinsic good is done when interests are satisfied, then the principle exactly captures these vital tenets of value theory and applies them appropriately to action. Certainly an appropriate account of 'like interests' is required, and depends for its application on a suitable account of what interests consist in. But unless some rival account of intrinsic good (perhaps a holistic one) is preferred, Singer's principle surely reflects a large part of the truth.

Many writers, of course, harness the issue of which items to take into consideration and the issue of which have rights (an approach at which holists protest just as they do at giving pride of place to interests). Thus Leonard Nelson holds that having interests is necessary and sufficient for a being to have rights,[7] and H. J. McCloskey, who used to take this view and who has all along rejected belief in animal rights, used also to claim that nonhuman animals lacked interests;[8] but more recently, having dropped this claim, he has also laid down much stronger requirements for the possession of rights than Nelson or than the slightly more cautious position adopted by Joel Feinberg.[9] R. G. Frey, despite a general scepticism about natural rights, has taken great pains to argue that animals lack interests in any relevant sense, lest this should be thought to give them rights;[10] and Tom Regan has contended that unless we ascribe to most humans and some animals rights which can only be overridden with very good reason, our reflective moral judgements cannot stand up.[11] (Regan seeks to avoid any consequentialist aggregation of good and evil and the resulting trade-offs, but seems to incur similar, if not worse, problems by according potentially conflicting rights to multitudes of creatures, especially as none of these rights is at all easily to be overridden.) Without endorsing the position of the holists, I do not regard it as necessary to locate rights where they belong before settling issues of priority of consideration: for, granted the value of benefits and the negative value of their counterpart evils wherever a beneficiary can be found, we can proceed direct to the requirement to take good and bad consequences into account if our actions are to be morally justifiable.

Now the issue of interspecific priorities between conflicting interests could be much simplified if it could either be accepted, with Frey, that nonhuman animals lack beliefs and desires and therefore lack interests, or with Ruth Cigman that for them death is no misfortune,[12] or, with Singer, that those beings lack interests which lack the capacity or potential for feeling pleasure or pain.[13] For in each case the possible area of conflict would be much diminished. But I am satisfied by the arguments of Joseph Margolis[14] that many nonhuman animals have both beliefs and desires, and thus the kinds of interests which go with them; the fact that death deprives many animals of the fulfilment of their specific potentials satisfies me that death can be an evil even where no concept of death is held; and I have argued above, especially in chapter 8, for the rejection of hedonism and for the belief that many nonsentient organisms have a good of their own, and therefore I cannot accept the view that interests stop where sentience does.

This being so, the Equality of Interests principle must be applied to a wider range of creatures than Singer intends, and to a greater variety of interests which one and the same creature may have. Thus humans have an interest in being able to make autonomous choices and to form friendships, and in preserving their self-respect, as well as in being free from pain; while nonhuman creatures, whether sentient or nonsentient, also have an interest in flourishing after their kind by developing their own specific capacities. Granted this plethora of interests, it is important to decide under what descriptions the interests of members of different species are to be identified and compared.

Classification of interests

One of the alternative classifications suggested by Devine[15] would turn on the intensity of the feelings which an organism stands to enjoy or suffer. This interpretation of Singer's principle is rejected by Devine because it omits interests, such as those of sleepers, which need not turn on feelings at all. But this objection does not make it inappropriate for an adherent of the principle to consider the interest of creatures in not being severely hurt. The real objection to classifying interests in that manner is that the role of the interest in the life of the creature concerned is ignored. The interest in not suffering acute pain is for some creatures just that; for others it also involves an interest in forgoing the fear and confusion which would accompany the pain; and for some humans it further involves an interest in being able to have unsullied memories and to form and implement future plans with confidence, and in being spared a sense of humiliation and rejection. Despite this objection, the interest in not being severely hurt remains an interest, but two creatures share it as a 'like interest' only where no other interests are at stake.

Another classification considered by Devine is by 'the general kind' of the interests: his example is the need for water, shared by plants and human beings. Devine's point here is that if this interest of a plant and a human is considered equally, the outcome (equal shares of water) is morally absurd. Singer, of course, would not acknowledge the example as a problem, as he holds sentience to be necessary for the possession of interests; but in this, as has been argued in chapter 8, he seems to be wrong. Accordingly interests must not be classified in a way which generates such acutely counter-intuitive judgements. But the problem does not lie in classifying interests by their general kind (such as the interest in exercising autonomous choice). Rather it lies in isolating an interest under a description such as 'the need for x' without mention of the other needs which depend on the fulfilment of the given need. For if the full range of interests which are at stake are taken into account, the Equality of Interests principle is not as obviously misguided as Devine supposes.

Nevertheless the difficulties just mentioned suggest that interests be somehow classified by their level of complexity or sophistication. Thus Aubrey Townsend, in the course of a critical notice of Clark's and Singer's books about the proper treatment of animals,[16] contends that morality is concerned with diverse kinds of interests, an interest in welfare (which he takes to concern the living of a pain-free happy life) and an interest in autonomy, and that autonomy normally trumps welfare. I have argued elsewhere against just such a claim,[17] but without accepting Townsend's priorities I can acknowledge that some moral responses are only possible towards an autonomous agent, and that in the sense of 'autonomy' which he derives from Stanley Benn[18] only humans (and only some of *them*) are autonomous. This sense involves the ability to make and execute decisions and plans in the light of more-or-less rational beliefs and preferences. Now on many occasions when there is an opportunity to recognize and foster such autonomy, this interest may well be accorded priority over any conflicting interests: but, as I shall argue, such a priority cannot be taken for granted, particularly where the basic interests of a beast clash with a peripheral interest of a human, like the broadening of the scope for autonomous action.

Benn himself, as I have pointed out in chapter 8, accepts the moral standing of 'works of nature', including even ecosystems: they are 'axiotima', things which it is appropriate to value or esteem. But he holds that the needs of humans, or at any rate persons, generally takes precedence over those of other *axiotima* because of their distinctive capacities; and that even if humans can only be saved from biological extinction by conserving the biosphere, nevertheless if this were to involve the 'institutional bridling of human creative intelligence', which is precisely 'the capacity which constitutes the human species a threat to the biosphere', these measures would not be justified.[19] Benn is here expressing moral opposition to totalitarianism at all costs; yet his determination to preserve creative intelligence from any measures of coercion necessary to prevent the extinction of humanity and the endangering of most *axiotima* too seems disproportionate and potentially self-frustrating. Creative intelligence, for one thing, would not need to be institutionally bridled in all respects, or all politically significant respects, in order to avert disastrous manipulation of the environment; for another thing, the only prospect for the survival of creative intelligence is probably some curtailment, voluntary or otherwise, of its exercise. Thus the choice with which Benn presents his readers between man and the biosphere is a misleading one. But in any case Benn does not make out his case for holding that urgent anthropocentric agendum-grounds (or reasons for action) should generally take precedence over urgent nonhuman needs. Even if it is granted that we have reason to cherish distinctive human capacities, this does not entitle us to prefer the interest in their realization in general over the nondistinctive interests of humans or the interests of nonhumans. Such a two-level theory of types of interest is excessively rigid, and obscures the genuine moral conflicts which exist over, for example, the eating of meat, over animal experiments, and over agricultural developments which contribute to the eclipse of wild species.

Self-consciousness

Another two-level theory of interests has, however, been put forward by Peter Singer himself. In his paper 'Killing Humans and Killing Animals' he argues that, while the suffering of nonhuman animals and of humans should be taken into consideration equally, where killing is concerned the possession of the capacity to see oneself as a distinct entity with a future marks a relevant difference between most humans (plus any other animals which have it) and all other animals, including some humans, which do not.[20] For those with this capacity, death involves the frustration of autonomous plans and projects, whereas the painless death of those who lack it spells at worst a loss of pleasure, and this can be made good by producing another animal which leads a pleasant life instead of the one which is killed. Thus entities lacking the concept of a self are replaceable, and where they are concerned we should simply seek to maximize the balance of pleasure over pain, as the Total theory of classical utilitarianism maintains; but entities which have this concept are in an important sense irreplaceable, and among such entities we should give precedence to existing ones, or ones which will exist in future independently of our decisions, rather as the Person-affecting principle enjoins.

I have already criticized this partial adoption of the Person-affecting principle (see chapter 6) over the discounting of possible people whose existence would depend on us. Here I have a different point to make, a point about capacities. Singer's recognition of the capacity of self-consciousness constitutes an enrichment of his hedonism, but he does not take enough capacities into account. This may be brought out in connection both with human infants and with nonhuman animals. Thus the killing of a human infant deprives it of much more than pleasure (and of the capacity for future enjoyment, remarked by Singer in 'Not for Humans Only'[21]). Unless it is very severely subnormal, it will have the potential for developing all the capacities characteristic of humans (including those for practical and theoretical reasoning, for autonomy, for forming friendships, for meaningful work and for self-respect), and its death deprives it of all prospect of the goods which consist in developing these potentials. As to nonhuman animals, Michael Lockwood adapts an example of Christina Hoff to give his readers pause over the replaceability thesis.[22] To suit the convenience of pet-owners who cannot take pets on holiday with them and prefer a new pet when they return, the company 'Disposapup Ltd' rears and supplies puppies, takes them back and kills them at holiday-time, and supplies replacements on demand. Though the activities of Disposapup are much less horrific than factory farming, we may well condemn them as immoral, even if we detach ourselves from the propensity to treat pets as humans. If so, I suggest, we should need to appeal to more than the puppies' loss of pleasure, and to point to the natural fulfilments of canine potentials of which all of the firm's puppies are deprived. (Others might express this protest as one directed at the manipulation of nature: but this protest would be ungrounded unless the development of natural potentials matters.)

So Singer's two-level theory of interests (those based on sentience and those based on self-consciousness) seems, like those of Townsend and Benn, to be unduly insensitive to the great variety of potentials among both humans and nonhumans, and the related goods constituted by developing them and flourishing after one's kind. As John Benson comments, even if animals in factory-farms were anaesthetized, and thus could not suffer, there would still be reason to protest at depriving them of natural fulfilments.[23] But Singer seems to lack the resources for sharing in the protest.

Two-factor Egalitarianism

A theory which supplies a more elaborate classification of interests, and thus takes account of a greater variety of types, has been put forward by Donald VanDeVeer.[24] In his theory of Two-factor Egalitarianism, two kinds of variable which have already been noted are brought to the fore, the role of an interest in a creature's life and the psychological capacities of the creature. Within any one creature's life, some interests are basic and some are peripheral, while others are serious interests, in that their neglect or frustration is costly to the creature's well-being without threatening its survival.

Thus because of their different importance, basic interests should in general be preferred to serious and peripheral interests, and serious interests, while not outweighing basic ones, take precedence over those which are peripheral. But this principle would require us to give equal weight to the basic interests of creatures with very different psychological capacities, (as in Devine's objection to Singer). To avoid such an outcome VanDeVeer adopts the 'Weighting principle',[25] on which, with some qualifications, 'the interests of beings with more complex psychological capacities deserve greater weight than those with lesser capacities'. As the former are preferred to the latter because of their capacities rather than their species, the charge of discrimination on the mere basis of species-membership is averted (or so VanDeVeer hopes).

The fully-fledged version of Two-factor Egalitarianism runs as follows:

Where there is an interspecies conflict of interests between two beings, A and B, it is morally permissible, *ceteris paribus*:
(1) to sacrifice the interest of A to promote a like interest of B if A lacks significant psychological capacities possessed by B;
(2) to sacrifice a basic interest of A to promote a serious interest of B if A substantially lacks significant psychological capacities possessed by B, [and]
(3) to sacrifice the peripheral interest to promote the more basic interest if the beings are similar with respect to psychological capacity (regardless of who possesses the interests).[26]

Now clearly this position relies heavily on the Weighting principle, and requires a very heavy weighting for significant psychological capacities. Accordingly it also rests on the assumption that some capacities (or their development or exercise) are more valuable than others. Can these principles be upheld?

VanDeVeer has three defences of the Weighting principle. Firstly humans are typically subject to certain kinds of suffering to which other animals are not subject, so the same treatment may harm a human more than a nonhuman because of the greater human ability to foresee the future. Preferring the human in such a case, we may remark, is in keeping with most interpretations of the Equality of Interests principle, as the interests at stake are unequal. Secondly some creatures are more prone than others to deferred suffering, and the difference is a function of the psychological capacities involved. This is again a utilitarian consideration which Singer could endorse. Thirdly the cost in opportunities foregone will be heavier in the case of, for example, human death than with nonhuman deaths, again because of the much greater human capabilities. To the extent that these capabilities are not confined to suffering and enjoyment, a hedonist cannot grant the relevance of this point; but adherents of the Equality of Interests principle clearly can. So also, in a way, does Bonnie Steinbock,[27] when she writes that freedom from suffering is a minimal condition for exercising capacities which humans have and animals do not, capacities for responsibility, altruistic reasons for action and self-respect; and that as we value these capacities human suffering is regarded as more deplorable than animal suffering. Since, however, not all humans in fact have these capacities and it is possible that not all nonhuman animals lack them, Steinbock could only maintain her position of valuing every human life more than any animal life on the basis of preference for humans as such.

Do those who accept VanDeVeer's reasons need to accept his Weighting principle and his Two-factor Egalitarianism? Only, I suggest, with some qualifications. Thus the more complex activities would be relevant only where their development or exercise is at stake; and though, in cases of conflict, this is usually so, particularly when the needs of the more sophisticated creature for survival are in question, it would not always be so. Thus in the case of a human who is deprived of meat from a factory-farm, though serious interests (the exercise of autonomy and the symbolic significance of a feast) may be at stake, it is unlikely that the prospects for a worthwhile life in the long-term are at risk, whereas the basic interests of the animals concerned (in avoiding suffering and premature death) are certainly at stake. Yet VanDeVeer's second principle would probably (and perhaps contrary to his intentions) allow most current forms of factory-farming to continue; and to this extent he is vulnerable to a charge of speciesism. His principles accordingly need modifying to ensure that one or other of his reasons for accepting the Weighting principle actually applies to each case of 'sacrifice' of basic or serious interests. This granted, however, the Equality of Interests principle is satisfied. (His principles are still not comprehensive, as they do not tell us the weight to be attached to the interests not related to psychological capacities at all, such as those of plants, apart from implying that interests which are related to such psychological capacities take precedence over those which are not, a principle which could be questioned.)

VanDeVeer's third reason, however, (the cost of the loss of valuable opportunities) turns, as Steinbock's views do, on the view that the exercise of some capacities is more valuable than that of others. A similar point seems to be envisaged when Devine talks of animal pain being deficient in 'conceptual richness';[28] while Singer, who would resist Devine's application of the idea, himself holds that 'it is not arbitrary to hold that the life of a self-aware being, capable of abstract thought, of planning for the future, of complex acts of communication, and so on, is more valuable than the life of a being without these capacities'.[29]

Benson, however, rejects any such claims about relative intrinsic value, holding that 'to make those characteristics which make human life valuable to a man into the standard to judge of the value of life seems to be a good example of speciesism'.[30] Such hierarchies are also opposed by Clark[31] and by John Rodman,[32] and these writers are certainly right in stressing the different forms of active life to which different nonhuman species are adapted, and how their interests plausibly depend on the capacity to achieve the relevant form of life.

Having rejected belief in the intrinsic value of lives of differing capacities, Benson develops a different account of the value of life in terms of its value *to the creature concerned*. A creature's life has value for the creature if it has self-awareness and the capacity to plan ahead, and it is wrong, for that reason, to kill that creature. Yet even creatures which lack these capacities may still have a point of view and lives of value for themselves, as long as they have the capacity to enjoy and go on enjoying the life proper to their kind; and it is at any rate possible to hold that killing such a creature is also wrong. What is apparent here is that Benson holds, where action is concerned, that some creatures' continued life constitutes an independent moral consideration (the continued life of those with self-awareness and the capacity to plan ahead), and that the continued life of other creatures may constitute such a ground, but not so clearly.

I submit that this position is no different from one on which the life proper to the kind of each of them is held to be of intrinsic value, but in different degrees. For something is of intrinsic value if there are nonderivative moral reasons for fostering, desiring or cherishing it, and this is just what Benson accepts about the continued lives of nonhuman animals: and he also accepts, in effect, that it is true of lives with different capacities to different degrees. Nor is this just an *ad hominem* reply to Benson. For anyone who counts as morally relevant the different degrees to which the continuation of the form of life to which it is adapted is of value to a creature, and/or the differences in opportunities for self-realization foregone by the deaths of different creatures, is thereby acknowledging that varying degrees of *intrinsic* value attach to lives in which different capacities are realized. This position is compatible with recognizing that, other things being equal, nonhuman animals should be allowed to develop the full range of capacities natural to themselves, and that wild (and domesticated) creatures are not substandard humans, of value only through embodying a pale reflection of human traits, but have fulfilments of their own which are other than ours.

The proposition that lives in which some capacities are available and realized are of more value than lives in which they are not can be criticized in other ways. Thus Cora Diamond holds that capacities such as that for suffering are not morally fundamental, but rather various relationships and the forms of (social) life of which they form part.[33] But if these relationships happen to exclude a creature the capacities of which are as a result disregarded, then the resulting practice is open to moral criticism; and the same applies if relationships bring it about that creatures with capacities of radically different types are treated as if they were of equal value. The same reply may serve for anyone who goes beyond Benson and refuses to count, say, the deaths of those creatures with self-awareness and the ability to plan ahead and of those without these capacities as of different moral significance; normal humans should not be treated like ants, nor, come to that, should intelligent chimpanzees, and this even though they all, ants included, have moral standing.[34]

There is also the possible criticism that the moral recognition of different capacities commits us to meritocracy and to favouring the intelligent within human society: but this objection has been effectively countered both by VanDeVeer and by Steinbock,[35] who point out that there may well be thresholds below which differences in capacity do not count, and that for most (though not all) purposes a certain minimum intelligence qualifies all humans for equal treatment. Accordingly I conclude that because of the good which the creatures concerned stand to gain or lose, lives in which some capacities are realized are more valuable than those in which they are not or cannot be, and that the Equality of Interests principle must be interpreted accordingly. Thus when the realization of these capacities is at stake, the basic and serious interest of beings which have them outweigh the basic and serious interests of those which lack them. To this (limited) extent VanDeVeer's Weighting principle may be accepted, but it should not be accepted in the less qualified way in which it was originally presented.

Acceptance of the Equality of Interests principle and of this form of the Weighting principle commits me to a version of VanDeVeer's Two-factor Egalitarianism. But it has to be understood that creatures with capacities for more valuable forms of life receive priority over others only where the ability to exercise those capacities is genuinely at stake; a clause to this effect needs to be inserted in (1) and (2) of VanDeVeer's formulation, so that B's interests can be preferred only where B's ability to exercise significant psychological capacities which are lacked by A would otherwise be forfeited or imperilled. It should be added that, as creatures incapable of consciousness lack a point of view and thus forfeit nothing of which they could have been aware even when they are killed, the interests of conscious creatures normally take precedence over theirs; but that, as they have moral standing (see chapter 8), when at any rate a large number of them are at stake (as when a forest is threatened), or when the possible existence of multitudes of future ones could be foreclosed (by the elimination of a species) their otherwise almost negligible intrinsic value as individuals amounts to a serious moral ground, quite apart from their inherent and instrumental value. At times, too, it will be wrong to damage or destroy a tree or plant because the mere pleasure which the act of destruction would give is of even slighter moral significance than the continuing life of a healthy plant. What all this amounts to is the basis for an expanded version of the Total theory; but this is not the place to attempt to expound such a theory further, for there are objections yet to be answered.

Discrimination

Any theory on which like interests merit like consideration has to face the objection that humans with like capacities and thus like interests to those of nonhumans may rightly be accorded priority, or so it may be claimed. This claim is sometimes based on consequentialist grounds, which consequentialist adherents of the Equality of Interests principle could accept. Thus, to Singer's contention that one should only be willing to inflict suffering on a nonhuman animal if one would also be willing to inflict it on a human of like intelligence, it may be replied that suffering will be caused in other humans who care about the human of severely subnormal intelligence,[36] and also that any experimentation on such humans would have the bad consequence of weakening people's inhibitions against the infliction of suffering on humans in normal cases. These effects upon third parties of the like treatment of like interests are on any account morally relevant, and do justify some differential treatment, without the principle (on which like interests merit like *consideration*) being overthrown. Indeed the importance of the preservation of inhibitions seems to be the most that can be said for the Overflow principle advanced by Devine:

Act towards that which, while not itself a person, is closely associated with personhood in a way coherent with an attitude of respect for persons.[37]

Common acceptance of this principle, or something like it, may indeed explain our respect for dead bodies; but, beyond the argument from inhibitions, it is hard to see how to justify the principle (except insofar as the interests of nonpersons are morally significant in their own right), and harder still to see why the Equality of Interests principle should be discarded in its favour.

A different kind of objection is propounded by those who hold that humans may be given preferential treatment because of the relationships in which they stand, a point employed by Benson[38] as well as by Diamond, and elaborated by Leslie Pickering Francis and Richard Norman.[39] I have already pointed out, though, that this principle discriminates against those who stand in few relationships or in none. It is further weakened by a salient observation of Francis and Norman themselves. Thus some so-called imbeciles, including some sufferers from Down's syndrome, have a much greater intelligence and capacity for communication than any nonhuman animals, and in such cases the value of their lives is generally recognized; but in other cases of severe subnormality, such as cases of anencephaly, the possibility that passive or even active euthanasia is justified is being seriously debated. Their point is that the only humans with whom the capacities of some animals will stand comparison are ones the value of whose lives is in doubt. But if it is in doubt despite the relationships in which they stand, then the existence of such relationships does not seem to make a crucial difference to the treatment which they should have, or indeed to be the crucial moral factor in their regard.

In any case the criterion of standing in particular relationships cannot in itself be other than arbitrary. Yet the point made by Francis and Norman that for most nonhuman animals various forms of relationship (linguistic, economic and political) are impossible is significant, and for the reason that it turns on the capacities of the various creatures concerned. Certainly what is good about capacities is their development or their exercise, but their mere possession is what makes it possible for others to deprive or facilitate such development, and thus to qualify them for differential treatment. But such points about capacities can be accepted by adherents of the Equality of Interests principle. It should be emphasized here that capacities here include potentials, and thus explain the priority which can rightly be given to normal newborn human infants over nonhuman animals with comparable current powers.

The other basis on which discriminating in favour of humans when nonhumans have like interests is sometimes defended is the need to draw a clear line. Even if, it is argued, severely retarded humans do not merit preferential treatment in their own right, it is still better to treat them as if they did, so as to have an easily applicable line to draw between beings to be treated as persons and others. Devine, who propounds this case, also holds that once the line has been drawn there is no injustice in giving priority to those who would not individually have qualified to be on the favourable side of it but happen to fall so nonetheless.[40] Now it is undoubtable that in some cases such drawing of lines prevents the undermining of morally important inhibitions, and this may partially justify our unwillingness to experiment on severely retarded humans who happen also to have no friends, guardians or relations who might suffer or object in consequence. On the other hand where a better line can be drawn, we may well be responsible for unnecessary suffering if we fail to draw it and opt for the criterion of being human instead. Thus VanDeVeer is surely right to deny that we should save the life of an infant human with Tay-Sachs disease by means of a kidney transplant from a healthy chimpanzee of greater capacities;[41] and if we strive to preserve all human life we might also inflict extra years of life on someone who would be better off dead. Thus the principle of giving priority to humans is not to be preferred to one on which all the interests concerned are duly considered, weighed up and served as best may be. (Far less should we prefer the interests of humans where, as over eating meat from factory-farms and over painful experiments on laboratory animals to test the safety of luxuries, far greater interests are at stake for the nonhuman than for the human.)

Holist priorities

Before closing this chapter I should remark the very different emphasis of ethical holists, and in particular of John Rodman and of J. Baird Callicott.[42] These writers find in the humanitarian ethic of

Singer little more than an extension of the privileged class with moral standing which is permitted to exploit all else besides; they are much more concerned with species and with the biosphere than with individual beings, and they regard domestic animals as so degenerate a form of life, and as so symbolically harmful as to discount their interests (as opposed to those of wild animals) and to favour phasing them out. They would probably welcome my acceptance of the moral standing of virtually all living creatures, but would still object to what they would regard as a homocentric hierarchy of values (this objection I have already considered) and to yet a further deployment of the 'Method of Argument from Human Analogy and Anomaly'.[43]

Now certainly if the sole moral criterion is the preservation of the integrity, stability and beauty of the biotic community then very different principles will be arrived at from the above and also from those of Singer. Thus suffering will only count as an evil where its effects are ecologically bad; and where they are held to be good (as over culling the white-tailed deer where its population is too large for the sustainability of the surrounding ecosystem) it will not even count as a negative moral factor at all. Again, neither individual creatures (human or otherwise) nor their states will be of intrinsic value, and their relative value will consist solely in their relative contribution to ecological stability. And since the present global human population is held to be a global disaster for the biotic community, it should be reduced (or so Callicott implies) to roughly twice that of bears.[44]

There is reason to be grateful to Rodman and Callicott for pointing out the fundamental divergences between the movement for more humane treatment of animals, with its emphasis on vegetarianism, whether as defended by Singer or (very differently) by Regan,[45] and the holistic land ethic of Aldo Leopold. This divergence has also been assessed from his own point of view in Singer's recent work.[46] Thus Singer is critical of environmentalists who support some forms of hunting; and, despite finding that environmentalists' campaigns to preserve rare species are often more effective in preventing, for example, whaling than campaigns against cruelty, maintains that rare nonsentient species should only be preserved where (as not always) the short-term or long-term interests of sentient animals are at stake, and also that even if whaling is carried on in a sustainable way, it is still objectionable because individual whales, 'sentient creatures with lives of their own to lead', would still be threatened.[47]

My disagreements with Singer over the extension of moral standing and intrinsic value will already be clear. Nor do I accept in full his case for vegetarianism, though I do accept his case against consuming the products of factory-farms and of other practices which cause significant animal suffering without sufficient reason. I am not convinced either that he has taken sufficient account of the need to limit some animal populations. But he is on entirely firm ground in stressing the evil of suffering, and the need to take strong measures to reduce it. Granted that the disruption of the biosphere would imperil the lives of all sentient creatures, we do not need for that reason (or any other) to treat its preservation as the sole ethical criterion, or to cease to regard suffering as evil in itself, or measures and attitudes aimed directly at its alleviation (attitudes such as sympathy, compassion, and respect for individuals who can suffer) as morally central. Further, if sentience and other capacities of individuals are morally significant (as has been maintained above) then it is morally imperative to extend moral consideration to nonhumans with such capacities — an instance this of the very method of reasoning at which Rodman protests. If, by contrast, the biosphere had moral standing and none of its individual members had such standing in their own right, matters would be different; but I have not discovered any arguments for holding this to be the case.

Callicott accuses Singer and others of a life-loathing philosophy, because of their opposition to avoidable pain and their concern to minimize such a natural and ecologically beneficent sensation. Singer probably understresses values beyond enjoyment, such as creativity, but, as Steinbock remarks, the ability to exercise such capacities is easily undermined by suffering.[48] Callicott also fears that his own position may appear to be gratuitous misanthropy.[49] Granted his own Leopoldian premise it is not gratuitous. But as this premise implies that human life, however worthwhile, is of no intrinsic value and has value only insofar as it preserves the biosphere, misanthropy is not an inappropriate description. There are ample grounds for preserving species and wilderness, based on the needs and the value of present and future creatures, and likewise for resisting 'the optimization of the biosphere' or the total use of the earth in the human interest:[50] but, although it is regrettable when some species are lost through wear and tear inflicted on the environment by humans, this alone in no way justifies holding that the lives of any of those humans are on balance an evil. Humans too have lives of their own to lead, with scope for valuable as well as pernicious trans-formations of the lands they have populated; and any criterion on which there are too many of them only begins to be plausible if it introduces something else of counterbalancing value. For some levels of population this can perhaps be done (see chapter 10), but the holists altogether fail to do it for any level.

Rodman for his part suspects that

the same principles are manifested in quite diverse forms — e.g. in damming a river and repressing an animal instinct (whether human or nonhuman), in clear-cutting a forest and bombing a city, in Dachau and a university research laboratory, in censoring an idea, liquidating a religious or racial group, and exterminating a species of flora or fauna.[51]

Like principles of oppression may be involved, and maybe all liberation movements are, as Rodman contends, natural allies (despite a clash alleged to exist by Francis and Norman between feminism and opposition to animals experiments).[52] But Rodman's examples cannot be regarded as comparable cases of oppression. Among interests there are priorities: I have tried above, in the modified version of Two-factor Egalitarianism which I have advanced, to delineate some which are rationally defensible.

NOTES

1 Arne Naess writes at p. 96 of 'The Shallow and the Deep, Long-Range Ecology Movement', *Inquiry,* 16, 1973, 95—100, of *'the equal right to live and blossom'* (his italics), and of biospherical egalitarianism.
2 'The Moral Basis of Vegetarianism', *Philosophy,* 53, 1978, 481—505, e.g. at p. 497.
3 Peter Singer, *Animal Liberation, A New Ethics for our Treatment of Animals,* London: Jonathan Cape, 1976, p. 9. The relevant chapter, entitled 'All Animals are Equal', is reprinted in Tom Regan and Peter Singer, *Animal Rights and Human Obligations,* Englewood Cliffs, NJ: Prentice-Hall, 1976.
4 Peter Singer, 'Utilitarianism and Vegetarianism', *Philosophy and Public Affairs*, 1980, 325—37, pp. 328f.
5 Thus John Rodman, 'The Liberation of Nature', *Inquiry,* 20, 1977, 83—145: similar views are present in Holmes Rolston III, 'Is There an Ecological Ethic?', *Ethics*, 85, 1974—75, 93—109; Kenneth Goodpaster, 'From Egoism to Environmentalism', in Goodpaster and Sayre (eds), *Ethics and Problems of the 21st Century*, 21—35; and in J. Baird Callicott, 'Animal Liberation: A Triangular Affair', *Environmental Ethics*, 2, 1980, 311—38.
6 Thus R. G. Frey, *Interests and Rights: The Case Against Animals,* Oxford: Clarendon Press, 1980.

7   *A System of Ethics,* trans. Norbert Gutermann, New Haven: Yale University Press, 1956, Part I, Section 2, chapter 7, 136—44; reprinted in Stanley and Roslind Godlovitch and John Harris (eds), *Animals, Men and Morals, An Enquiry into the Maltreatment of Non-humans,* New York: Taplinger Publishing Co., 1972, 149—55.

8   'Rights', *The Philosophical Quarterly,* 15, 1965, 115—27.

9   A transition is apparent in McCloskey's 'The Right to Life', *Mind,* 84, 1975, 403—25, where autonomy is required for the possession of rights. The newer position is more explicit in 'Moral Rights and Animals', *Inquiry,* 22, 1979, 23—54. For Feinberg's position see 'The Rights of Animals and Unborn Generations', in *Philosophy and Environmental Crisis,* 43—68, especially pp. 50f.

10 *Interests and Rights,* chapters II, V, VI and VIII. Frey's scepticism about natural rights is expressed in his Postscript, pp. 168—70.

11 'Animal Rights, Human Wrongs', *Environmental Ethics,* 2, 1980, 99—120; 'Utilitarianism, Vegetarianism and Animal Rights', *Philosophy and Public Affairs,* 9, 1979–80, 305—24. These papers develop the argument of his earlier paper, 'The Moral Basis of Vegetarianism', *Canadian Journal of Philosophy,* 5, 1975, 181—214.

12 'Death, Misfortune and Species Inequality', *Philosophy and Public Affairs,* 10, 1980—81, 47—64. (Cigman rejects belief in any non-human animals' right to life, but accepts that they have moral standing.)

13 'Not for Humans Only: The Place of Nonhumans in Environmental Issues', in Goodpaster and Sayre (eds), *Ethics and Problems of the 21st Century,* 191—206, at pp. 194f.

14 *Persons and Minds: The Prospects for Nonreductive Materialism,* Dordrecht, Boston and London: Reidel, 1977, chapters 8 and 9.

15 'The Moral Basis of Vegetarianism', p. 490.

16 Aubrey Townsend, 'Radical Vegetarians', *Australasian Journal of Philosophy,* 57, 1979, 85—93, p. 91.

17 'Supererogation and Double Standards', *Mind,* 88, 1979, 481—99, pp. 493f.

18 'Freedom, Autonomy and the Concept of a Person', *Proceedings of the Aristotelian Society,* 76, 1975—76, 109—30.

19 'Personal Freedom and Environmental Ethics: The Moral Inequality of Species', in Gray Dorsey (ed.), *Equality and Freedom,* Vol. II, New York: Oceana Publications and Leiden: A. W. Sijthoff, 1977, 401—24, especially at pp. 416—20.

20 'Killing Humans and Killing Animals', *Inquiry,* 22, 1979, 145—56.

21 'Not for Humans Only', p. 199.

22 Michael Lockwood, 'Killing and the Preference for Life', *Inquiry,* 22, 1979, 157—70, p. 168.

23 'Duty and the Beast', *Philosophy,* 53, 1978, 529—49, pp. 63ff.

24 'Interspecific Justice', *Inquiry,* 22, 1979, 55—79, pp. 63ff.

25 Ibid. p. 70. A similar point is made by L. W. Sumner, 'A Matter of Life and Death', *Noûs,* 10, 1976, 145—71, pp. 164f.

26 'Interspecific Justice', p. 64.
27 'Speciesism and the Idea of Equality', *Philosophy*, 53, 1978, 247—63, p. 254.
28 'The Moral Basis of Vegetarianism', p. 486.
29 *Animal Liberation*, p. 22. A similar view, couched in more speciesist terms, is expressed by Joel Feinberg at pp. 66f of 'Human Duties and Animal Rights', in Richard Knowles Morris and Michael W. Fox (eds), *On The Fifth Day, Animal Rights and Human Ethics*, Washington: Acropolis Books, 1978, 45—69.
30 'Duty and the Beast', p. 533.
31 *The Moral Status of Animals*, pp. 169—71.
32 'The Liberation of Nature', p. 94f.
33 'Eating Meat and Eating People', *Philosophy*, 53, 1978, 465—79, pp. 470f.
34 Cf. A. M. McIver, 'Ethics and the Beetle', *Analysis*, 8, 1948, 65—70.
35 VanDeVeer, 'Interspecific Justice', pp. 74f; Steinbock, 'Speciesism and the Idea of Equality', pp. 254f.
36 Leslie Pickering Francis and Richard Norman, 'Some Animals are More Equal than Others', *Philosophy*, 53, 1978, 507—27, p. 510.
37 'The Moral Basis of Vegetarianism', p. 503.
38 'Duty and the Beast', pp. 536f.
39 'Some Animals are More Equal than Others', pp. 518—27.
40 'The Moral Basis of Vegetarianism', p. 497.
41 'Interspecific Justice', p. 65 and p. 77, n. 15.
42 See n. 5 (above).
43 Rodman, 'The Liberation of Nature', p. 87. I defend this method in 'Methods of Ecological Ethics'.
44 Callicott, 'Animal Liberation', pp. 320, 332—3, 324—6.
45 Singer's and Regan's different bases for vegetarianism are explored in Regan's 'Utilitarianism, Vegetarianism and Animal Rights' (see n. 11 above), and Singer's 'Utilitarianism and Vegetarianism' (see n. 4 above).
46 In 'Not for Humans Only', especially at pp. 201—5.
47 Ibid. pp. 204f.
48 See n. 27 (above).
49 'Animal Liberation', p. 326.
50 See further Robin Attfield, 'Western Traditions and Environmental Ethics'.
51 'The Liberation of Nature', pp. 89f.
52 'Some Animals are More Equal than Others', p. 516.

10
Problems and Principles: Is a New Ethic Required?

In this chapter I shall briefly review the way the principles arrived at in the four preceding chapters bear on the problems of pollution, resources, population and preservation, and discuss their adequacy and the extent of such revisions as may be required to our moral traditions.

Pollution

Though I did not adopt the 'Polluters Stop' principle of Lippit and Hamada, a case was made out for the containment of pollution and the prevention of its escalation. The example given was the need to curtail the emission of waste heat; but there are many other cases where pollution can threaten the impoverishment or the actual poisoning of human and nonhuman life in the short term or the long term. In general I favour Kavka's Lockean standard by which each generation is required to leave equivalent opportunities to its successor; indeed even the technology the introduction of which Kavka urges to compensate succeeding generations for expended resources would need to be as free of pollution as possible, or it would fall foul of its own justification. I accepted Kavka's own qualification about the need for the present generation to invest in Third World development so that population levels can be stabilized and the Lockean standard become capable of fulfilment on the part of future generations; as the consequent activity would involve some pollution, it is all the more important to stress that pollutant processes which are unacceptable in developed countries should not be exported to the Third World.

I have also endorsed Hubbard's proposal for a consumption maximum for the use of nonrenewable resources, which would prevent exponential increases in pollution. The same qualification as above would apply again: the case for development in poor countries justifies a greater consumption than would otherwise be the fair share of the current generation. The consumption maximum is justified by the needs of future people, whether their existence is brought about by ourselves or otherwise. Already the principles adduced exceed those of the 'shallow ecology movement', but they stretch traditional morality only to the extent that it sometimes permits discounting the future. Yet concern for posterity is a keynote both of the Old Testament and of the Enlightment philosophers (see chapter 5). So there is no clear departure involved even in the principle also adopted that the generation of nuclear energy should not proceed until safe storage methods for the waste products have been discovered.

Where Passmore now finds Western traditions in need of supplementation is over pollution which damages or destroys natural beauty or nonhuman species.[1] In this area I have accepted, with Singer, the moral standing and significance of sentient nonhuman animals, and also, against Singer, the moral standing of nonsentient living creatures too. Human interests probably suffice to show that ecosystems such as the forests of Africa should not be imperilled by being sprayed with pesticides;[2] but human interests can also clash with those of wild (and of domesticated) living creatures, and even when it pays people to eradicate wild habitats there is still a moral case (and sometimes an overriding one) against doing so. The recognition of this would indeed stretch accepted practice, but it is in keeping with the teaching of the Bible and with the concern, expressed in the Stewardship tradition, for the care of the earth (see chapters 2 and 3). What would need to be revised would be the widespread presupposition that nonhumans have only instrumental value and that they are dispensable. In much current reflection, as when we accept our kinship with nonhumans, we reject this mechanistic view, and this rejection sometimes affects our practice; so the necessary revision is sufficiently familiar and acceptable to allow it to win acceptance.

Resources

There are problems here over the depletion of the stocks of non-renewable resources, over the imperilling of renewable resources, and over the gap between the availability of resources (of whatever sort) and expected levels of demand. These descriptions of the problem do not prejudge solutions. Thus, as Kenneth Sayre points out,[3] the energy problem may be solved either by increasing the rate of generation or by decreasing the level of consumption. The principles favoured above fall in fact somewhere in between.

Thus the use of non-renewable resources should be justly distributed between generations, depletions being counterbalanced by the devising of new techniques so that succeeding generations have opportunities matching those of their predecessors. This would require a consumption maximum, so pitched as to be more-or-less stable across the generations: expected levels of consumption in excess of the maximum would need to be curtailed in favour of simpler, less energy-intensive styles of life, though the use of renewable sources of energy would also have a major contribution to make. At the same time each generation would as far as possible be guaranteed a minimum of resources, including food (and to that end agricultural land and fisheries), energy (partly through the savings of earlier generations) and clean air and water. Once population levels have been stabilized, each generation should be provided for equally, and allow equal future provision by taking no more non-renewable resources than its share. If also each generation preserves vulnerable renewable resources (forests and natural cycles), the Lockean standard is observed by which each leaves enough and as good for its successor.

Forests too are resources in that they are usable by man, but they and other areas of wilderness are not just resources. There is a moral case, or so I have argued, against the felling of trees relating both to their intrinsic value and to their value to nonhuman animals. This case constrains the uninhibited use of what may otherwise fairly be construed as resources, and tells strongly against practices such as clear-cutting. It also requires sensitivity in the adoption of such otherwise ecologically sound principles as that of aiming at maximum sustainable yield, especially where the yield or harvest consists of sentient creatures.[4] Indeed some practices in which animals or plants are treated merely as resources are ruled out by Two-factor Egalitarianism as interpreted above, such as the hunting of whales, and indeed hunting in general, except where it is genuinely justified by necessity.

The main extension of our moral traditions called for in the area of resources, however, concerns the recognition of obligations to people of the distant future. Passmore is, I believe, mistaken to claim that utilitarianism (and cognate consequentialist theories) preclude such a recognition through their readiness to discount uncertain benefits.[5] Nor do we ordinarily assume that justice is only possible to those who, unlike future people, have bargaining power. So our traditions, including that of Stewardship, which involves handing over the earth in as good a state as we received it, provide for the recognition of these obligations much more than Passmore supposes. What is needed is an extension of sympathies to match our moral beliefs, on which time is as irrelevant as place. Education about how current actions and omissions can affect future people should help, as it can over effects on people who are geographically distant: ecological discoveries in the former case mirror the dawning realization in the latter that it is within our power to make a considerable difference for good or ill, and their dissemination could well, as education is beginning to do in the matter of world poverty, facilitate a change in attitudes.

Population

Though each worthwhile life is of value and there is nothing wrong with population growth as such, there is a great deal amiss when it takes place in a world where hundreds of millions of people already suffer the miseries of absolute poverty. The world population of humans is certain to grow in any case, even though the rate of growth is falling; and it is imperative that growth should cease at some sustainable level. Zero growth cannot and should not be introduced abruptly, but should be phased in. Only if population is stabilized can succeeding generations be provided for by constant rather than ever-increasing consumption: and accordingly the problems of pollution and resource depletion will *in the end* become unmanageable unless population growth is brought to a halt.

Some of the same considerations suggest that the lower the level at which stability is reached, the better. But I also concluded against the view that the level of the world population ought to be lower than at present, granted that it is possible to feed the current population and that every worthwhile life has its own intrinsic value. On the other hand if population eventually ceases to grow only when it has reached a level which generates too much pollution and exhausts remaining resources too rapidly, there would then be a case for a policy of gradual downward movement towards a level which can be sustained indefinitely without those who live being poisoned by pollution or impoverished through lack of resources.

That level, though not lower than the present one of 4,000 million, may well be less than the level at which population eventually ceases to grow.

The interests of nonhumans must also be taken into account in matters of population. At some very high levels of human population, planetary life-support systems could be fundamentally disrupted both for humans and for all other forms of life; if this were seriously in prospect, there would be conclusive moral reasons, despite what Stanley Benn seems to imply,[6] for calling a halt. (In fact this degree of disruption is threatened not so much by population growth as by the threat of nuclear war and nuclear accidents.) But there must also be somewhat lower levels of population than these which would be bound to threaten a great number of wild species and their habitats without the biosphere as a whole being ruined. (Such threats, e.g. to the Amazonian rain-forest, are already with us, but not as an inevitable outcome of current population levels.) The increased area which would need to be put under cultivation if population were, say, trebled could displace most of the larger nonhuman animals; and in addition it could easily fail to sustain its fertility, so that ever more desperate attempts at cultivating poorer and poorer land would have to be made, with yet worse ecological effects. So a stage could be reached where feeding an extra human involved accelerated ecological stress, including the loss not just of many existing nonhumans but also of all future ones of several kinds, through the extinction of their species. On the theory presented above, the interests of nonhumans count for enough to curtail the growth of the human population before that point is reached.

A more drastic conclusion would of course be reached on any theory of radical biotic egalitarianism[7] which counted as of equal significance not like capacities but animals, whatever their species, human or nonhuman. On such a theory there is no more value — even in general — in human than in nonhuman lives; so, granted the inherent value of diversity, and granted similar population densities for humans and nonhumans, we should halt population growth before any animal species became extinct. (Where lives are of equal value, diversity could serve as a tie-breaker.) Moreover, as the extinction of other species began long ago when the human population was much smaller and has become more frequent with the growth of human numbers, we should probably have to reduce the human population so as to avert the extinction of further species. I have however rejected such theories above. On the

modified form of Two-factor Egalitarianism accepted in chapter 9
no such conclusions follow, though nonhumans should not be killed
nor their species extinguished for the sake of peripheral human
interests. But the constraints upon the growth of the human
population added by this principle do not exceed those mentioned
in the last paragraph.

The principle does, however, in the form in which I have accepted
it, imply that it is wrong to perpetuate factory-farms by consuming
their products. Though I am not committed to vegetarianism, a
criticism could here be raised which is sometimes directed at
vegetarians.[8] For if the principle here commended were universally
adopted not only would many fewer animals be reared but also
vegetarian diets would become much more common, and food-
chains would become shorter and therewith more efficient. The
criticism which may therefore be raised is that this would lead to an
extra increase in the human population, with consequent ecological
damage. I reply as follows. First, the likelihood of the principle
being adopted widely enough for its adoption to have *these* effects is
slight. Second, the prospect of ecological damage would still
constitute a reason for restricting the human population, even if
food-chains allowed of an increase. Third, so would the misery for
humans which would result if population growth were not restricted.
Fourth, shorter and more efficient food-chains would make it
possible to feed adequately a much greater proportion of the actual
human population; and as long as population growth was
discouraged for the reasons just given, a very great deal of good
could thus be done without the evils supervening which are predicted
in the criticism. Indeed the possibility of feeding the earth's current
human population is a central reason for the widespread adoption
of a much more vegetarian diet.

Thus the principles adopted neither urge a drop in the world
human population nor allow of an exponential increase, but counsel
stabilization at a level which can be sustained indefinitely without
progressive ecological deterioration. This reinforces Kavka's point
that the current generation is justified in investing a share of
resources greater that the consumption maximum would otherwise
allow in the alleviation of poverty in the Third World, an effort
without which the rate of population growth is unlikely to decrease
sufficiently. This extra deployment of resources could lead to some
ecological stress in the short run, but must be endured if the
problem of population growth is to be reduced to manageable

proportions (and likewise the other ecological problems which it exacerbates).[9]

The moral innovations which Passmore now accepts in the matter of population are of two sorts. One is the need for people in largely non-Christian countries such as India to revise the tradition of 'early marriages and mandatory fruitfulness'.[10] This I do not dispute; but the revision is manifestly one which Indians have widely accepted, if not widely enough, and thus one which is clearly in keeping with some of the strands of morality as it is already understood in India, as Indian newspapers and my Indian relations attest. The other is the need to overcome objections, usually raised in the West, to publicity for contraceptives, and also to annul the injunction on males to procreate children. These changes too can be accommodated within existing moral traditions, Roman Catholic ones included. But, though Passmore is doubtless right in holding that not all males (or females) have an obligation to produce children, I have contended above, with Sikora and Anglin, that many people do have such an obligation; and thus I cannot support as extensive a revision as Passmore favours in this case. Rather people should be encouraged to have no more children than are required to replace themselves, because of the extra strains on resources, and in particular the extra impact on those in poor countries least able to buy food, resulting from each addition to the total population of the developed countries of the West. (In a world with severe undernourishment the Extra Person Obligation has its upper limits.)

With the population problem, as with the problem of resources, though there are large implications for both humans and nonhumans now alive, the main extension of our moral traditions which is required lies, in fact, in the matter of taking into account the interests of the people of the next several centuries hence.[11] In the matter of population the acceptance of this longer perspective has already become widespread, and not only in the West; but in areas of poverty, economic change is required before attention can be focused on the long-term future. Thus the alleviation of poverty remains the prerequisite for solutions to the population problem.

Preservation

Conservation is not only a matter of the husbanding of non-renewable resources and the protection of renewable ones, but extends also to the preservation of wild species and their habitats and of planetary life-support systems in general. As Passmore acknowledges, wanton destruction has long been condemned, and this condemnation can apply where natural organisms, species or their habitats are destroyed as much as over works of art.[12] Even when this recognition is not matched by an awareness of what it implies, i.e. the value of what ought to be saved from destruction, it allows the precarious position of wildlife and of wilderness to be seen as a problem.[13] Concern for animal welfare adds emphasis to this perception; and the scope of the problem is enlarged when it is realized that the habitats of all life on earth, humans included, are potentially at risk, and that life-support systems in general need to be preserved.

Long-term human interests are obviously at stake over life-support systems, including those relevant to agriculture and those which maintain the cleanness of air and water. The interests of present and future humans in medical and agricultural research, scientific investigation, recreation and the aesthetic appreciation of nature also constitute strong grounds for preserving most species and the terrains and ecosystems in which they participate. Nor should the symbolic significance of wild nature for our sanity and sense of perspective be overlooked. To these considerations Singer rightly adds the interests of nonhuman animals; like Goodpaster I believe that nonsentient creatures also have moral standing, since in most cases they too have interests. I have also pointed out that those future creatures which would otherwise realize their proper capacities but which we can blight or debar from existence must be taken into account, and that when this is done there is a much strengthened case for the preservation of even inelegant and unprofitable species.

The various interests just mentioned can, of course, conflict, and just as humans must eat to live, so must predation on the part of wild animals be allowed to continue if but the predators' interests are to count. In general, intervention with the natural order can often preserve or even enhance it, but the likely consequences (long-term ones included) must, as Byerly points out,[14] be taken fully into consideration. Positive action may however be necessary to preserve life-support systems: as just mentioned, the human population must not be allowed to reach a level which subverts them, and the same can be true with the populations of nonhuman species liable to ruin their own habitats. But except where this is true, or food is not to be had otherwise, the hunting and culling of wild animals is gratuitously cruel and to be condemned as such. In terms of Two-factor

Egalitarianism it involves the sacrifice of the animals' basic interests where no serious or basic interests of humans (or other species of greater psychological capacities than the hunted or culled animals) are at risk.

I have not adopted the view that what matters is the biosphere as a whole, or that its components matter only as they contribute to its stability: such a view involves a complete break with accepted ethical norms, and I do not see how to argue from them to it. Ecosystems should be preserved rather for the sake of the creatures which they support. Thus there is no decision to make between humans and the biosphere: the reason for preserving the latter lies in the interests of humans and of other creatures — and there could hardly be a stronger one.[15] The moral significance of individual nonsentient creatures is admittedly slight, but it is as well to be aware of it, especially where large numbers of present or future organisms are in question (as where a forest may be eradicated or a species eliminated).

Taking into account the interests of future people and of nonhuman living creatures in matters of preservation extends the range of obligations conventionally acknowledged. Thus the obligation to provide for future people (in the weak sense in which it was accepted in connection with Sterba's suggestions in chapter 7) probably involves preserving the greatest possible range of species; and the interests of future humans and nonhumans alike add strength to the need to institute a consumption maximum for every generation to abide by. Again, the interests of existing nonhuman animals in continuing to lead the kind of life to which they are adapted impose limitations on the conditions in which they may be reared or killed for food or for laboratory experiments, or exterminated as a by-product of modern agricultural or industrial techniques. All the more obviously all these interests reveal strong obligations not to overheat or poison the atmosphere or blight all future life with nuclear fallout.

Moral traditions

But all these recently mentioned obligations are recognizable extensions of acknowledged ones, either through a broader range of consequences being recognized or through interests analogous to already recognized ones being taken into account. They also accord with the tradition of Stewardship, and with its Old Testament origins in which wild creatures are regarded as valuable in their own right and subject to God's care. This tradition requires humans to care for the earth on which they live, and nothing more or less is involved in the extension of obligations delineated here.

Passmore now finds our attitudes to nature to stand badly in need of revision in matters of preservation.[16] This cannot be denied with any cogency. Like him, I do not reject cost/benefit analysis, but when most future costs and benefits are discounted and those of nonhumans disregarded, the exercise attracts an entirely specious authority. Worse still is the lust for short-term returns, common to East and West alike, with which, whether by companies, politicians or administrators, decisions are usually made, and the confidence in progress which seems to give assurance that all other considerations can look after themselves. Again, all unqualifiedly mechanistic and instrumental views of nature need to be overcome, as also does the view on which it is worthless until tamed and humanized by ourselves. But these metaphysical views can be countered from within existing bodies of accepted belief; thus neither of them sits easily with acceptance (on the basis of the theory of evolution) of our kinship with nonhuman animals, nor with the Stewardship interpretation of the Judaeo-Christian belief in man's dominion over nature. Similarly there already exist the moral resources to challenge and condemn the malpractices which lead to the despoliation of nature.

Here, as with other problems, education and the broadening of imagination both have a key role to play. So do pressure groups and political parties. But if these parts are to be played, a sound ethical theory is needed. This and the four previous chapters are a contribution towards presenting such an ethical theory and exhibiting its bearing on ecological matters; a theory which, as I argued in Part One, is implicit already in some of our more long-standing traditions, and in particular in the tradition of Stewardship.

NOTES

1 'Ecological Problems and Persuasion' in Gray Dorsey (ed.), *Equality and Freedom,* Vol. II, New York: Oceana Publications and Leiden: A. W. Sijthoff, 1977, 431—42, p. 438.
2 Several relevant articles appear in *Vole*, 4, (3), March 1981.
3 'Morality, Energy and the Environment', *Environmental Ethics,* 3, 1981, 5—18, p. 7.
4 Cf. Singer, 'Nor for Humans Only', in K. E. Goodpaster and K. M. Sayre (eds), *Ethics and Problems of the 21st Century*, pp. 201f.
5 'Ecological Problems and Persuasion', p. 439; *MRN*, pp. 84f. Passmore

has been criticized on this score in R. and V. Routley, 'Nuclear Energy and Obligations to the Future', *Inquiry*, 21, 1978, 133—79, and in chapter 6 above.

6 'Personal Freedom and Environmental Ethics: The Moral Inequality of Species', in Gray Dorsey (ed.), *Equality and Freedom.*

7 William T. Blackstone, 'The Search for an Environmental Ethic', in Tom Regan (ed.), *Matters of Life and Death,* Philadelphia: Temple University Press, 1980, 299—335, p. 303.

8 Callicott criticizes Singer on related grounds at 'Animal Liberation: A Triangular Affair', *Environmental Ethics,* 2, 1980, 311—38, p. 331.

9 It is notable that Dennis C. Pirages and Paul R. Ehrlich, despite Ehrlich's earlier views, now favour efforts directed at Third World development even at the expense of the West holding back over resource consumption, partly from the belief that it could assist the introduction of a steady-state world economy of the kind proposed by Herman Daly. See their *Ark II: Social Response to Environmental Imperatives,* San Francisco: W. H. Freeman, 1974, p. 243.

10 'Ecological Problems and Persuasion', p. 440.

11 Here at any rate I am in agreement with Robert Young, 'Population Policies, Coercion and Morality', in *Environmental Philosophy,* 356—75.

12 'Ecological Problems and Persuasion', p. 441; *MRN,* p. 124.

13 Thus the *World Conservation Strategy* (published in 1980 jointly by the International Union for Conservation of Nature and Natural Resources, the United Nations Environmental Programme and the World Wildlife Fund), though admirable in relating conservation to development, confines its arguments to ones based solely on human interests.

14 In 'Principles of Noninterference with Nature in Ecological Ethics', in *Ethics: Foundations, Problems and Applications, Proceedings of the Fifth International Wittgenstein Symposium,* Vienna: Verlag Hölder-Pichler-Tempsky, 1981, 318—20.

15 Cf. the case for conservation presented in W. H. Murdy, 'Anthropocentrism: A Modern Version', *Science,* 187, March 1975, 1168—72.

16 'Ecological Problems and Persuasion', p. 441.

References

Articles, essays and reviews

Anglin, William, 'The Repugnant Conclusion', *Canadian Journal of Philosophy*, 7, 1977, 745—54

Anglin, William, 'In Defense of the Potentiality Principle', in R. I. Sikora and Brian Barry (eds), *Obligations to Future Generations*, 31—7

Attfield, Robin, 'The Logical Status of Moral Utterances', *Journal of Critical Analysis*, 4 (2), 1972, 70—84

Attfield, Robin, 'On Being Human', *Inquiry*, 17, 1974, 175—92

Attfield, Robin, 'Toward a Defence of Teleology', *Ethics*, 85, 1975, 123—35

Attfield, Robin, 'Against Incomparabilism', *Philosophy*, 50, 1975, 230—4

Attfield, Robin, 'Racialism, Justice and Teleology', *Ethics*, 87, 1977, 186—8

Attfield, Robin, 'Supererogation and Double Standards', *Mind*, 88, 1979, 481—99

Attfield, Robin, 'How Not to be a Moral Relativist', *The Monist*, 62, 1979, 510—21

Attfield, Robin, Review of Renford Bambrough, *Moral Scepticism and Moral Knowledge*, *The Philosophical Quarterly*, 31, 1981, 177—8

Attfield, Robin, 'The Good of Trees', *Journal of Value Inquiry*, 15, 1981, 35—54

Attfield, Robin, 'Christian Attitudes to Nature', *Journal of the History of Ideas*, 44, 1983

Attfield, Robin, 'Western Traditions and Environmental Ethics', in Robert Elliot and Aaron Gair (eds), *Environmental Philosophy: A Collection of Readings*

Attfield, Robin, 'Methods of Ecological Ethics', forthcoming in *Metaphilosophy*

Auxter, Thomas, 'The Right not to be Eaten', *Inquiry*, 22, 1979, 221—30

Ayers, Michael, 'Mechanism, Superaddition and the Proof of God's Existence in Locke's *Essay*', *Philosophical Review*, 90, 1981, 210—51

Baier, Annette, 'The Rights of Past and Future Persons', in Ernest Partridge (ed.), *Responsibilities to Future Generations*, 171—83

Baker, John Austin, 'Biblical Attitudes to Nature', in Hugh Montefiore (ed.), *Man and Nature*, 87—109

Barbour, Ian G., 'Attitudes Toward Nature and Technology', in Ian G. Barbour (ed.), *Earth Might Be Fair*, 146—68

Barr, James, 'Man and Nature: The Ecological Controversy in the Old Testament', *Bulletin of the John Rylands Library,* 55, 1972, 9—32

Barry, Brian, 'Justice Between Generations', in P. M. S. Hacker and J. Raz (eds), *Law, Morality and Society,* 268—84

Barry, Brian, 'Circumstances of Justice and Future Generations', in R. I. Sikora and Brian Barry (eds), *Obligations to Future Generations,* 204—48

Bayles, Michael, 'Harm to the Unconceived', *Philosophy and Public Affairs,* 5, 1975—76, 292—304

Bayles, Michael, 'Famine or Food: Sacrificing for Future or Present Generations', in Ernest Partridge (ed.), *Responsibilities to Future Generations,* 239—45

Benn, Stanley, 'Freedom, Autonomy and the Concept of a Person', *Proceedings of the Aristotelian Society,* 76, 1975—76, 109—30

Benn, Stanley, 'Personal Freedom and Environmental Ethics: the Moral Inequality of Species', in Gray Dorsey (ed.), *Equality and Freedom,* Vol. II, 401—24

Bennett, Jonathan, 'On Maximizing Happiness', in R. I. Sikora and Brian Barry (eds), *Obligations to Future Generations,* 61—73

Benson, John, 'Duty and the Beast', *Philosophy,* 53, 1978, 529—49

Bickham, Stephen, 'Future Generations and Contemporary Ethical Theory', *Journal of Value Inquiry,* 15, 1981, 169—77

Blackstone, William T., 'The Search for an Environmental Ethic', in Tom Regan (ed.), *Matters of Life and Death,* 299—335

Boulding, Kenneth, 'The Economics of the Coming Spaceship Earth', in John Barr (ed.), *The Environmental Handbook,* 77—82

Breslaw, John, 'Economics and Ecosystems', in John Barr (ed.), *The Environmental Handbook,* 83—93

Brumbaugh, Robert S., 'Of Man, Animals and Morals: A Brief History', in Richard Knowles Morris and Michael W. Fox (eds), *On the Fifth Day, Animal Rights and Human Ethics,* 6—25

Burton, Robert G., 'A Philosopher Looks at the Population Bomb', in William T. Blackstone (ed.), *Philosophy and Environmental Crisis,* 105—16

Byerly, Henry, 'Principles of Noninterference with Nature in Ecological Ethics', in Edgar Morscher and Rudolf Stranzinger (eds), *Ethics: Foundations, Problems and Applications, Proceedings of the Fifth International Wittgenstein Symposium,* 318—20

Callahan, Daniel, 'What Obligations do we have to Future Generations?', *American Ecclesiastical Review,* 164, 1971, 265—80; reprinted in Ernest Partridge (ed.), *Responsibilities to Future Generations,* 73—85

Callicott, J. Baird, 'Elements of an Environmental Ethic: Moral Considerability and the Biotic Community', *Environmental Ethics,* 1, 1979, 71—81

Callicott, J. Baird, 'Animal Liberation: A Triangular Affair', *Environmental Ethics,* 2, 1980, 311—38

Cigman, Ruth, 'Death, Misfortune and Species Inequality', *Philosophy and Public Affairs,* 10, 1980—81, 47—64

Clark, Stephen, Review of K. E Goodpaster and K. M. Sayre, (eds), *Ethics and Problems of the 21st Century, Philosophical Books,* 21, 1980, 237—40

Coleman, William, 'Providence, Capitalism and Environmental Degradation', *Journal of the History of Ideas,* 37, 1976, 27—44

Craig, Leon H., 'Contra Contract: A Brief Against Rawls' Theory of Justice', *Canadian Journal of Political Science,* 8, 1975, 63—81

de George, Richard T., 'The Environment, Rights and Future Generations', in Ernest Partridge (ed.), *Responsibilities to Future Generations,* 157—65

Delattre, Edwin, 'Rights, Responsibilities and Future Persons', *Ethics,* 82, 1972, 254—8

Devine, Philip, 'The Moral Basis of Vegetarianism', *Philosophy,* 53, 1978, 481—505

Diamond, Cora, 'Eating Meat and Eating People', *Philosophy,* 53, 1978, 465—79

Dubos, René, 'Franciscan Conservation and Benedictine Stewardship', in David and Eileen Spring (eds), *Ecology and Religion in History,* 114—36

Elliot, Robert, 'Why Preserve Species?' in Don Mannison, Michael McRobbie and Richard Routley (eds), *Environmental Philosophy,* 8—29

Feinberg, Joel, 'The Rights of Animals and Unborn Generations', in William T. Blackstone (ed.), *Philosophy and Environmental Crisis,* 43—68. Also in Richard A. Wasserstrom (ed.), *Today's Moral Problems,* 581—601; and in Ernest Partridge (ed.), *Responsibilities to Future Generations,* 139—50

Feinberg, Joel, 'Human Duties and Animal Rights', in Richard Knowles Morris and Michael W. Fox (eds), *On the Fifth Day, Animal Rights and Human Ethics,* 45—69

Fiering, Norman S., 'Irresistible Compassion: An Aspect of Eighteenth Century Humanitarianism', *Journal of the History of Ideas,* 37, 1976, 195—218

Francis, Leslie Pickering and Norman, Richard, 'Some Animals are More Equal than Others', *Philosophy,* 53, 1978, 507—27

Frankena, William K., 'Ethics and the Environment', in K. E. Goodpaster and K. M. Sayre (eds), *Ethics and Problems of the 21st Century,* 3—20

Fyodorov, Yevgeny and Novik, Ilya, 'Ecological Aspects of Social Progress', in *Society and the Environment: a Soviet View,* (ed. anon.), 37—55

Gerasimov, Innokenty, 'Man, Society and the Geographical Environment', in *Society and the Environment: a Soviet View* (ed. anon.), 25—36

Golding, Martin, 'Obligations to Future Generations', *The Monist,* 56, 1972, 85—99; also in Ernest Partridge (ed.), *Responsibilities to Future Generations,* 61—72

Golding, M. P. and Golding, N. H., 'Why Preserve Landmarks? A Preliminary Inquiry', in K. E. Goodpaster and K. M. Sayre (eds), *Ethics and Problems of the 21st Century*, 175—90

Goodin, Robert E., 'No Moral Nukes', *Ethics*, 90, 1980, 417—49

Goodman, David C., 'The Enlightenment: Deists and "Rationalists"', in David C. Goodman *et al.*, *Scientific Progress and Religious Dissent*, 33—68

Goodman, David C., 'God and Nature in the Philosophy of Descartes', in David C. Goodman *et al.*, *Towards a Mechanistic Philosophy*, 5—43

Goodpaster, Kenneth, 'On Being Morally Considerable', *Journal of Philosophy*, 75, 1978, 308—25

Goodpaster, Kenneth, 'From Egoism to Environmentalism', in K. E. Goodpaster and K. M. Sayre (eds), *Ethics and Problems of the 21st Century*, 21—35

Goodpaster, Kenneth, 'On Stopping at Everything: A Reply to W. M. Hunt', *Environmental Ethics*, 2, 1980, 281—4

Govier, Trudy, 'What Should We Do About Future People?' *American Philosophical Quarterly*, 16, 1979, 105—13

Gunn, Alastair, S., 'Why Should We Care about Rare Species?' *Environmental Ethics*, 2, 1980, 17—37

Gunter, Pete A. Y., 'The Big Thicket: A Case Study in Attitudes toward Environment', in William T. Blackstone (ed.), *Philosophy and Environmental Crisis*, 117—37

Hare, R. M., 'Abortion and the Golden Rule', *Philosophy and Public Affairs*, 4, 1974—75, 201—22

Hare, R. M., 'Survival of the Weakest', in Samuel Gorovitz *et al.* (eds), *Moral Problems in Medicine*, 364—9

Haworth, Lawrence, 'Rights, Wrongs and Animals', *Ethics*, 88, 1977—78, 95—105

Helton, David, 'Tsetse Fly and Ecology', *Vole*, 4 (3), March 1981, 16

Hesse, Mary, 'On the Alleged Incompatibility between Christianity and Science', in Hugh Montefiore (ed.), *Man and Nature*, 121—31

Hilton, R. H. and Sawyer, P. H., Review of Lynn White Jnr, *Medieval Technology and Social Change, Past and Present*, 24, 1963, 90—100

Hubbard, F. Patrick, 'Justice, Limits to Growth, and an Equilibrium State', *Philosophy and Public Affairs*, 7, 1977—78, 326—45

Hubin, D. Clayton, 'Justice and Future Generations', *Philosophy and Public Affairs*, 6, 1976—77, 70—83

Hunt, W. Murray, 'Are *Mere Things* Morally Considerable?', *Environmental Ethics*, 2, 1980, 59—65

Kavka, Gregory, 'The Futurity Problem', in R. I. Sikora and Brian Barry (eds), *Obligations to Future Generations*, 186—203. Also in Ernest Partridge (ed.), *Responsibilities to Future Generations*, 109—22

Laslett, Peter, 'The Conversation Between the Generations', in Royal Institute of Philosophy (ed.), *The Proper Study*, 172—89

Linear, Marcus, 'Zapping Africa's Flies', *Vole*, 4 (3), March 1981, 14—15

Lippit, Victor D., and Hamada, Koichi, 'Efficiency and Equity in Inter-generational Distribution', in Dennis Clark Pirages (ed.), *The Sustainable Society,* 285—99

Lockwood, Michael, 'Killing Humans and Killing Animals', *Inquiry,* 22, 1979, 157—70

Lovelock, J. and Epton, S., 'The Quest for Gaia', *The New Scientist,* 65, 1975, 304—9

McCabe, Herbert, 'The Immortality of the Soul', in Anthony Kenny (ed.), *Aquinas: A Collection of Critical Essays,* 297—306

McCloskey, H. J., 'Rights', *The Philosophical Quarterly,* 15, 1965, 115—27

McCloskey, H. J., 'The Right to Life', *Mind,* 84, 1975, 403—25

McCloskey, H. J., 'Moral Rights and Animals', *Inquiry,* 22, 1979, 23—54

McIver, A. M., 'Ethics and the Beetle', *Analysis,* 8, 1948, 65—70

Macklin, Ruth, 'Can Future Generations Correctly Be Said to Have Rights?', in Ernest Partridge (ed.), *Responsibilities to Future Generations,* 151—5

McMahan, Jefferson, 'Problems of Population Theory', *Ethics,* 92, 1981—82, 96—127

McRobie, George, 'The Inappropriate Pesticide', *Vole,* 4 (3), March 1981, 1

Midgley, Mary, 'Duties Concerning Islands' in Robert Elliot and Aaron Gair (eds), *Environmental Philosophy: A Collection of Readings*

Midgley, Mary, 'The Limits of Individualism' (forthcoming paper)

Moncrief, Lewis W., 'The Cultural Basis of our Environmental Crisis', *Science,* 170, 508—12; reprinted in David and Eileen Spring (eds), *Ecology and Religion in History,* 76—90

Murdy, W. H., 'Anthropocentrism: A Modern Version', *Science,* 187, March 1975, 1168—72

Naess, Arne, 'The Shallow and the Deep, Long-range Ecology Movement. A Summary', *Inquiry,* 16, 1973, 95—100

Narveson, Jan, 'Utilitarianism and New Generations', *Mind,* 76, 1967, 62—72

Narveson, Jan, 'Moral Problems of Population', in Michael D. Bayles (ed.), *Ethics and Population,* 59—80

Narveson, Jan, 'Animal Rights', *Canadian Journal of Philosophy,* 7, 1977, 161—78

Narveson, Jan, 'Future People and Us', in R. I. Sikora and Brian Barry (eds), *Obligations to Future Generations,* 38—60

Nell, Onora, 'Lifeboat Earth', *Philosophy and Public Affairs,* 4, 1974—75, 273—92

New Internationalist, editorial, 79, September 1979

O'Briant, Walter H., 'Man, Nature and the History of Philosophy', in William T. Blackstone (ed.), *Philosophy and Environmental Crisis,* 79—89

Oldak, Pavel, 'The Environment and Social Production', in *Society and the Environment: a Soviet View,* (ed. anon.), 56—68

Parfit, Derek, 'Rights, Interests and Possible People', in Samuel Gorovitz *et al.* (eds), *Moral Problems in Medicine,* 369—75

Parfit, Derek, 'On Doing the Best for Our Children', in Michael D. Bayles
    (ed.), *Ethics and Population*, 100—15
Parfit, Derek, 'Innumerate Ethics', *Philosophy and Public Affairs*, 7,
    1977—78, 285—301
Parfit, Derek, 'Energy Policy and the Further Future', forthcoming in Peter
    Brown and Douglas MacLean (eds), *Energy Policy and Future
    Generations*
Parfit, Derek, 'Overpopulation, Part One' (unpublished paper)
Parfit, Derek, 'Future Generations: Further Problems', *Philosophy and
    Public Affairs*, 11, 1981—2, 113—72
Passmore, John, 'Attitudes to Nature', in Royal Institute of Philosophy
    (ed.), *Nature and Conduct*, 251—64
Passmore, John, 'The Treatment of Animals', *Journal of the History of
    Ideas*, 36, 1975, 195—218
Passmore, John, 'Ecological Problems and Persuasion', in Gray Dorsey
    (ed.), *Equality and Freedom*, Vol. II, 431—42
Pletcher, Galen K., 'The Rights of Future Generations', in Ernest Partridge
    (ed.), *Responsibilities to Future Generations*, 167—70
Pritchard, Michael S. and Robison, Wade L., 'Justice and the Treatment
    of Animals: A Critique of Rawls', *Environmental Ethics*, 3, 1981,
    55—61
Regan, Tom, 'The Moral Basis of Vegetarianism', *Canadian Journal of
    Philosophy*, 5, 1975, 181—214
Regan, Tom, 'Feinberg on What Sorts of Beings Can Have Rights', in
    Southern Journal of Philosophy, 14, 1976, 485—98
Regan, Tom, 'Narveson on Egoism and the Rights of Animals', *Canadian
    Journal of Philosophy*, 7, 1977, 179—86
Regan, Tom, 'An Examination and Defense of One Argument Concerning
    Animal Rights', *Inquiry*, 22, 1979, 189—219
Regan, Tom, 'Animal Rights and Human Wrongs', *Environmental Ethics*,
    2, 1980, 99—120
Regan, Tom, 'Utilitarianism, Vegetarianism and Animal Rights', *Philosophy
    and Public Affairs*, 9, 1979—80, 305—24
Regan, Tom, 'The Nature and Possibility of an Environmental Ethic',
    Environmental Ethics, 3, 1981, 16—31
Rodman, John, 'The Liberation of Nature', *Inquiry*, 20, 1977, 83—145
Rodman, John, 'Animal Justice: The Counter-revolution in Natural Right
    and Law', *Inquiry*, 22, 1979, 3—22
Rolston, Holmes, III, 'Is There an Ecological Ethic?', *Ethics*, 85, 1975,
    93—109
Roupas, T. G., 'The Value of Life', *Philosophy and Public Affairs*, 7,
    1977—78, 154—83
Routley, Richard, 'Is There a Need for a New, an Environmental Ethic?',
    Proceedings of the XVth World Congress of Philosophy, Varna, 1973,
    205—10.
Routley, Richard and Routley, Val, 'Nuclear Energy and Obligations to the
    Future', *Inquiry*, 21, 1978, 133—79

Routley, Richard and Routley, Val, 'Against the Inevitability of Human Chauvinism', in K. E. Goodpaster and K. M. Sayre (eds), *Ethics and Problems of the 21st Century,* 36—59

Routley, Val, Critical Notice of John Passmore, *Man's Responsibility for Nature, Australasian Journal of Philosophy,* 53, 1975, 171—85

Routley, Val and Routley, Richard, 'Human Chauvinism and Environmental Ethics', in Don Mannison, Michael McRobbie and Richard Routley (eds), *Environmental Philosophy,* 96—189

Routley, Val and Routley, Richard, 'Social Theories, Self Management and Environmental Problems', in Don Mannison, Michael McRobbie and Richard Routley (eds), *Environmental Philosophy,* 217—332

Sagoff, Mark, 'On Preserving the Natural Environment', *Yale Law Journal,* 84, 1974, 205—67

Sayre, Kenneth, 'Morality, Energy and the Environment', *Environmental Ethics,* 3, 1981, 5—18

Schwartz, Thomas, 'Obligations to Posterity', in R. I. Sikora and Brian Barry (eds), *Obligations to Future Generations,* 3—13

Scott, Robert, Jnr, 'Environmental Ethics and Obligations to Future Generations', in R. I. Sikora and Brian Barry (eds), *Obligations to Future Generations,* 74—90

Semenov, Nicolai, 'Energetics for the Future', in *Society and the Environment: a Soviet View,* (ed. anon.), 69—98

Sher, George, 'Hare, Abortion and the Golden Rule', in *Philosophy and Public Affairs,* 6, 1976—77, 185—90

Sikora, R. I., 'Utilitarianism: The Classical Principle and the Average Principle', *Canadian Journal of Philosophy,* 1975, 409—19

Sikora, R. I., 'Is it Wrong to Prevent the Existence of Future Generations?', in R. I. Sikora and Brian Barry (eds), *Obligations to Future Generations,* 112—66

Sikora, R. I., 'Utilitarianism and Future Generations', *Canadian Journal of Philosophy,* 9, 1979, 461—6

Sikora, R. I., 'Classical Utilitarianism and Parfit's Repugnant Conclusion: A Reply to McMahan', *Ethics,* 92, 1981—82, 128—33

Singer, Peter, 'Famine, Affluence and Morality', *Philosophy and Public Affairs,* 1, 1971—72, 229—43

Singer, Peter, 'A Utilitarian Population Principle', in Michael D. Bayles (ed.), *Ethics and Population,* 81—99

Singer, Peter, 'Reconsidering the Famine Relief Argument', in P. G. Brown and H. Shue (eds), *Food Policy,* 36—53

Singer, Peter, 'Killing Humans and Killing Animals', *Inquiry,* 22, 1979, 145—56

Singer, Peter, 'Not for Humans Only: The Place of Nonhumans in Environmental Issues', in K. E. Goodpaster and K. M. Sayre (eds), *Ethics and Problems of the 21st Century,* 191—206

Singer, Peter, 'Animals and the Value of Life', in Tom Regan (ed.), *Matters of Life and Death,* 218—59

Singer, Peter, 'Utilitarianism and Vegetarianism', *Philosophy and Public Affairs*, 9, 1979—80, 325—37

Sprigge, Timothy L. S., 'Professor Narveson's Utilitarianism', *Inquiry*, 11, 1968, 337—41

Stearns, J. Brenton, 'Ecology and the Indefinite Unborn', *The Monist*, 56, 1972, 612—25; reprinted in Richard A. Wasserstrom (ed.), *Today's Moral Problems*, 602—13

Steinbock, Bonnie, 'Speciesism and the Idea of Equality', *Philosophy*, 53, 1978, 247—63

Sterba, James P., 'Abortion, Distant Peoples and Future Generations', *Journal of Philosophy*, 77, 1980, 424—40

Sumner, L. W., 'A Matter of Life and Death', *Noûs*, 10, 1976, 145—71

Sumner, L. W., 'Classical Utilitarianism and the Population Optimum', in R. I. Sikora and Brian Barry (eds), *Obligations to Future Generations*, 91—111

Surber, Jere Paul, 'Obligations to Future Generations: Explorations and Problemata', *Journal of Value Inquiry*, 11, 1977, 104—16

Townsend, Aubrey, 'Radical Vegetarians', *Australasian Journal of Philosophy*, 57, 1979, 85—93

Tribe, Laurence H., 'Ways not to Think about Plastic Trees', *Yale Law Journal*, 83, 1974, 1315—48

VanDeVeer, Donald, 'Interspecific Justice', *Inquiry*, 22, 1979, 55—79

Warren, Mary, 'Do Potential People Have Moral Rights?', in R. I. Sikora and Brian Barry (eds), *Obligations to Future Generations*, 14—30

Welbourn, F. B., 'Man's Dominion', *Theology*, 78, 1975, 561—8

White, Lynn Jnr, 'The Historical Roots of our Ecological Crisis', *Science*, 155 (37), 10 March 1967, 1203—7; reprinted in John Barr (ed.), *The Environmental Handbook*, 3—16

Williams, Mary B., 'Discounting Versus Maximum Sustainable Yield', in R. I. Sikora and Brian Barry (eds), *Obligations to Future Generations*, 169—85

Young, Robert, 'Population Policies, Coercion and Morality', in Don Mannison, Michael McRobbie and Richard Routley (eds), *Environmental Philosophy*, 356—75

Books

Aiken, William and La Follette, Hugh (eds), *World Hunger and Moral Obligation*, Englewood Cliffs, NJ: Prentice-Hall, 1977

Alexander, H. G. (ed.), *The Clarke—Leibniz Correspondence*, Manchester: Manchester University Press, 1956

Allchin, A. M., *Wholeness and Transfiguration Illustrated in the Lives of St Francis of Assisi and St Seraphim of Sarov*, Oxford: SLG Press, 1974

Aquinas, Thomas, *Summa Contra Gentiles*, trans. Anton Pegis *et al.*, (5 Vols.), Garden City, NY: Image Books, 1955—57

Aquinas, Thomas, *Summa Theologiae,* (60 Vols.), London: Eyre and Spottiswoode, and New York: McGraw-Hill, 1964

Aristotle, *De Anima,* trans. Kenelm Foster and Silvester Humphries, London: Routledge & Kegan Paul, 1951

Arseniev, Nicholas, *Mysticism and the Eastern Church* (1925), trans. Arthur Chambers, London and Oxford: Mowbray, 1979

Attfield, Robin, *God and The Secular: A Philosophical Assessment of Secular Reasoning from Bacon to Kant,* Cardiff: University College Cardiff Press, 1978

Bacon, Francis, *The New Organon,* ed. Fulton H. Anderson, Indianapolis and New York: Bobbs-Merrill, 1960

Bacon, Francis, *The Advancement of Learning and the New Atlantis,* ed. Arthur Johnston, Oxford: Clarendon Press, 1974

Baillie, John, *The Belief in Progress,* London, Glasgow and Toronto: Oxford University Press, 1950

Bambrough, Renford, *Moral Scepticism and Moral Knowledge,* London and Henley: Routledge & Kegan Paul, 1979

Baptist Hymn Book, The, London: Psalms and Hymns Trust, 1962

Barbour, Ian G., *Earth Might Be Fair,* Englewood Cliffs, NJ: Prentice-Hall, 1972

Barr, John (ed.), *The Environmental Handbook* (British Version), London: Ballantine and Friends of the Earth, 1971

Bayle, Pierre, *Historical and Critical Dictionary* (1697), trans. and ed. Richard H. Popkin, Indianapolis and New York: Bobbs-Merrill, 1965

Bayles, Michael D. (ed.), *Ethics and Population,* Cambridge, Mass.: Schenkman, 1976

Becker, Carl, *The Heavenly City of the Eighteenth-Century Philosophers,* New Haven and London: Yale University Press, 1932

Bieler, André, *La Pensée economique et sociale de Calvin,* Geneva: Georg, 1959

Birch, L. Charles, *Nature and God,* London: SCM Press, 1965

Black, John, *Man's Dominion,* Edinburgh: Edinburgh University Press, 1970

Blackstone, William T. (ed.), *Philosophy and Environmental Crisis,* Athens, University of Georgia Press, 1974

Boyle, Robert, *The Christian Virtuoso,* London, 1690

Brown, Peter and MacLean, Douglas (eds), *Energy Policy and Future Generations,* Tottowa, NJ: Rowman and Littlefield, forthcoming

Brown, P. G. and Shue, H. (eds), *Food Policy,* New York: Free Press, 1977

Bury, J. B., *The Idea of Progress,* London: Macmillan Press, 1920

Calvin, Jean, *Commentaries on the First Book of Moses, called Genesis,* trans. John King (2 Vols.), London, 1847

Catherwood, Sir Frederick, *A Better Way, The Case for a Christian Social Order,* Leicester: Inter-Varsity Press, 1975

Christian Faith and Practice in the Experience of the Society of Friends, London: London Yearly Meeting of the Society of Friends, 1960

Clark, Stephen R. L., *The Moral Status of Animals,* Oxford: Clarendon Press, 1977

Clarke, Samuel, *Letter to Dodwell, Etc.* (1706), (6th edn) London, 1731

Cole, H. *et al., Thinking About the Future: A Critique of The Limits to Growth,* London: Chatto & Windus and Sussex University Press, 1973

Collins, F. Howard, *Epitome of the Synthetic Philosophy of Herbert Spencer,* London: Williams & Northgate, 1889

Commoner, Barry, *The Closing Circle,* London: Jonathan Cape, 1972

Cowper, William, *The Task,* Ilkley and London: Scolar Press, 1973

Cudworth, Ralph, *The True Intellectual System of the Universe,* (2nd edn), London, 1743

Derr, Thomas Sieger, *Ecology and Human Liberation,* Geneva: WSCF Books, 1973

Descartes, René, *The Philosophical Works of Descartes,* trans. Elizabeth S. Haldane and G. R. T. Ross (2 Vols.), Cambridge: Cambridge University Press, 1967

Donaldson, Peter, *Worlds Apart,* London: BBC, 1971

Dorsey, Gray (ed.), *Equality and Freedom* (3 Vols.), New York: Oceana Publications and Leiden: A. W. Sijthoff, 1977

Ehrlich, Paul R., *The Population Bomb,* London: Pan Books/Ballantine, 1971

Ehrlich, Paul R. and Ehrlich, Anne H., *Population, Resources, Environment: Issues in Human Ecology,* San Francisco: W. H. Freeman, (2nd edn) 1972

Elliot, Robert and Gair, Aaron (eds), *Environmental Philosophy: A Collection of Readings,* Brisbane: University of Queensland Press, due to appear in 1983

Engels, F., *Dialectics of Nature,* New York: International Publishers, 1954

Engels, F., *Anti-Dühring,* Moscow, 1975

Frey, R. G., *Interests and Rights: The Case Against Animals,* Oxford: Clarendon Press, 1980

George, Susan, *How the Other Half Dies,* Harmondsworth: Penguin Books, 1976

Ginsberg, Morris, *The Idea of Progress: A Revaluation,* Westport, Conn.: Greenwood Press, 1953

Glacken, C. J., *Traces on the Rhodian Shore, Nature and Culture in Western Thought from Ancient Times to the End of the Eighteenth Century,* Berkeley, LA and London: University of California Press, 1967

Glover, Jonathan, *Causing Death and Saving Lives,* Harmondsworth: Penguin Books, 1977

Godlovitch, Stanley, Godlovitch, Roslind and Harris, John (eds), *Animals, Men and Morals. An Enquiry into the Maltreatment of Non-humans,* New York: Taplinger Publishing Co., 1972

Goodman, David C. *et al., Scientific Progress and Religious Dissent,* Milton Keynes: Open University Press, 1974

Goodman, David C. *et al., Towards a Mechanistic Philosophy,* Milton Keynes: Open University Press, 1974

Goodpaster, K. E. and Sayre, K. M. (eds), *Ethics and Problems of the 21st Century,* Notre Dame and London: Notre Dame University Press, 1979

Gorovitz, Samuel *et al.* (eds), *Moral Problems in Medicine,* Englewood Cliffs, NJ: Prentice-Hall, 1976

Hacker, P. M. S. and Raz, J. (eds), *Law, Morality and Society,* Oxford: Clarendon Press, 1977

Hale, Sir Matthew, *The Primitive Origination of Mankind,* London, 1677

Hardin, Garrett, *The Limits of Altruism,* Bloomington: Indiana University Press, 1977

Hardin, Garrett and Baden, John (eds), *Managing the Commons,* San Francisco: W. H. Freeman, 1977

Hart, Judith, *Aid and Liberation,* London: Gollancz, 1973

Heilbroner, Robert L., *An Inquiry into the Human Prospect,* London: Calder & Boyars, 1975

Hughes, J. Donald, *Ecology in Ancient Civilizations,* Albuquerque: University of New Mexico Press, 1975

Hume, C. W., *The Status of Animals in the Christian Religion,* London: Universities Federation for Animal Welfare, 1957

Hume, David, *The Philosophical Works,* ed. T. H. Green and T. H. Grose, London: Longmans, Green, 1974—75

Jaki, Stanley L., *Science and Creation,* Edinburgh: Scottish Academic Press, 1974

Kant, Immanuel, *Lectures on Ethics,* trans. Louis Infield, New York: Harper & Row, 1963

Karrer, Otto (ed.), *St Francis of Assisi, The Legends and the Lauds,* trans. N. Wydenbruck, London: Sheed & Ward, 1977

Kelly, J. N. D., *Early Christian Doctrines,* London: Adam & Charles Black, (4th edn) 1968

Kenny, Anthony (ed.), *Aquinas: A Collection of Critical Essays,* London: Macmillan Press, 1969

King-Farlow, John, *Self-Knowledge and Social Relations,* New York: Science History Publications, 1978

La Mettrie, Offray de, J., *Les Animaux plus que machines,* La Haye, 1751

Lecky, W. E. H., *History of European Morals from Augustus to Charlemagne* (2 Vols.) (1869), London: Longmans, Green, 1913

Leopold, Aldo, *A Sand County Almanac and Sketches Here and There,* New York: Oxford University Press, 1949

Leopold, Aldo, *A Sand County Almanac with Other Essays on Conservation,* New York: Oxford University Press (2nd edn of the above), 1966

Linzey, Andrew, *Animal Rights: A Christian Assessment of Man's Treatment of Animals,* London: SCM Press, 1976

Locke, John, *Works,* ed. T. Tegg *et al.* (10 Vols.), London, 1823

Lovejoy, A. O., *The Great Chain of Being,* Harvard: Harvard University Press, 1936

Lovelock, J. E., *Gaia, A New Look at Life on Earth,* Oxford: Oxford University Press, 1979

Mannison, Don, McRobbie, Michael and Routley, Richard (eds), *Environmental Philosophy,* Canberra: Australian National University, 1980

Margolis, Joseph, *Persons and Minds: The Prospects for Nonreductive Materialism,* Dordrecht, Boston and London: Reidel, 1977

Marx, Karl, *Selected Works* (2 Vols.), Moscow, 1949 and London, 1950

Marx, Karl, *Capital,* (3 Vols.), ed. F. Engels, New York: International Publishers, 1967

Marx, Leo, *The Machine in the Garden: Technology and the Pastoral Ideal,* New York: Oxford University Press, 1964

Meadows, Donella H. *et al., The Limits to Growth,* a report for the Club of Rome's Project on the Predicament of Mankind (1972), London and Sydney: Pan Books, 1974

Mesarovic, Mihajlo D. and Pestel, Eduard, *Mankind at the Turning Point,* the second report to the Club of Rome, London: Hutchinson, 1975

Midgley, Mary, *Beast and Man: The Roots of Human Nature,* Hassocks: Harvester Press, 1979

Milman, H. II., *The History of Christianity from the Birth of Christ to the Abolition of Paganism in the Roman Empire* (3 Vols.), London: John Murray, 1840

Mishan, Edward J., *The Costs of Economic Growth,* Harmondsworth: Penguin Books, 1969

Montefiore, Hugh (ed.), *Man and Nature,* London: Collins, 1975

Morris, Richard Knowles and Fox, Michael W. (eds), *On the Fifth Day, Animal Rights and Human Ethics,* Washington, DC: Acropolis Books, 1978

Morscher, Edgar and Stranzinger, Rudolf (eds), *Ethics: Foundations, Problems and Applications, Proceedings of the Fifth International Wittgenstein Symposium,* Vienna: Verlag Hölder-Pichler-Tempsky, 1981

Narveson, Jan, *Morality and Utility,* Baltimore: John Hopkins Press, 1967

Nash, Roderick, *Wilderness and the American Mind,* New Haven: Yale University Press, 1967

Nelson, Leonard, *A System of Ethics,* trans. Norbert Guterman, New Haven: Yale University Press, 1956

Neuhaus, Richard, *In Defense of People, Ecology and the Seduction of Radicalism,* New York: Macmillan and London: Collier-Macmillan, 1971

Nisbet, Robert, *The Social Philosophers,* London: Heinemann, 1974

Nisbet, Robert, *History of the Idea of Progress,* London: Heinemann, 1980

Nozick, Robert, *Anarchy, State and Society,* Oxford: Blackwell, and New York: Basic Books, 1974

Parsons, Howard L., *Marx and Engels on Ecology,* Westport, Conn. and

London: Greenwood Press, 1977

Partridge, Ernest (ed.), *Responsibilities to Future Generations,* New York: Prometheus Books, 1981

Passmore, John, *The Perfectibility of Man [PM],* London: Duckworth, 1970

Passmore, John, *Man's Responsibility for Nature [MRN],* London: Duckworth, 1974; 2nd edn, 1980

Peacocke, A. R., *Creation and the World of Science,* Oxford: Oxford University Press, 1979

Pirages, Dennis C. and Ehrlich, Paul R., *Ark II: Social Response to Environmental Imperatives,* San Francisco: W. H. Freeman, 1974

Pirages, Dennis Clark (ed.), *The Sustainable Society,* New York and London: Praeger Publishers, 1977

Price, Richard, *A Free Discussion of Materialism and Philosophical Necessity in a Correspondence between Dr Price and Dr Priestley, Etc.,* London, 1778

Price, Richard, *Sermons,* London, c. 1790

Priestley, Joseph, *An Essay on the First Principles of Government and on Political, Civil and Religious Liberty,* (2nd edn) London, 1771

Purver, Margery, *The Royal Society: Concept and Creation,* London: Routledge & Kegan Paul, 1967

Rawls, John, *A Theory of Justice,* London, Oxford, New York: Oxford University Press, 1972

Ray, John, *The Wisdom of God Manifested in the Works of Creation,* 11th edn, London, 1743

Regan, Tom (ed.), *Matters of Life and Death,* Philadelphia: Temple University Press, 1980

Regan, Tom and Singer, Peter (eds), *Animal Rights and Human Obligations,* Englewood Cliffs, NJ: Prentice-Hall, 1976

Richardson, Alan (ed.), *A Theological Wordbook of the Bible,* London: SCM Press, 1957

Rivers, Patrick, *Living Better on Less,* London: Turnstone Books, 1977

Robinson, J. A. T., *The Body,* London: SCM Press, 1952

Routley, Richard and Routley, Val, *The Fight for the Forests,* Canberra: Australian National University Press, 1974

Royal Institute of Philosophy (ed.), *The Proper Study*, London and Basingstoke: Macmillan Press, 1971

Royal Institute of Philosophy (ed.), *Nature and Conduct,* London and Basingstoke: Macmillan Press, 1975

Schmidt, Alfred, *The Concept of Nature in Marx,* New York: Humanities Press, 1972

Schweitzer, Albert, *Civilisation and Ethics,* trans. C. T. Campion, London: Adam & Charles Black, 3rd edn, 1946

Shrader-Frechette, K. S., *Nuclear Power and Public Policy,* Dordrecht, Boston and London: Reidel, 1980

Sikora, R. I. and Barry, Brian (eds), *Obligations to Future Generations,* Philadelphia: Temple University Press, 1978

Singer, Peter, *Animal Liberation, A New Ethic for Our Treatment of Animals,* London: Jonathan Cape, 1976

Singer, Peter, *Practical Ethics,* Cambridge: Cambridge University Press, 1979

Skolimowski, Henryk, *Eco-Philosophy,* Boston and London: Marion Boyars, 1981

Society and the Environment: a Soviet View, (ed. anon.), Moscow: Progress Publishers, 1977

Spinoza, *Ethics,* trans. Andrew Boyle, London: Dent, Everyman's Library, 1910

Spring, David and Spring, Eileen (eds), *Ecology and Religion in History*, New York, Evanston, San Francisco and London: Harper & Row, 1974

Stone, Christopher, *Should Trees Have Standing?,* Los Altos, Cal.: William Kaufman, 1974

Stone, Lawrence, *The Family, Sex and Marriage in England, 1500—1800,* London: Weidenfeld & Nicolson, 1977

Turner, E. S., *All Heaven in a Rage,* London: Michael Joseph, 1964

Vesey, Godfrey (ed.), *The Proper Study,* Royal Institute of Philosophy Lectures, 4, 1969—70, London and Basingstoke: Macmillan Press, 1971

Warnock, Geoffrey, *The Object of Morality,* New York: Methuen Press, 1971

Wasserstrom, Richard A. (ed.), *Today's Moral Problems* (2nd edn), New York: Macmillan Publishing Co. and London: Collier-Macmillan, 1979

Westermann, Claus, *Creation,* London: SPCK, 1974

White, Lynn Jnr, *Medieval Technology and Social Change,* Oxford: Clarendon Press, 1962

White, T. H. (trans. and ed.), *The Book of Beasts,* London: Jonathan Cape, 1954

Whitehead, A. N., *Science and the Modern World,* Cambridge: Cambridge University Press, 1926

Wiles, Maurice and Santer, Mark (eds), *Documents in Early Christian Thought,* Cambridge: Cambridge University Press, 1975

Williams, Bernard and Smart, J. C. C., *Utilitarianism, For and Against,* London and New York: Cambridge University Press, 1973

World Conservation Strategy, (ed. anon.), New York: International Union for Conservation of Nature and Natural Resources, United Nations Environmental Programme and World Wildlife Fund, 1980

Index

Editors who are not referred to also as authors are omitted here, as also are works the titles of which are not presented in the main text. Bold type in subject entries indicates references of greatest importance.